The Primary School Management Book

A PRACTICAL HANDBOOK FOR HEADS AND TEACHERS

David Playfoot
Martin Skelton
Geoff Southworth

MARY GLASGOW PUBLICATIONS

© Mary Glasgow Publications Limited 1989

First published in 1989 by
Mary Glasgow Publications Limited
131–133 Holland Park Avenue
London W11 4UT

Illustrated by Martin Salisbury
Designed by Eric Drewery
Typeset by Anneset, Weston-super-Mare, Avon
Printed by Hollen Street Press, Slough, Berks

British Library Cataloguing in Publication Data
Playfoot, David
  The primary school management book.
  1. Great Britain. Primary Schools. Management
  I. Title II. Skelton, Martin III. Southworth, Geoff
  372.12'00941

ISBN 1-85234-265-X

345043

CONTENTS

5 *Issues into Practice* 101

Contents

Primary schools are increasingly complex places. Those involved in running them are responsible for overseeing a range of social, intellectual and emotional aims within a context of diverging views, staff shortages, major curriculum changes, often unsatisfactory buildings and, sometimes, doubtful public confidence.

Yet primary schools which are well run – where staff, parents and governors share common aims for their children, where human beings are respected, where agreed policies are in operation and where confidence is high – can be marvellous places.

In management terms, primary schools have often been seen as the poor relations of education: small, cosy places where children are simply prepared for some later and more important stage. In recent years this view has been challenged. The primary stage of education is now acknowledged as vitally important for children; the range of the primary curriculum has extended enormously; the involvement of parents in the work of schools, both formally and informally, has brought major benefits and some problems; the devolution of responsibility from the local authorities to schools has increased the administrative workload. The National Curriculum has brought yet more changes.

The Primary School Management Book has been written to help all those responsible for the day-to-day education of primary children to understand and organise their schools as effectively as possible. It is a positive and, above all, a realistic book which can be read and used by everyone concerned about and responsible for the development of primary schools in these challenging times.

1 INTRODUCTION

1.1 *What this book is about*

We have written this book together because we get on well together. We think alike in many ways although, naturally, we have our differences. The most important educational idea we share in common is that we are all interested in what happens in the day-to-day practice of schools.

That's not to say that theory and research is of no interest to us. Anyone thinking that would be a long way from the truth. You only have to look at the bibliography at the end of this book to see how seriously we take theory and research. In the end, though, what matters to us is what happens in practice.

We have a feeling that many educational books are full of excellent theory which either doesn't reflect the day-to-day life of primary schools or which cannot be translated into actual practice.

We welcome moves by recent researchers to look at schools and classrooms first and then develop theories which help us from their observations. If such a move continues primary schools must surely benefit over the next decade. On the other hand, we reject the use of theories from industry (many of which haven't really been judged in real life there) applied to education as though the problem of transfer from an industrial setting to an educational one was quite simple.

If anything requires an understanding of what happens in practice rather than what happens in theory, it is management. Whether we are managing ourselves, our classrooms, our colleagues or our schools a failure to understand the practical complexities of management can be disastrous. So, this book is about the practical management of important aspects of primary schools.

All three of us have been classroom teachers; all three of us have been headteachers; at the time of writing one of us is a practising headteacher, one is a director of an INSET agency and one works for the Cambridge Institute as a tutor in primary management.

We have a broad experience of the real practice of primary schools and we have colleagues, friends and contacts with even more. Whatever else you obtain from this book, we hope that you will recognise how firmly it is rooted in the realities that many of us face each day.

The book is divided into a range of themes, around which we have grouped a number of topics. Some of these topics provide background information to the practice of managing primary schools into the 1990s; the rest deal head-on with the issues regularly faced by teachers and headteachers.

Section 1, part of which you are reading now, provides an introduction to the book and describes in general terms the nature of the schools we work in.

Section 2, People in Management, is important because it establishes that education is essentially a human occupation. The theme of this section is that understanding ourselves and others is the key to providing a •
challenging environment in schools for both children and adults.

Section 3, Schools as Organisations,

provides some background ideas relevant to primary schools as organisations.

Section 4, Key Management Issues, presents some of the most frequently encountered ideas about primary school management.

Section 5, Issues into Practice, expands on the first four sections by relating them to the day-to-day practice of modern primary schools. This section is sub-divided into five further sections, each of which relates to a particular aspect of the management of primary schools – the staff, the children and classrooms, analysing the organisation, financial management and buildings, and external relations.

We have tried to make this book as accessible and clearly written as possible. The issues we are talking about are too important to be clouded by unnecessary complexity. The book is aimed at everyone who works in primary schools; we know just how busy those people are.

We hope the book will make you think. We hope it will give you insights into some of the issues of primary school management. We want it to provide some ways forward which we know have worked. The most important of these solutions is to understand the context in which we work and not just to observe it.

If you want to delve further into any of the subjects you can either follow the brief reading lists we have given on some pages or turn to the bibliography at the back of the book. With an understanding of the realities of your own school and how it operates, and with a willingness to look critically at everything you read in the light of your own practice, any other reading can only help.

Finally, we would like you to see this book as a way in to understanding the management of primary schools, which accurately reflects your own experiences. Only then will it be really useful.

1.2 *The School Constituency*

In addition to being 'the whole body of voters represented by a member of parliament or the like' (*Chambers Concise Dictionary,* 1985) a constituency is also the 'set of people, supporting, patronising or forming a power-base for a business organisation, pressure group, etc.' (ibid.).

However, that which giveth also taketh away. The constituency which provides support for an organisation is also the constituency which can orchestrate its downfall, cause difficulties, hinder development, and create shifts in focus.

The constituency of schools is particularly wide, as the diagram shows, and the more potent a topic education becomes in the national and political agendas, the broader its constituency grows.

Those who work in school should be aware of the effects the constituency members can have upon the school, as well as the effects the school can have on the constituency. There is also a need to be fully aware of how much even a small school can affect, or be affected by, a constituency which is much larger than is realised on a day-by-day basis.

The diagram is largely self-explanatory and it is quite possible to make local, national and international additions to it. It isn't intended to be comprehensive; it is meant to give a flavour of the range of influences acting on schools at any one moment. To realise that governmental and local authority funding for the development of science or INSET in general is affected by international shifts in currency or deficits in trade balances is to build upon that which otherwise risks becoming understandably parochial.

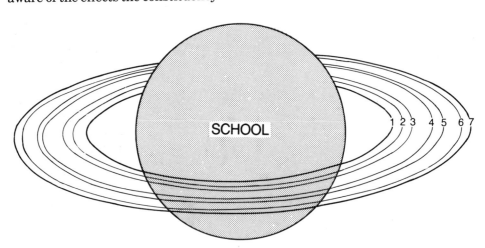

1   Children
2   Staff (teaching and non teaching), parents
3   Governors, the LEA, National Curriculum, contributing schools,
      Government, the law
4   Neighbours, local media
5   Community groups
6   National media
7   International events

Because schools are so busy it is easy to miss the importance to outsiders of a variety of things which appear to be relatively harmless within the organisation itself.

The teachers of a primary school had, over the years, grown more and more dissatisfied with the format of the annual Sports Day. Each summer, grumbles could be heard about too many children sitting around doing nothing while others ran races which took only seconds to complete, about the potential discipline problems (and therefore extra work) which that caused for watching staff, about the over-competitiveness of some children, about the parallel attitudes of some parents, and about the upset caused to young children who 'lost' races without really understanding the nature of the Sports Day at all.

Eventually, they decided to do something about it. A group of staff met on a number of occasions to consider other possibilities. After visits to other schools, the presentation of a report to their colleagues and much further discussion it was decided to change Sports Day to a less competitive non-team event which could take place at the same time as the Summer Fair. Twenty different mini-events would be organised and each child could, if they wished, enter any six of them at any time during the afternoon. Points would be allocated to individual children based on how they performed in each event. The events were to be chosen to suit children of very different abilities.

The staff of the school worked hard to organise the event and details were sent to parents about a fortnight before the Summer Fair was due to take place.

Immediately:

- Letters were received from a number of parents whose "children had been looking forward to a Sports Day all year"
- Governors were contacted and three of them expressed surprise that they had not been consulted about such a major change in the school's annual activities
- The Inspector for Physical Education within the authority visited the school and reminded the headteacher of the recently issued statement of support for competitive games issued by the Education Committee. In the light of this, the Inspector was particularly incensed at not having been informed
- A number of parents came to the Summer Fair with the express intention of causing a fuss. In doing so, they became involved in public arguments with other, supportive parents which members of staff had to try to sort out
- The annual report of the Governors to parents, normally a quiet affair, ended up in a four-way argument between supportive and antagonistic parents, the headteacher and some of the Governors
- As a result of that meeting and things that were said, three members of the PTA committee – including the secretary and treasurer – resigned
- A local newspaper picked up the story and spread banner headlines on its front page about the whole story. Some time later, a national newspaper used the school in a feature about the neglect of competitive sport by Britain's teachers
- A number of parents whose children were due to begin at the school in the following year went elsewhere at the last minute, bringing the school's staffing and financial policies under severe strain.

The example on page 13 is an amalgam of events which have actually taken place in three different schools. We are not suggesting that the staff of this composite school were wrong in wanting to change the nature of Sports Day; we have had very similar feelings ourselves! Neither are we suggesting that such a change exhibits an overall non-competitiveness; one of the three schools won both of the local football and netball tournaments that year. What the story – and many similar ones which appear in local newspapers across the land each year – does underline is that schools are rarely in a position to take unilateral action. Schools are a central feature of a broad, active and influential constituency. Every public decision taken by a school needs to reflect an understanding of the range of responses the constituency is likely to make and the effects those responses will have.

The school in our illustration may well have made the 'right' educational and administrative decision about Sports Day but it would have suffered less if as much care had been taken in presenting the decision as had been taken in reaching it.

The diagram on page 12 suggests, too, the dual nature of schools. In one sense schools are responsible to the members of their particular constituency; in another, equally important sense, they exist only as a result of the interactions and perceptions which that constituency brings to bear. Schools are created from their constituency, to which they are then responsible.

1.3 The Purpose of Schools (and the Purpose of Managing Them)

There are a number of common assumptions about the purpose of schools. Few of us would disagree with a view which suggested that schools should develop the intellectual, social, emotional and physical abilities of children and support their needs.

Within these simply defined purposes, though, real life turns out to be very varied.

- *'Intellectual' purposes* can involve facilitating the abilities of children already working three or four years ahead of levels thought to be normal for their age; it can also mean supporting the very slow development of children for whom 'academic' work will remain non-existent for most of their lives
- *'Social' purposes* can mean allowing children of considerable social maturity the opportunity to act out that maturity in a secure environment which saves them from being negatively labelled as precocious; it can also mean working over a period of years with children who are unable to enter the playground without ruining every game they encounter
- *'Emotional' purposes* can mean providing time for children who want to talk at some length and depth about their feelings; it can also mean providing extravagant security to children whose emotional equilibrium has already been unbalanced at a young age
- *'Physical' purposes* can mean restraining the desire of physically gifted and enthusiastic children to over-exert themselves at too young an age; it can also mean helping one child take three months to begin to manipulate a pair of scissors.

The division of these purposes into apparently distinct categories hides the real-world complexities of their interdependence.

Which of these purposes is pre-eminent at any one time depends upon a number of factors. Governments, for example, may try and determine the importance of one rather than the others by their use of public funding. Educationalists may create a debate which emphasises one purpose rather than another. Parents in certain schools may appear to adopt a viewpoint which encourages their children's schools to concentrate on particular aspects of the service they offer. Teachers in classrooms may feel more disposed towards some aspects of a child's development rather than others.

The problems

There are three obvious problems with the notion of a school's 'purpose'. First, as we have seen above, we cannot always be sure what we mean when we accept an apparently simple definition of the purposes of schools as 'intellectual', 'social', 'emotional' and 'physical'. Each 'purpose' has its own confusion of meanings which often interact with other 'purposes', too.

Second, as Charles Handy has pointed out in *Understanding Schools as Organisations*, the existence of such a broad range of purposes invites clashes in the demands placed upon schools and the extent to which schools are able to achieve them. Maximising the intellectual capabilities of a child may mean diminishing the opportunities to develop social skills; maximising a child's physical skills may involve reducing the extent to which intellectual purposes can be realised.

Inevitably, schools have to effect a compromise. What that compromise is and how it should be realised can be a source of friction between the various interest groups involved.

The third problem is slightly different. Put at its most simple, we can say that *schools don't have purposes; the people concerned with them do.*

The technical term for attributing human values to non-human things is 'reification'. Reification reminds us that it is nonsensical in real life to talk of schools as having purposes. 'Schools' exist out of the varied interests and qualities of the people and resources in them which are in turn affected by the influences acting upon them.

If we were able to deny the existence of these differing interests, qualities and resources and simply describe identical schools as having the same purposes (and probably the same aims) there would be little difficulty in establishing the same performance. Indeed, those who argue that a consistent performance can be reproduced in schools of widely differing characters seem to base their arguments on exactly the premise that everyone agrees on the nature and priorities of the purposes of their work. To us, this seems to be one of the major mistakes in understanding schools as organisations.

The purpose of management

We shall see elsewhere in the book how both the individuals and the groups who work in schools or who are connected with schooling are likely to have a range of views about almost anything – including the purposes of the institution with which they are particularly concerned. This is a normal, even healthy, state of affairs.

What those involved in management are trying to do is to manage these diverse attitudes into something more coherent, something shared to the greatest possible extent by those involved in the life of the school. This does not mean creating a situation in which everyone holds the same views or in which there is no disagreement about the nature of the tasks to hand; on the other hand, there is little doubt that 'good' schools share in common the ability to work towards a set of declared purposes which are reasonable to most of the people involved.

It is our view that this aspect of management is unlikely to be carried out successfully by those intent on sticking solely to a 'top-down' style of management. Much more likely is that success will be achieved by those who have a variety of strategies at their disposal (including, where appropriate, a top-down approach) which respond to the differing needs of everyone involved but which, in the end, allow the discussion of views and the creation and acceptance of defined purposes to take place in the open.

2 PEOPLE IN MANAGEMENT

2.1 *Managing Yourself – 1*

There is a growing feeling that the way in which we manage our 'outer worlds' is intimately connected with the way in which we manage our 'inner worlds'. Put at its simplest, we work better as managers when we are able to manage – to understand, know, cope with, direct – our own selves.

Day-to-day life provides us with plenty of examples. Yesterday we were able to stay calm when the window broke in the classroom, while at the same time two children were sent from the playground, a parent telephoned with a complaint, a colleague reported that the video wasn't working and the caretaker reported overflowing toilets. Today, we can barely cope with the first incident let alone all the others.

Why is this? The actual incidents were the same or very similar. What has changed in the situation? The most likely answer is that we have changed and that the difference in our own equilibrium is the key to the difference in our reactions.

Our ability to manage is not dependent wholly, or even mostly, on the situations we are faced with but on our own level of self-competencies and self-understandings when we face those situations. We manage others by managing ourselves. Knowing ourselves before we try and know others is an important part of the management process.

'Knowing yourself' doesn't mean achieving a permanent Buddha-like calm (however desirable that may be as a long-term aim!). What it does mean is accepting who you are, understanding your own potential for development, knowing your strengths and working within them.

There is another reason why knowing ourselves is important as managers. Understanding the motivations, drives and enthusiasms of others is equally a part of the management task. But understanding others is difficult; we cannot really know what others think or why others behave as they do. The only clues we can obtain are through the assumption that others behave at least similarly to us; understanding our own motivations, attitudes, and strengths and weaknesses provides us with a better opportunity to understand those of others.

Even though understanding ourselves and others can be mystifying, managers of schools and classroom need to make the effort. As D Bannister said,

> To try and understand oneself is not simply an interesting pastime, it is a necessity of life. In order to plan our future and to make choices we have to be able to anticipate our behaviour in future situations. This makes self-knowledge a practical guide, not a self-indulgence.

This isn't a book about developing self-knowledge and we can do no more in the first few pages than suggest its importance and one or two areas which you might like to consider. To further your understanding you will have to go elsewhere; there are some suggestions in the bibliography at the back of this book. It is a book about management, though, and management without a degree of self-knowledge is likely to be less effective than it might otherwise be.

What basic type of person are you?

Any broad distinction of people into types is difficult; no one fits into any single category very neatly. Also, there seem to be an unlimited number of categories into which one might divide a group of people. We are going to ask you to decide whether you are a 'process' or a 'product' type of person. Neither is right or wrong but each category has its consequences in managerial action. Knowing which you are will help you to see which kind of manager you are 'naturally' more likely to be. Of course, you won't be wholly one or the other. Read the list of characteristics of each and try and decide where you fit on the product . . . process line.

Product   Process

A product person
- is most interested in achieving the final result
- likes to get things done; planning is seen as less (but not un-) important
- has an overview but can miss some important details
- takes a more single-minded approach
- is likely to be more definitive about how things should be done
- is more impatient with delays.

A process person
- enjoys the 'doing' of things as much as the end result
- likes ideas and theories
- accepts a diversity of response
- enjoys human interaction
- often wheels and deals
- sees complexity.

Understanding which of these feels most like you should help you to begin to understand your immediate potential for managing different situations.

Even though you may be able to identify yourself generally as a 'product' or 'process' person and understand the overall implications, it quickly becomes clear that certain aspects of management benefit from one approach rather than another. You might want to think about the aspects of management in which being a 'process' or 'product' person presents difficulties.

You will find on page 20 a list of some managerial tasks. Which benefit from 'process' or 'product'? Which approach do you take to those tasks now?

What matters to you?

Each of us carries round a group of ideas which we use to interpret the world. We may immediately begin to think of people as 'aggressive/compliant', 'dedicated/scroungers', 'bright/stupid' and situations as 'welcoming/threatening', 'dynamic/moribund' and so on. These have been called our 'constructs'.

Kelly, who formulated the Personal Construct theory, expanded his ideas. He suggested that we also have 'super-ordinate' constructs and 'sub-ordinate' constructs. The former are those of central concern to us; the latter are those of lesser importance. 'Fashion', for example, might be a 'super-ordinate' construct. What we wear at any given time, however, may be 'sub-ordinate' construct; as long as it is in fashion, we don't mind what it is. Equally, though, 'fashion' may be a sub-ordinate construct in our lives; we are not that concerned about it one way or another.

Our constructs determine what matters to us and, in turn, our attitudes and behaviour to key aspects of our lives. Managing education is affected by the constructs we hold. If education is not a 'super-ordinate' construct in our everyday lives we are unlikely to think about it or be as careful in our management of it as we would be if it were. Even when education is a 'super-ordinate' construct, though, it is likely to contain its own super and sub-ordinate constructs. "I prefer the sciences to the arts", "I'm only interested in children being happy", "I think all the children are naughty until I have trained them" will all have a considerable effect upon the teaching which takes place in classrooms.

> What is important to you in your everyday life? Write down up to six things, scoring them 1–10 for their level of importance to you.
>
> What is important to you in education? Write down up to six things, scoring them 1–10 for their level of importance to you.
>
> Spend a few minutes thinking about your scores. How are they being (or have they been) reflected in your personal and professional lives?

2.2 Managing Yourself – 2

What are your strengths and weaknesses?

Each of us has strengths and weaknesses. Identifying them as accurately as possible helps us to determine the base line from which we begin and plan for our future development. We have listed opposite a number of qualities and skills which managers in schools require. Think about each one carefully and try to assess your own competency. If you feel yourself to be excellent score yourself six; if you feel yourself to be quite poor score yourself one. As you consider each in turn, try and bring to mind recent examples which support your judgement.

Some Qualities and Skills of Management

	+					−
Thinking creatively	1	2	3	4	5	6
Thinking logically	1	2	3	4	5	6
Keeping abreast of developments	1	2	3	4	5	6
Translating theory into practice	1	2	3	4	5	6
Setting targets	1	2	3	4	5	6
Creating plans of action	1	2	3	4	5	6
Evaluation	1	2	3	4	5	6
Budgetary control	1	2	3	4	5	6
Managing time	1	2	3	4	5	6
Coping with stress	1	2	3	4	5	6
Adjusting to change	1	2	3	4	5	6
Selecting staff	1	2	3	4	5	6
Motivating people	1	2	3	4	5	6
Leading	1	2	3	4	5	6
Negotiating	1	2	3	4	5	6
Controlling	1	2	3	4	5	6
Handling conflict	1	2	3	4	5	6
Making presentations	1	2	3	4	5	6
Appraising	1	2	3	4	5	6
Developing people	1	2	3	4	5	6
Conducting meetings	1	2	3	4	5	6
Record keeping	1	2	3	4	5	6

What can you develop?

Some people believe that there is always the opportunity for self-development; others that self-development is unlikely, that their personalities and abilities are more or less static. We very much take the former view. Of course, some aspects of our lives will remain the same but we are conscious of changes which have occurred in our own lives and of friends and colleagues we have known. Change, or more accurately, development is possible.

We need to identify those areas in our own lives where development is important to us. Look at the range of weaknesses you identified elsewhere on these pages and fill them in on the chart below. Mark on the chart those in which you feel development to be urgent and those in which you feel it to be non-urgent.

Then mark those in which development seems more immediately possible and those in which it seems possible only in the longer term. (Why not start with success?) If you can identify a weakness where development is both urgent and possible you have found a starting point.

Possible areas of development	Urgent	Non-urgent	Possible	More difficult

Because development is possible this doesn't always make it easy. Some aspects of change and development can be very threatening. We are, after all, likely to be disturbing a reasonably comfortable notion of 'who we are'. Sometimes, too, the threat of development causes us to entrench ourselves in even more inflexibility.

At other times, though, development is enhancing in itself. The feeling that comes from being able to do something better can be very exciting, spurring us on to further development and sparking otherwise dormant aspects of our selves.

It has been suggested that there are three stages to self-development. They are:

- a picture in our minds of what it will be like when we have changed
- acting out the 'role' of a person like that (without quite believing it to be 'me')
- after a period of time, the assimilation of that acted behaviour into our everyday 'selves'.

This idea certainly makes sense when we think of aspects of adolescent behaviour. How does it match with your own experiences? Can you think of parallels in your own personal and professional lives which prove this to be the case? Looking at one of the possibilities you identified for development earlier, try and use this strategy as a way of planning your own self-development.

What do you need compensating for?

Few of us will achieve a state of competency in everything. We will always have our own strengths and weaknesses. Having weaknesses is not a failure but simply a description of the situation. As a manager (and as a person) our task is to find ways of coming to terms with these weaknesses and, where possible, of compensating for them.

The concept of teamwork is important. The task is to identify those aspects of our own selves for which compensation is important. Such identification may come from the list we compiled earlier; the list of abilities which it is urgent for us to develop but which present greater immediate difficulties. Having such a list helps us to define who to turn to for help, what qualities to look for in others and what it is possible or less possible to do. Try and answer the following questions.

- How easy do you find it to accept and admit areas within your 'self' which need development?
- How easy is it to admit those to other people?
- What areas have you identified which might be compensated for?
- Who is there around you who might be of help?
- Which areas remain?
- What can be done about them?

What do others think of you?

We mentioned above that our self-knowledge comes in part from the messages we pick up from others about our abilities and performance. What happens in practice is a continual interaction between your 'self', the interpretations your 'self' makes of the responses of others and the actual views of those others.

The research that is available suggests that we are less aware of others' perceptions than we think. Sometimes our interpretations of what we *think* they are thinking are inappropriate; at other times our natural reserve precludes open discussion amongst even close friends or colleagues.

Yet the views of others are important; they represent an important part of our 'selves' in action. Self-knowledge is concerned with how we feel about our 'selves' but also about how our 'selves' are perceived by others.

Although there are formal situations in which others' awareness of our 'selves' can be explored, they are not easy to arrange on a day-by-day basis. Finding out the views of others is difficult. As a beginning, try the following.

- Identify any obvious mis-match between your perception of your 'self' in a situation and someone else's perception. Does it reveal a misunderstanding or a different viewpoint?
- Consider the different viewpoint carefully
- Find someone sympathetic to what you are doing and begin to explore perceptions of each other. Allow the opportunity for either of you to stop at any time.

'Starting from where people are' is in danger of becoming one of *the* hypocritical management statements; we all seem to say it a lot and do it very little. The truth is we often feel frustrated by the very existence of individual differences.

Starting from where people are is fine until where people are is the very thing which slows us down, gets in the way, causes frustration. Suddenly, we don't want to start from where people are; we want them to be where we are.

In spite of the frustration we need to accept that the speed of change is governed as much by the individual perspectives of others as it is by our own. The fact that we are generally less than satisfactory at starting from where people are doesn't make it less important to do so.

The simple fact that people are different seems very hard to take on board sometimes and even harder to remember. It is, however, self-evident.

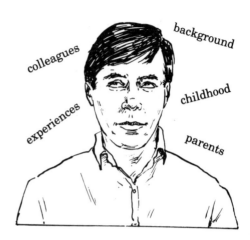

Think of your own views about

- footballers hugging each other after a goal has been scored
- Heavy Metal rock music
- eating meat
- being called by your first name as a teacher
- eating in class
- the balance between skills and knowledge in science
- whether teachers should strike.

The chances are high that you will have a view about most of these. The chances are high, too, that it won't take you long to find a colleague who thinks differently from you.

The kinds of views we have are based on a number of factors and the inter-relationship of those factors:

- our own interests and commitment
- the amount of knowledge and understanding we have of a subject
- our background
- our personality
- our influences.

The problem, and the excitement, of education is that most of the really important decisions cannot be made definitively. Consider the following questions:

- Is science a good thing for primary children?
- Should we abandon our reading schemes?
- How much calculator work should we do in mathematics?
- Should children be allowed into school before the official starting time?
- How much money should be allocated to each curriculum area this year?
- Does the way we do playground duty contribute to a good atmosphere in the school?

Opinions and views about such questions are too diverse for simple decisions to be made, precisely because the issues are so very important. The only decisions in a school which can be taken quickly and with more or less full agreement are those which are important for the moment but not for the longer term. For example, "Is it a wet playtime?", "Is the lavatory seat broken?" or "Were you in the playground ten minutes before school began?"

Many of the real issues which affect children's learning are more complex than that and are open – quite rightly and naturally – to different points of view.

> One of the tasks of management is to know when individual viewpoints can be held without damage to the school and when individual viewpoints need to be merged into generally acceptable policies.

To make these management decisions we have to be concerned with

- knowing what people think
- how strongly they feel things
- the likelihood of change within them.

Near Zones and Far Zones

Two Americans, Glaser and Strauss, have suggested that our ideas and beliefs fall into 'near zones' and 'far zones'. Those which fall into our near zones mean much more to us than those which fall into our far zones.

However, our feelings, ideas and commitments don't always fit consistently into the same category. Different factors can cause them to change.

> "Towards the end of a hot sunny day when we are all tired I just don't want to make them work as hard as I otherwise would."

Here 'hard work' has moved from a near zone to a far zone.

> "I suppose the National Curriculum has made me take more interest in science. I mean, if we have to do it I'd better get clued up."

Here, science has moved from a far zone towards a near(er) zone.

'Near zones' and 'far zones' are good tools for trying to assess the strength and importance of the ideas, feelings and understandings of colleagues and of ourselves.

Whether we choose to admit it or not the group of people with whom we work will have a different range of ideas, viewpoints, commitments and abilities.

It is hardly surprising that things should go awry if we begin to manage ourselves and our colleagues as if we were all the same. We can only hope to manage situations involving people competently by starting from the basis of our differences – and finding out as much about them as possible. As Robert Zend said, "People have one thing in common: they are all different."

2.4 Group Perspectives

The previous pages quite rightly concentrated on the importance of understanding how we each think, what our interests are, what we know and what we want to do as individuals.

Schools, though, are more than a collection of individuals. Whether it is in the classroom or staffroom, people group together for all sorts of reasons. For example

- being in a group often helps people feel better, feel more secure
- group members can help each other by using strengths and supporting weaknesses
- groups can unite in opposition to ideas which are unpopular.

Groups will form in different ways, too. They may

- unite around a single common idea
- form around a strong leader
- form for self-protection.

Near zones and far zones (see page 24) are as important for groups as they are for individuals.

One of us spent some time a few years ago in a particular primary school which everyone who visited it described as 'very good', 'marvellous' and so on. The children and staff worked hard, the relationships between staff and children were good, the quality of the school's policies was very high and the buildings were well-cared for. On any normal judgement of a 'good school' this one was respected by the majority of teachers who knew it and the majority of parents whose children attended there.

One of the noticeable things about the school was how everyone, staff and children, used the word 'we' rather than 'I'. The staff, in particular, had a very strong group feeling; they always talked of 'we'.

Interestingly, when each of the staff were spoken to on their own their independence from each other was revealed quite clearly. They all had different individual views from each other, liked each other more or less and had all sorts of differing hopes for their future.

The distinctions and divisions between them could have pulled them apart. In some schools they most certainly would have.

What held that staff together – what was in their near zones – was the collective view that they could best help the children there by having common policies which really worked. They were prepared to fight for what they thought was right, but once a decision was made they all accepted that their own personal views had to be held in suspension.

Although they understood that they were different from each other they were able to use the group feeling to immense benefit both for them and the children in the school.

Positive and negative power

The power of group feelings can be both positive and negative. In the case of the school described in the box the power the staff group gave to the school was both strong and positive; in another instance the group could have exerted an equally strong negative power. Later in the book, we will examine this a little more.

Group membership

We can often belong to a range of groups simultaneously. In Richard's school he is a member of different groups. They include

- the group of staff members interested in sport. Sport takes up much of the social discussion in the staffroom and many of the teachers in this group often support a school team together
- the group who visit the pub on a Friday evening. These are people who like a drink and use the pub as a safe place to vent their feelings. Sometimes Richard agrees with all the grumbles but sometimes he doesn't agree with any – but he still enjoys being in the group
- the group interested in teaching science. Richard holds a post of responsibility for science, is very keen and has a number of colleagues who continually come to him for advice. This group attend INSET together.

There may be other groups of which Richard is a member too. At different times each group will have a different degree of importance to him because of his own individual perspectives. The groups, too, will have different levels of importance at different times. The first hint of the National Curriculum probably increased the strength of the 'pub group'. The realisation that science had to be taught as a third component of the core curriculum and is the first subject to be assessed probably increased the importance of the science group.

As with individual perspectives, those of us managing classrooms or schools ignore group perspectives at our peril. Groups can react both positively or negatively. They can act in public or they can act anonymously.

Kate told us:

"We had made all the decisions about our maths teaching and we all agreed that problem-solving was important. It was only about six months later that I realised that two or three of the staff hadn't really wanted it and just hadn't done anything about it. They said they had, but it only became clear when the children changed classes and their new teachers said that they didn't seem to have any idea about problem-solving at all."

We will look in more detail at working with groups later in the book when we discuss consensus, collegiality and analysing our own organisations.

2.5 Teacher Perspectives

We began this book by stressing the importance of knowing our 'selves' as much as possible and managing our 'selves' on the basis of that knowledge. Such an understanding helps us to work more effectively and to understand that those with whom we work have different, but similar, 'selves', too.

One of the ways in which those 'selves' are revealed is through the perspectives we hold. Teachers in schools hold both individual perspectives and group perspectives; it is important to understand what they are and that there will always be a range of them with which we have to be concerned.

On these pages we are going to explore briefly some of the views which teachers hold. We are indebted for the basic classification to Units 9 and 10 of an Open University Course 'Educational Studies' E202. If you can get hold of this course book it will repay much re-reading.

The dimensions of teachers' views

The dimensions come directly from the Open University course book. The comments which illuminate each are from teachers with whom we have spoken.

1 Definition of the teacher's role

a) **authoritative role . . . no distinct role**

"I rue the day when most of these parents were allowed into schools. They don't know what they are talking about when it comes to education."

"Well, I see my job as . . . more or less the parent in the classroom. I don't think there's much that I do which couldn't be done by anyone else."

b) **curriculum . . . method**

"I don't care how, but by the end of this term I'm going to make sure these children know everything they have to know."

"The skills of history are just so important. We've spent years teaching children facts. How they do it is so important."

c) **narrow . . . wide**

"This 'caring' thing is all a bit of nonsense, really. We can't be expected to do that. Let's just teach them what we have to."

"Caring's not nonsense at all. Education is about the whole child. How can we ignore that?"

d) **high teacher control . . . low teacher control**

"To find two classes like that in the same school was amazing. In Mrs L's class no one could move without her permission. She literally moved her eyelids to let them go out to lunch. In Mrs M 's class they just seemed to know when it was time, packed their things away and went out."

e) **universalism . . . particularism**

"I know some people make excuses, but I don't. They've all got to achieve the same things as far as I am concerned."

"It's not surprising that William underachieves. Just look at the background he has had."

f) **product . . . process**

"They got twenty out of twenty in the maths test I've just given them. I'm really pleased."

"Yes, that's good. But how were they working things out? Was there anything interesting or unusual?"

2   *Conceptualising pupil action*

a) **childhood continuous . . . childhood unique**

"It seems to me that we have to prepare children as soon as possible for the world of work. There's no getting away from it."

"Young children just aren't ready to be treated like miniature adults. They need things arranging especially for them."

b) **pessimistic . . . optimistic theories of human nature**

"Look, if we let children stay in at lunchtime, you know what will happen. They'll wreck the place."

"If we give them the responsibility they won't. They enjoy taking responsibility and being trusted. You know that."

3   *Conceptualising knowledge*

a) **objective knowledge . . . personal knowledge tied to particular purpose or culture**

"There are certain facts about the first World War. That's what we ought to teach."

"I disagree. Children ought to be thinking about their own responses

and why different people behaved as they did."

b) **hierarchical structure . . . little hierarchy**

"At least with maths schemes what they have to learn is ordered for you. It's all there, done for you."

"That's why so many children have difficulties. Who says you have to learn this before that, anyway? Lots of children come to school with all sorts of understandings we just ignore. They're not in any order at all."

c) **discipline-bound . . . general**

"All this topic work is just flim-flam. Why can't we get back to history and geography as separate lessons?"

"All through my secondary school I never realised that so much of the geography we were doing had an effect upon our history, too. Look at the Norman Invasion, for example. Why weren't history and geography brought together? It would have made much more sense."

4   *Conceptualising learning*

a) **collective . . . individual**

"One of the advantages of working in groups is that the children can share what they are doing. They learn from and stimulate each other."

"Well, I don't think they should talk. It might not be their work and it has got to be all their own work, hasn't it?"

b) **extrinsic . . . intrinsic motivation**

"The only way I can get my class to

learn anything is to promise them a test on Friday. It's the only thing which works."

"The trouble is, children only learn when the interest really comes from inside them. That's when learning really takes place."

c) learning by hearing about . . . learning by doing

"What's the point of all this doing? If I want them to know something I tell them. Simple."

"Doing things is so important for young children. They can't abstract very well and doing it makes it mean so much more to them."

5 Preferred techniques

a) imperative mode of control . . . reliance based on personal appeals

"If you are not ready by the time I count to ten then we'll all stay in at playtime."

"Look, how often do you see me do that? What happened last week when Susan did it to you? You were upset, weren't you?"

b) class tests . . . assessment compared to past performance

"It's not good enough. Only six out of ten is below the pass mark. See me later."

"Well done, Billy. Really good this week. A big improvement on your last piece of work. Keep it up!"

The range of views we have highlighted is not comprehensive and you will certainly be able to think of others we might have included. This doesn't matter at the moment. Neither does your own agreement or disagreement with the views expressed.

What does matter is to illuminate and acknowledge the range of views which does exist and within which and from which children's learning and schools have to be organised and managed.

Teachers are not a uniform group of people who all think the same, although many management 'techniques' seem to assume that they are. The differences are not only between individual teachers, either; often they are within individual teachers. It might seem easy to create groupings of views which seem to hold together. Resist the temptation. There is little evidence that our views are logically coherent.

What is important is that we understand the views of those with whom we work. This understanding is another important component in effective management.

2.6 Other Perspectives

The previous section gave a flavour of the range of teacher perspectives and underlined the importance of understanding the perspectives of those with whom you work.

The working group of those who manage classrooms or schools is not restricted to teachers, however, and it is equally important that you work towards understanding as much as possible the perspectives held by all the others who are likely to influence the working of the school.

This is a large group. It comprises at least:

- children
- supply teachers
- ancillary helpers
- midday supervisors
- support staff (psychologists, doctors, etc.)
- administrative staff
- parents
- governors
- visitors
- LEA officers
- councillors
- neighbours
- community officials
- PTA committee members.

Each group, and each individual within each group, shares the same breadth of perspectives we saw teachers sharing. (Not the same perspectives, of course, but the same breadth.)

So, midday supervisors are no more an homogenous group than are teachers. You will probably be aware of that through talking and listening to those with whom you work; it is the extent of that breadth of points of view which needs exploring and understanding.

Teaching involves as much human interaction as any other job you care to name. Each action you take or decision you make in your classroom and school will ultimately be filtered through, interpreted by and acted upon by others. Understanding the perspectives of others enables us to:

- make decisions about which actions are likely to be successful or unsuccessful
- reveal the 'backstage' work which needs to be undertaken with groups or individuals before action takes place
- present what we have to say or what we want to do appropriately to different audiences
- respect as honestly held the views of those with whom we work (even though we might not be in agreement)
- reduce the level of tension inspired by surprise opposition
- challenge the views we hold by presenting opposing attitudes
- help develop teamwork and collegiality by accepting the validity of others' viewpoints.

Each of the groups, and each member of the groups, will have their own super-ordinate and sub-ordinate constructs, near zones and far zones, too. So, of all the points of view we come to understand, some of them will matter far more than others to their holders.

In other words, if you ask a midday supervisor for a view about history teaching in the primary school you will probably receive one. This doesn't mean that the particular view expressed ranks in importance in the mind of the midday supervisor with the level of disciplinary back-up available at lunchtime. You need to be able to assess the weighting of the perspectives you gather.

Look back to the groups listed above. Ask yourself what you think is of importance to them. How do you know? Does this apply to the particular group with whom you work, since this is the group of greatest importance to you?

Listen carefully to members of each of those groups over the next month. If you have time, jot down views which agree and views which are contradictory within each group. Continue to gather as much evidence as you can.

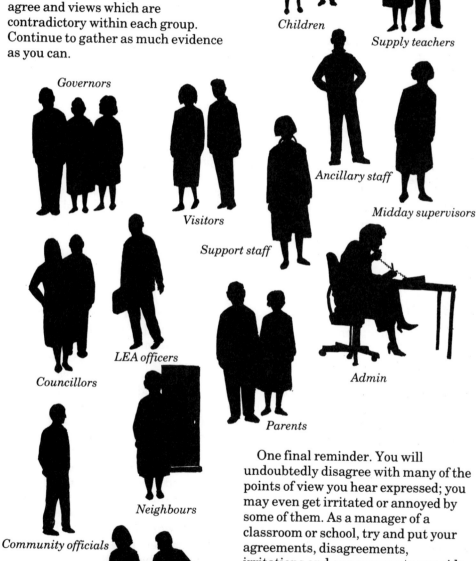

Children

Supply teachers

Governors

Ancillary staff

Midday supervisors

Visitors

Support staff

Councillors

LEA officers

Admin

Parents

Neighbours

Community officials

PTA Committee members

One final reminder. You will undoubtedly disagree with many of the points of view you hear expressed; you may even get irritated or annoyed by some of them. As a manager of a classroom or school, try and put your agreements, disagreements, irritations and annoyances to one side. They are not the issue.

What is important is that you both understand and accept these points of view as being important in defining the context within which you have to work and, therefore, manage.

2.7 Dealing with Differences

Differences of opinion and attitude are inevitable in schools. All organisations have them. Organisations such as schools are particularly open to differences since so much of what they do is, at the very least, problematic. The first sections of this book have considered some of the perspectives teachers and others hold toward schools and education. The variety is enormous. So you are going to have differences within and between colleagues, parents, governors and children.

Dealing with differences, sorting them out, co-ordinating them is one of management's main tasks. We can carry out this task in two ways, by creating situations in which the number of differences is reduced and by dealing with those which remain.

Reducing the Differences

1   Treat differences as inevitable

The only way that differences won't occur in your school is if you pretend that they don't exist. Some differences will certainly be solved if you turn a blind eye, but others will simply grow worse and worse.

Becoming irritated about differences is equally unrewarding however. Anyone who tries to sort out a quarrel by displaying their own irritation at it is likely to either make the original quarrel worse or transfer its focus onto themselves.

Treating differences as inevitable should enable us to stay calmer about them, to be more able to think carefully about the situation which has caused them and what action we can take to help solve them.

It will also provide a good model from which children in your school can learn. There is little point conducting five assemblies each week on the theme of 'The world is full of differences' and then becoming obviously irritated each time they occur in your own school. Actions speak louder than words.

2   Treat differences differently

Not all differences have the same importance as each other. Their importance is often connected to the situation in which they occur and the perspectives of those involved.

December in primary schools often seems to bring out a rash of differences which are forgotten by January, but two teachers of conflicting styles and personalities working next to each other in an open-plan school may require more significant handling than the after-school sherry provided following the infant carol service.

We need to be sensitive to the level of importance differences have for the participants and for the school.

3   Reduce the likelihood of differences happening

Though differences are inevitable, some can certainly be avoided. School policies and job descriptions (well-negotiated) are good tools for allowing people to know what is expected of them and where they stand. They can't neutralise every difference but they can forestall the development of many common differences in schools.

Good interviewing can prevent differences occurring for years ahead. Allowing candidates to find out whether they really want to work in your school, and assessing their character and abilities to make sure they will contribute to team building rather than team disintegration, are both positive steps towards reducing differences.

4 Create an atmosphere in which differences are accepted

One of the key things leaders appear to do is to create atmospheres. If, as a leader, you want to work in a classroom or school where differences are both tolerated and dealt with properly then you have to take some of the responsibility for creating the situation within which that can happen.

Ways of doing this include:

- always discussing differences with children and colleagues
- showing delight in the appreciation of different arguments
- genuinely valuing the different contributions colleagues and children make
- revealing strengths and weaknesses in your own personality
- setting up structures and meetings in the school where differences can be revealed formally.

Whichever route you take, schools are about more than telling people things. At a quite profound level differences are fundamental to the educational process. Schools should reflect this.

Dealing with those which remain

1 Identify the problem

Don't try and solve differences unless you are sure of the problem. As with analysing your school, analysing differences requires sufficient evidence for a decision to be made. Insufficient evidence will exacerbate the problem. Gather as much evidence as you can before you step in to help.

Differences may be due to

- personal problems
- staleness
- significant disagreements
- lack of understanding
- disappointments
- insecurity

2 Negotiate between the parties

Negotiation is a very difficult skill and there are no hard and fast rules despite the large amount of research which has taken place in the last few years. Nevertheless, there is reasonable agreement that all negotiators need

- to be as neutral as possible. Differences are unlikely to be resolved if one party feels out of favour with the negotiator
- to understand and present the case relating to each of the different arguments as fully as possible. Nothing should be omitted
- to present solutions which are viable. Solutions which clearly won't work increase rather than decrease differences and reduce the status of the negotiator who suggested them
- to know that those who hold the differences are willing for agreement to be reached. Agreements which are rejected as soon as the meeting is over are useless
- to have a strategy which enables a logical, understandable and fair sequence of events to take place during the negotiation.

A negotiating strategy

There is no perfect negotiating strategy and, because those involved in the negotiations may behave less than calmly occasionally, negotiators may have to temporarily abandon any strategy they have. Nevertheless, certain factors seem to be useful.

1 Try and create as little other tension as possible. The room setting, introductory remarks, tone of voice are all important.
2 Allow each party to state its case uninterrupted. Repeat and confirm each case when both parties have finished speaking.
3 Iron out different interpretations of the facts.

4 Identify those areas where agreement is most likely and try to achieve this early on.
5 Introduce the notion of compromise for the remaining, and most difficult, issues. Like differences themselves, compromise is almost inevitable. Use real examples of compromise in action.
6 Try to ensure that one party's compromise is met by another from the other side. Don't allow one party to do all the work.
7 Agree on what has been agreed. Both parties must be clear about what has been agreed and what hasn't. If they aren't, the agreement is unlikely to last.

3 SCHOOLS AS ORGANISATIONS

3.1 *Introducing some Basic Concepts of Organisation*

Schools are organisations. As such many of the ideas developed by organisational theorists can be usefully applied to schools to help us understand them. However, there are two cautionary notes to sound: first, there is a bewildering array of concepts so we need to be selective; second, most organisational concepts are derived from institutions other than primary schools so we need to think about applicability. The following concepts, therefore, have been selected because they are applicable. The concepts are first outlined in a general sense, though we have chosen to raise them as questions in order to provoke the reader into applying them. Second, we have also tried to apply the concepts to primary schools specifically.

Basic organisational concepts

1 *Objectives*
What are the aims of the organisation? Why is it there? What is the organisation planning to do?

Any organisation has aims, intentions, expectations and, perhaps, a mission.

2 *Structure*
What are the roles, responsibilities, tasks and duties of the members? How are communications organised? How are tasks coordinated? How are decisions taken? Who works with whom?

3 *Leadership*
Who provides leadership? Who 'gets things going'? Who has responsibility and offers direction?

4 *Power*
Who has authority to do things? Who uses power positively or negatively? Who has overt and/or covert influence? Is the informal power network matched/mismatched with the formal power network?

5 *Culture*
Each organisation has its own culture. Culture is determined by the organisation's underlying beliefs and values. What are the core values of your organisation? What are the ways of doing things which are taken for granted?

Some organisations have a single culture, others have several sub-cultures; organisations can be mono-cultural or multi-cultural.

6 *Environmental relationships*
Any organisation exists in an environment. To what extent does the environment affect the organisation? What links does the organisation have with the environment?

Applying these concepts to primary schools

1 Objectives

What is the school trying to achieve? Curriculum aims and statements of interest to parents in brochures, prospectuses, etc. often provide insight into a school's objectives. However, another concern arises in respect of the extent to which these aims are shared, both within the school and between the school and groups 'outside' it (for example parents, governors, the community).

2 Structures

Primary schools are full of structures: class groupings of children, teams/departments of teachers, staffing quotas, responsibility posts (for example incentive allowances, curriculum posts), timetables, meetings, roles of ancillary and secretarial staff. The list could go on and on. However, one important feature of primary school structure is to consider those structures which are determined externally (for example salary scales, admission and leaving ages) and those decided internally (for example allocation of allowance posts, use of time, meetings).

3 Leadership

Usually leadership is visible in respect of the roles of the headteacher, deputy head, coordinators and/or allowance postholders. But recent studies (Nias et al. 1989) suggest that leadership is also exercised by secretaries, ancillaries, individual teachers. The chairperson of governors may also exercise leadership.

4 Power

Power in primary schools might be located in many persons. Formal and informal power might underpin any of the aforementioned leaders. Similarly, authority (which is legitimate power) might stem from an individual's expertise (in art, music, science or with reception infants) or experience (through long acquaintance with the school, age group, or profession). Even from this brief outline power can be seen to be, potentially, widely and differentially distributed. Of course, the principal source of power in a primary school is usually the headteacher.

5 Culture

A primary school's culture is an amalgamation of social, moral and academic values. How do staff and children relate to one another? What are the values which define these relationships (for example courtesy, care, consideration, competition, individuality, mutual dependence)? What is considered right and proper (for example helpfulness, winning, cooperation, respect for others, single-mindedness)? What are the beliefs upon which the academic curriculum is based (group work, individualised programmes, subjects, cross-curricular projects)?

The answers to these questions begin to map out a school's culture (see also pp. 40–42).

6 Environmental Relationships

All primary schools are affected by their contexts. The context relates to:

- school type: infant, junior, JMI, first, lower, Church of England, County, Roman Catholic, Community

- catchment area: eg. the area from which the children are drawn – rural, suburban, urban; housing conditions; socio-economic factors

- the LEA: eg. policies and procedures of the Local Education Authority in respect, for example, of LMS and its formulae; curriculum policies; school inspections and reviews; teacher appraisal; support agencies and groups; admissions; suspensions; special needs

- school governors: eg. their expectations, involvement, ambitions and general views and means of working with the school

- central government (and its agencies): statutory policies in respect of National Curriculum Council, Schools Examination and Assessment Council, Employment Law, rules of School Governors.

We have expanded on some of these concepts elsewhere in the book: leadership pp. 51–56; culture p. 40–42; environmental contexts pp. 43–44.

If you would like to follow-up any of the ideas introduced here we suggest the following texts as useful starting points:

T Bush *Theories of Educational Management* (Harper & Row, London, 1986)

C Handy *Understanding Organisations* Second edition (Penguin Books, London, 1981)

D J Pugh, D J Hickson & C R Hinings *Writers on Organisations* Third edition (Penguin Books, London, 1983)

3.2 Types of Organisation

Organisational theorists have promoted many ideas for examining and understanding organisations. However, we felt it might be best to look at some of the factors which most directly affect the nature of any particular primary school. We have chosen to look at the following factors.

1 Hierarchy

All primary schools are hierarchical. There is always a headteacher and staff either teaching or non-teaching – usually both. In all but the smallest schools there are deputy heads and in medium sized and larger schools there are staff with specified responsibilities and incentive allowances. Some schools will be very hierarchical, others will be more collegial.

2 Size

A factor relating to hierarchy is school size. Hierarchies tend to be more pronounced the larger the school. Moreover, with larger schools the presence of structure also tends to increase. Large schools have departments, teams, coordinators, etc.

School size is a big factor and, in common parlance, there are really only three types of school – small, medium and large.

3 Design

School design plays a major role in affecting the type of organisation. Two obvious school types are cellular (for example, enclosed classrooms) and open-plan (for example, open teaching spaces or bays). However, the effects of having or not having any of the following appears to influence the school as an organisation:

- split site
- corridors
- dining hall
- assembly hall
- gymnasium
- sinks
- headteacher's office
- staffroom
- temporary classrooms
- community use
- specialist areas

4 Designation

The title of the school is very important; nursery, infant, junior, JMI, primary, middle (deemed primary) denominational (either controlled or aided), community. One or more of these will have a considerable impact on the school as an organisation.

5 Culture

The ways of doing things in a school which are taken for granted affect how the school 'works' (see pp. 38–40). Culture is often a product of history, the building and patterns of interaction. Culture also reminds us that what matters most in a school is how *people* relate to one another. Schools have a subjective, interpersonal dimension.

6 Cohesion

This refers to the extent to which people and policies work together. Any primary school, even a small one, is really an amalgam of many parts. The extent to which these parts cohere or fragment indicates the extent to which the school is a whole or not (see Southworth, 1987).

As a result of these factors a school might be described as:

ST. ELSEWHERE C. of E. (Aided) Community Primary School. A large, open-plan school with collegial relationships which occupies a single site. The building is modern and purpose-built. The staff work together in a collaborative culture and ensure that all programmes of work are congruent with the whole school's policies.

Sounds too good to be true! In effect what St. Elsewhere really shows is that a primary school is a mix and blend of a number of factors and concepts. Consequently, when we describe a school we are already classifying it as some type of organisation, but the *type* rests on the precise placement of the school along a series of continua:

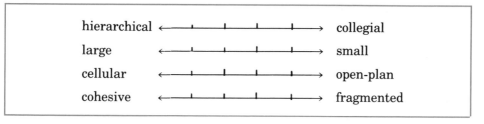

Thus to recognise a school's type we need first to plot it on each continuum and then look at the profile. To illustrate this we have done this for two schools:

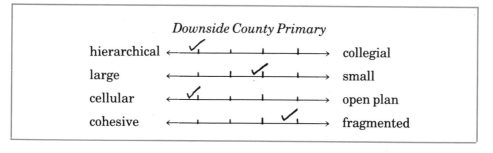

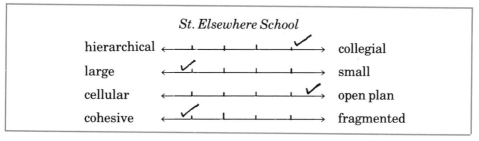

Thinking about primary schools as organisations

Before looking at basic concepts of organisation and school types we need to ask, "What is an organisation?" Rather than answer this ourselves we have drawn on Reid, Bullock & Howarth (1988) who have also attempted to answer the question. They show that primary schools are organisations, that we need to treat with care some of the concepts organisationalists use, and that primary schools have some specific differences from other kinds of organisation. These ideas will be taken up on some of the following pages.

3.3 Organisational Culture

What is organisational culture?

Here are two attempts at defining organisational culture.

> Culture is an informal understanding of the 'way we do things around here.' The elements of culture are shared values and beliefs, rituals and ceremonies and an informal network of storytellers, spies and gossip.
>
> (Deal & Kennedy, 1983)
>
> Central to the concept of culture is the idea of value, that which is regarded as worthwhile by members of some group. These values are manifest in the norms which govern behaviour and the symbols – language, actions, artefacts – which express these values. Thus in a school with an academic culture there will be norms which emphasise academic endeavour perhaps symbolised through dress, honours boards, staff qualifications etc.
>
> (Hoyle, 1986)

It can be seen from these two quotations that culture is about values which are both implicit and explicit to the school.

What makes a culture?

Obviously people make a culture, but culture is really the way people interact. Interactions are affected by several things.

1 Buildings
They affect how staff interact and work together. Temporary classrooms, split sites, corridors, halls, staffrooms, cellular classrooms, open-plan areas – all of these influence how staff meet and what opportunities they have to learn about each other.

2 Coordination
Arrangements to coordinate the work of staff affect the culture. By deciding how far headteachers want to coordinate the work of colleagues they are affecting the extent and nature of formal interaction.

3 Social events and incidents
The ways in which staff interact socially have a bearing upon the general ways in which they 'work' together. Over a period of time patterns can be detected which are frequently highly stable. Social encounters are concentrated at playtimes, lunch-times, and before and after school. Therefore, who meets with whom, when and where are matters which might reveal patterns.

4 History
A school's history and traditions affect and often explain behaviour. Things we have tried in the past, crises we have survived, adversity we have overcome, all have an influence on the way we do things now.
Traditions are most visible at

Christmas but also at other times of the year (for example, May Day, Fayres, Easter and other festivals, Sports Day, charity events).

5   Rituals and ceremonies
Often these are linked to eating and drinking: staff meals, cakes (for birthdays or saying thank you), glasses of wine, tea and coffee arrangements, going to the pub.

School assemblies are significant events – often when the unity and community of the school is implicitly celebrated.

Leave-takings and farewells (to staff moving on or retiring) are also important ceremonies.

How do you find out about culture?

It takes time to find out about a school's culture, not least because it is often implicit. However, newcomers often 'blunder' into the culture and are most sensitive to it because they and the culture are strange to one another.

Culture can be seen through in-jokes, mottoes, sayings, stories about the school's past, the values which are celebrated in assemblies, and what staff say to each other (see Nias, Southworth & Yeomans, 1989).

Nevertheless, culture is difficult to see since it is both a process and product. You may be interested to look at some of the exercises suggested by Pollard & Tann (1987), which provide useful ways of looking and thinking about culture. The best way is to try to observe one's own school's culture.

Why is culture important?

Two responses might serve as answers to this. First, since culture is to do with values, it is important to try and discern what a school's culture is since the values which underpin the culture are likely to affect not only how the staff behave but also the children. Although the connection between culture and curriculum is likely to be indirect, children will nevertheless learn things from the school's culture (for example, how adults relate to each other; consideration and courtesy).

Second, there is a belief that when a school's culture is strong and positive this will contribute to the effectiveness of the school. Mortimore et al. (1988) say: 'an effective school has a positive ethos. Overall, we found the atmosphere to be more pleasant in the effective schools.'

This is also supported by Deal (1985) who has devised a chart comparing the characteristics of effective schools with strong organisational cultures. Deal's chart is shown overleaf.

Characteristics of Effective Schools	Characteristics of Strong Organisational Cultures
Coherent ethos with agreed-upon ways of doing things: agreement on instructional goals	Strong culture with shared values and a consensus on "how we do things around here"
Importance of principal as leader	Importance of principal as hero or heroine who embodies core values or who anoints other heroic figures
Strong beliefs about teaching and learning	Widely shared beliefs reflected in distinctive practices or rituals
Teachers as role models: students with positions of responsibility	Employees as situational heroes or heroines who represent core values
Staff training on schoolwide basis	Rituals of acculturation and cultural renewal
Effective meetings to plan jointly and solve problems	Potent rituals to celebrate and transform core values
Orderly atmosphere without rigidity, guilt without oppression	Balance between innovation and tradition, autonomy and authority
Joint participation in technical decision making	Widespread participation in cultural rituals

Finally, culture also shows us that although schools can be structured and planned it is how the people inside them interact together and what they value and believe, which really makes the place distinctive and alive. Schools are organisations full of people, not robots. Schools are value-laden places.

Every school exists in an environment. Environment can be thought of in terms of *level*: the macro level which is common to all schools, and the micro level which is more closely linked to the individual school. Factors which affect the environment include:

Macro level:
Department of Education and Science (DES), National Curriculum Council (NCC), Schools Examination and Assessment Council (SEAC), central government legislation, teachers' salaries, unions and associations, H.M. Inspectors

Micro level:
School's catchment and local community, policies of LEA, school site and buildings, community use and involvements, governors.

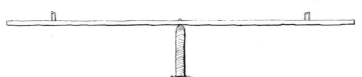

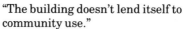

A school is, in part, influenced by the environment in which it is situated. This is most obvious in terms of the micro context. Individual governors may affect the school's aims; fundraising schemes and PTA/PA support generate greater or lesser financial help. Thus, staff are usually well aware of the micro context:

"Our parents are very keen to support us."

"The governors are closely involved in the work of the school."

"The building doesn't lend itself to community use."

"The LEA has emphasised the importance of nursery education for a long time."

This awareness is possibly because staff perceive themselves as able to affect the micro level. The constituents of the micro level are things we know, people we meet, groups we can contact and negotiate with. By comparison, the macro level is much more remote.

Two things are interesting about the environmental context. The first is the way in which each school is a product of both levels. For example, staffing quotas will be determined by LEA policies whilst, at the same time, salaries and allowances are determined at the macro level. Any school is a blend of macro and micro environmental contexts. Since schools have greater opportunity to 'negotiate' with the micro level, schools might also be able to affect, and in a sense manage, the environment in which they exist. The section on External Relations (pp. 206–219) picks up this theme with its attention to school image, and 'selling' the school. Second, the context is always changing. At the micro level this might be the influx of 'new' parents because of housing developments, because of alterations in LEA policies or changes in national policies. Indeed, schools are most likely to be most sensitive to the environment when it is changing.

Turbulent environment

The 1980s were a time of considerable environmental change. The 1980, 1981, 1986 and 1988 Education Acts show just how turbulent the macro level became. Moreover, the turbulence was made greater because each of these Acts altered the micro context, especially in respect of school governance and accountabilities and the role of the LEA (see Sallis 1988).

Turbulent environments make life more difficult for those inside the school. For one thing staff cannot focus purely on the internal organisation – they must also be alert to the external. This dual focus is something headteachers have had to develop.

However, headteachers are not unique in having to remain alert to the school and its context. Most managers in most organisations also have to do so. What headteachers (and others) need to recognise as a result of the 1980s, is that the post-1988 period makes it imperative that they are as knowledgeable about and as sensitive to the environment as possible. Headteachers work at the interface of the school and its environmental context. While, previously, headteachers needed only to manage the environment in a token way, today they need to see the school's environmental context as one of their main arenas of activity.

4 KEY MANAGEMENT ISSUES

4.1 Ancillary Staff

In recent years there has been an increasing emphasis on the need for primary schools to function as *whole* schools. Usually this has caused headteachers and deputy heads to consider issues of coordination or continuity, while many schools have worked hard to improve staff communication and to increase the amount of teacher collaboration. Although much valuable work has taken place, the bulk of the work appears to have either emphasised or been aimed at *teachers*. Therefore, while in many schools teachers have become less independent and more collaborative, there may also have been an underemphasis, perhaps even an underestimation, of the roles and responsibilities of ancillary staff. If whole schools are to be a reality we need to think seriously about how all staff – both teachers and ancillaries – work together.

Who are ancillary staff?

Naming these people is something of a problem because their titles sometimes vary from LEA to LEA. We list below some of the more common titles (with alternatives in brackets):

- school secretary (clerical assistant)
- welfare assistants (non-teaching assistants)
- Section 11 assistants (dealing with ethnic minorities; mother tongue teaching; EFL)
- caretakers (school keeper/cleaner-in-charge)
- cleaners
- midday supervisors (midday assistants/dinner ladies)
- kitchen staff (cook, meals staff)
- National Nursery Education Board Assistants (NNEB assistants).

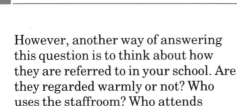

However, another way of answering this question is to think about how they are referred to in your school. Are they regarded warmly or not? Who uses the staffroom? Who attends meetings? How many teachers do they talk to? How do the children regard them? How has the school kept them informed about recent changes and developments? Does the caretaker know about LMS, for example? Which of these individuals are *naturally* regarded as members of staff and which (if any) are perhaps marginalised?

How are they involved in the school?

One thing seems quite obvious from looking at this list of ancillary staff: they undertake a range of tasks and make very significant contributions to the work of the teachers, the children's work and the life of the school as a whole. One way of illustrating this is to list just some examples of what these individuals actually do:

- act as receptionist/telephonist/ typist (secretaries/ancillary assistants)
- manage school finances and funds (secretaries)
- control stock and paper resources (ancillary assistants)
- provide classroom support (ancillary/NNEB assistants)
- work with individual children (ancillary/NNEB assistants/midday supervisors)
- support children with special educational needs (ancillary/NNEB assistants/midday supervisors)
- deal with behaviour problems (ancillary/NNEB assistants/midday supervisors/kitchen staff).

And these are only a few examples! In fact, what emerges from drawing up such a list is the realisation that all these ancillary staff deal with children. For example, all will have important conversations with children, and in this way the adults will affect the children's language development because all these adults play a part, albeit 'informally', in the school's language curriculum. Yet how far has the school involved these important members of staff in the planning, implementation, review and development of the language curriculum? Questions like this need to be asked for all aspects of the curriculum, especially social, moral and personal education. How, for example, do ancillary staff influence the school's policies on equal opportunities?

Some schools ignore such staff altogether; this seems to be unsound management. Some schools involve such staff very well; we know of schools where caretakers, secretaries and ancillaries take part in staff meetings and/or attend regular meetings with the headteacher and deputy; schools where welfare assistants for children with special educational needs are offered regular meetings to talk about their work and how they feel they and the children are getting on; schools where ancillary staff are offered in-service and development activities.

Looking forward

When schools undertake development plans (see pp. 143–148) they need to think about how to make best use of the ancillary staff. When schools look forward they need to try to embrace *all* the staff. That is fairly obvious but what about how their roles and responsibilities might change? Two things come to mind here.

First, over the last 15 years the 'number' of ancillary staff in schools has generally increased: either in terms of the numbers of persons in school or the amounts of time in school. There are now more midday supervisors, Section 11 assistants,, welfare helpers (especially for children with special educational needs). In acknowledging that there has been an increase in ancillary support, we are not saying whether this is sufficient or adequate – only that there are more today than there used to be yesterday! However, we also believe that this increase will continue. As LMS is applied to more and more schools we anticipate that some schools will expand their ancillary staff force. In which case it becomes even more imperative that they are fully integrated into the life of the school and perform roles which truly support the intentions of the school.

Secondly, LMS is likely to affect the work of secretaries quite significantly. During the 1990s school secretaries will become, in part at least, *bursars*. Of course they will need help in this – they may also need to work longer (paid!) hours. Also, since some LMS schemes rely on computerised programmes, secretaries will need to be increasingly familiar with information technology. For some secretaries this will be a dramatic change.

Moreover, if secretaries are to spend more time as bursars, who will take on their typing or receptionist work? They surely cannot be expected to absorb all the 'new' work while continuing with all their previous work. Thus the secretary's new role will have implications for others.

A final point to bear in mind when thinking about ancillary staff concerns the fact that they are often part-time workers – present on site for only a part of each day or week. Some will not see others because they are never present at the same time. Some may not see the headteacher or deputy head if their timetables never coincide. In a sense, one challenge for schools is to try to ensure that part-time workers *feel* they are full members of staff.

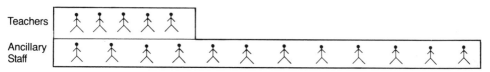

Relative numbers of teachers and ancillary staff in a typical primary school

4.2 Teacher Appraisal

The formal appraisal of teachers, on a widespread scale, has been a relatively recent development in education. While some individual schools have operated appraisal schemes for several years, it was not until the Department of Education and Science commissioned pilot work in teacher appraisal in 1987 that LEAs became involved. Prior to this activity appraisal tended to be informal and covert. With the government requiring all LEAs to introduce appraisal schemes from September 1989 appraisal has the opportunity to become more formal, open and systematic.

Although each LEA will have adopted a scheme best suited to its perceived needs and preferences, there are certain principles, aims and elements which schools need to keep in mind and, from time to time, apply to their own practices and the LEA's.

Basic Principles

a) Teacher appraisal is on-going. It is a continuous process, not an isolated (even if regularly-repeated) event. Teacher appraisal is not 'hit and run'.

b) Teacher appraisal is only a part of staff development (see pp. 116–118); it is neither the whole of staff development nor a substitute for it.

c) Teacher appraisal should make a positive difference to each teacher's classroom practice. Although appraisal will review other aspects of a teacher's work, appraisal should affect for the better teaching and learning in the school.

d) Teacher appraisal should be a supportive process for *all* teachers.

Appraisal is not simply for those whose performance is deemed to be poor; appraisal should also help the creative, imaginative and gifted teachers.

e) Teacher appraisal should be 'two way': it should benefit the school and the individual.

f) Resource implications should be reviewed periodically. Local Education Authority Training Grant Schemes, LMS, INSET and time spent on the process of appraisal should all be given full consideration and synchronised so as to facilitate the best possible approach to teacher appraisal and staff development.

Aims of teacher appraisal

Different schemes may have differing aims but the following might be common to many schemes. They are offered since it may be helpful to compare them against those adopted by the school. Appraisal should seek to:

a) help teachers develop as teachers and as professionals;

b) encourage teachers to engage in self-appraisal and in the discussion of their work;

c) enable teachers to know how they are doing;

d) .clarify the teacher's responsibilities and tasks in the light of present and changing circumstances;

e) identify the support the teacher may need inside and beyond the school.

Key elements of an appraisal process

(N.B. The sequence of these elements is, at best, notional and not prescribed.)

Preparation: appraisal should not be a surprise event. Prior to a teacher's appraisal there should be a rather informal (but not casual) meeting to discuss the appraisal process. A time schedule and specific focus might be agreed and a review reflecting upon the previous appraisal shared.

Job descriptions: appraisal should be related to the teacher's job description which, in turn, must be fully negotiated, understood and agreed in detail by both appraisee and appraiser. The job description is effectively a working document and should be a tool for considering teachers' responsibilities in their various tasks (curricular, managerial, pastoral, etc.).

Classroom observation: there is a clear need to observe the teacher's work in the classroom. Suitable times for observation should be mutually agreed. More than a single session and activity should be observed (see pp. 176–181).

Self-appraisal: teachers should undertake a review of the period since the last appraisal. Using an agreed approach (for example, checklist, prompt list) successes, failures, developments and disappointments could be itemised prior to discussion with the appraiser.

Initial review discussion: some days before the appraisal discussion an agenda for this discussion should be agreed and any relevant notes exchanged (for example, the appraiser could receive the teacher's self-appraisal; the teacher might receive the appraiser's review of the same period and classroom observation notes).

The appraisal discussion or interview: a time for formalised sharing of points of view, information, hopes, aspirations, expectations and targets for the future (see pp. 116– 118).

The appraisal report: this should be produced by the appraiser and be a concise summary of the appraisal discussion based upon notes taken during the discussion.

Follow-up: there is a need to check that agreed actions do happen and for the appraiser to ensure that individual teachers' professional development takes place.

Some further questions which each scheme and perhaps school will need to answer:

- Who appraises whom?
- How frequently should each individual teacher be appraised?
- How much classroom observation should take place?
- Are there any special circumstances to take into account (for example, children with special needs, critical incidents in the teacher's life)?

- What happens if judgements cannot be mutually agreed?
- What happens to the report?
- How long is the shelf life of a teacher's record?

Appraisal is not a guaranteed method of improving relationships, abilities, self-esteem or the health of your school. There is a real danger that education will follow sections of industry in believing that the existence of an appraisal scheme is enough in itself and that, once set up, the scheme will be self-running and self-determining.

Unfortunately, nothing could be further from the truth. The problems involved in talking with colleagues about strengths and weaknesses, about making classroom visits, about being the appraiser without apparently ever being the appraisee, about linking promotion and the allocation of posts with appraisal interviews and so on are enormous.

There is some evidence which indicates that in the majority of cases where appraisal has been introduced in organisations performance, relationships and self-confidence have all taken a dive.

If education is to avoid this, then both those conducting the appraisal and those being appraised need to work out beforehand exactly what is going to happen and need to feel confident that the theoretical benefits of appraisal have at least a chance of materialising in the real day-to-day life of their schools.

Those conducting the appraisal need to be particularly self-critical. An appraisal is – and should be – more than a friendly chat, but it requires skill and understanding to operate successfully. It requires the understanding of all participants, crucial abilities in the appraisers and a process which is clear to all.

So, don't take appraisal for granted. Organised effectively within your school it *can* bring dramatic improvements. However, it will only be effective if the process of appraisal is itself continually appraised.

A considerable number of studies have been conducted into leadership. Consequently there is no shortage of analyses and theories which attempt to portray what leaders do, what makes some leaders more effective than others and which factors influence leaders. Leadership has been studied in commercial and industrial organisations as well as education; we can all benefit from this research.

The key elements

Let's look at six key elements:

- leaders provide structures
- leaders need to be considerate
- leaders affect the way decisions are taken
- leaders provide an example
- leaders work in particular contexts
- leaders provide their organisation with a mission.

1 Leaders provide structures

Strucures are the basic organisational building blocks of your school. When we act as leaders in schools we set up structures. For example, there are timetables, communication networks and the organisation of colleagues and children into various groups.

Timetables can set up structures concerning the use of space – particularly shared space such as halls or specialist areas.

Communication networks relate to staff meetings, curriculum working parties, record keeping, liaison meetings, community links and so on.

Structures for staff and children mean the setting up of class groups, allocation of teachers to classes, teaching teams, departments, use of specialist and support staff such as ancillaries, peripatetic teachers and special needs staff.

Those of us who act as leaders (and that will almost certainly be all of us at one time or another) are involved in

- providing structures
- maintaining structures
- re-designing structures
- adapting structures.

2 Leaders need to be considerate

Being considerate is a necessary quality of leadership but consideration is not a simple once-and-for-all quality. Being considerate means that we understand the views and attitudes of those with whom we have to work.

If we accept that people are different then the consideration we show them needs to be different. For example, if someone wants to be involved in decision-making, it may not be considerate to tell them exactly what to do. If someone is by nature hierarchical, asking them to take part in the process of each and every decision may be counter-productive.

By considering each individual and trying to understand their perspectives and by considering each situation we stand a good chance of improving motivation and commitment to the work and life of the school.

As leaders we also need an understanding of individual circumstances. People can be affected by bereavement, illness, family crises and so on. At such times it's not a good idea to ask a teacher to help you run three nights' rehearsals for the school play!

Whatever leadership role you have, it is quite usual for that role to be observed and commented on by colleagues. If you show consideration, fairness and understanding it will be noticed.

3 Leaders affect the way decisions are made

'Centralised' and 'de-centralised' decision making depends very much on the way a leader chooses to delegate or structure the process. The diagram below sets this out graphically.

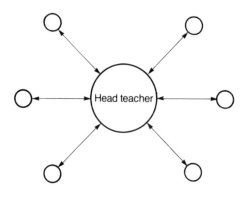

Centralised

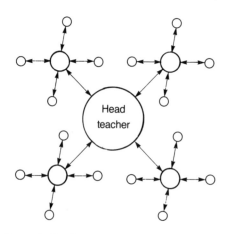

De-centralised

You may choose to lead in a centralised or de-centralised way as a result of

- your own personality
- the needs of the particular situation.

When you examine your own leadership style try and make sure that you don't delude yourself into thinking you've made a decision based on the second when really it's the first! Centralised or de-centralised styles of leadership do have a lot to do with who you are but they must also have something to do with the demands of each particular situation.

4 Leaders provide an example

In every facet of school life – in teaching, in policy-making, in pastoral work – leaders set an example. Depending on the point of view of those working with you, the example you set may be a positive or negative one. Over time and through a whole series of issues and decisions a balanced judgement may be forthcoming. No one is going to be viewed positively all the time; in the end, it's the consensus opinion that counts.

Setting an example is complex. It can involve a whole host of personal qualities as well as professional ones. So energy, delegation, trust, consideration, personal organisation, dealing with differences, handling disputes, sense of humour, and temperament can all play a part!

5 Leaders work in particular contexts

As leaders affect schools, so schools affect leaders. To be head of a small, rural school in a purpose-built, modern building with supportive parents and energetic staff is different from being head of a large, inner-city school in a dilapidated, vandalised building with disaffected parents and a staff whose morale is depressed.

But there is more to context than the buildings and the parents. Other contextual factors include

- the way priorities are decided
- the private and professional relationships among the staff
- the resources available to the school
- the level of staff development
- the effectiveness of the headteacher
- the level of support from the LEA.

The context affects the work of all leaders in schools. From time to time leaders need to assess how their *present* context is affecting their work as well as how *they* are affecting the context.

6　Leaders provide their organisation with a mission

Mission means establishing a sense of direction, a feeling of going somewhere, of aiming at something. Mission does not imply a military exactness nor a religious fervour. Rather, it is commonly agreed that leaders have a vision of how they would like to see the school working, and use this vision or mission to stimulate other teachers, parents, children and governors.

4.4 *Leadership – 2*

One consequence of a leader's work and responsibility is to remain self-critical. If leadership is concerned with six key elements (see pp. 51) it is also necessary for the leader to keep these dimensions under review.

The following questions are aimed at headteachers as leaders. They might also serve to suggest similar questions for deputy heads and curriculum leaders.

Questions for headteachers to ask themselves

It may also be helpful for headteachers to keep a detailed diary for a given period, say a fortnight, and then to ask themselves the following questions:

1 Time

a) How often did I
   - go into classes on one day
   - greet children and parents at the beginning or end of the school day
   - work with children?

b) What time did I give to meeting staff individually and in groups?

c)i) How much time did I spend out of school:
   - at County Hall/Town Hall etc.
   - at divisional meetings
   - at other schools
   - at conferences or in service courses
   - elsewhere?

  ii) Was this time:
   - necessary
   - useful to the school or LEA?

d) How much time did I spend on administration and meetings in and out of school hours?

e) How much time did I give to visitors including parents, governors, inspectors and LEA officers?

f) Do I need to try to change the time distribution revealed by answers to the above questions?

2 Objectives and organisation

a) What do I see as the priorities for the school in the next term/year/five years?

b) Do I know to what extent my view is shared by others?

c) What constraints exist?

d) Are any organisational changes desirable or necessary?

e) Which areas of the curriculum need attention and who can give this attention?

f) How do I ensure that resources are distributed in a balanced way to sustain current priorities and support new developments?

3 Internal relations

a) How available am I – formally and informally?

b)i) What steps do I take to ensure that the staff feel that I am interested in their professional development, advancement and personal welfare?

  ii) When, for example, did I last speak to:
   - a part-time teacher
   - a cleaner
   - a member of the non-teaching staff
   - a new teacher?

c)i) How satisfied am I that postholders are able to influence their colleagues in the area for which they have responsibility?

ii) How could their influence be extended?

d) How accurate is my awareness of the load carried by different individual teachers:
  - throughout the working day
  - in voluntary activities
  - in helping children and colleagues?

e) How accurate is my awareness of the load carried by non-teaching staff?

4 External relations

a) What is the first impact of the school on visitors?

b) Do I know what impression is given to telephone callers?

c) Have I satisfied myself that parents from all ethnic groups know to whom they can turn for help and that it will be forthcoming?

d) Are relationships with governors positive and fruitful? Do I keep them fully informed about developments in the school?

e) Have I sufficient knowledge of the LEA administrative structure and inspectors to ensure the school is properly supported?

f) Do I make good use of the Education Welfare Service and the Schools' Psychological Service?

g) Do I make good professional and personal relationships with:
  - local primary school headteachers
  - nearby secondary school headteachers
  - principals of local colleges of further and higher education?

h) Do I know, and am I known by:
  - local community leaders
  - police and welfare agencies
  - local shopkeepers
  - neighbours of the school?

i) Do parents feel at ease with me? How do I know?

5 General

a) Do I listen without interrupting when people are talking to me about what is important to them, however pressed I am for time?

b) Am I ready to learn from other people and other institutions?

c) Do I praise and thank people whenever they deserve it?

d) Do I know myself well enough to be able to make important decisions or judgements when I am under stress?

e) Do staff and children know what I feel strongly about in matters of curriculum, organisation and personal relationships?

f) In spite of everything, do I still find being a headteacher exciting?

6 The future

a) Are we clear about what we have been trying to do? How far are we meeting those intentions?

b) What are the priorities for action:
  - next term
  - in the coming year?

c) Who will initiate this action?

d) Do we need any outside support and advice? If so, what?

Ironically, leadership is not always defined by doing things. It is just as important to *be* someone and for the perception of what you are to be shared by those you are responsible for leading. If those you are leading don't carry around with them a perception of your capacity to lead as well as a perception of your willingness just to act then it is unlikely that your leadership will be as effective as it could be.

The ways in which such perceptions of leaders are created is difficult to define. One of the benefits of 'management by walking about' is that it enables those who depend on your leadership to see you engaging in informal as well as formal leadership, of allowing your own views, attitudes and aspirations to emerge in day-to-day life. It gives everyone a chance to see that the practice matches with the theory.

Finally, your effective leadership of others is defined as much in *their* perceptions of your leadership as it is in your own. The questions in this chapter are important in helping you consider the effectiveness of your leadership. Early on in the book we talked of the huge importance of understanding the range of perceptions carried by those around us. Try to make sure that the answers you give to these questions are not simply your own but include the honest responses of others, too. No good leader should become a victim of their own imagination!

4.5 Headteachers and Children

That the role of headteacher in a school is changing is not open to doubt. Headteachers in primary schools are responsible for an increasing number of administrative and management tasks; the contents of a book such as this indicate how much has changed in recent years.

The influence of a headteacher on a school is a powerful one, constantly referred to in descriptions of good or bad schools. That influence extends to the curriculum offered to children, the organisational systems, the public reputation, inter-staff relationships and much more.

It also extends to the children in a more direct way; while a class teacher is often the central adult in each child's school day, the headteacher can exert powerful influences for good or ill upon many children.

Many headteachers enjoy contact with children and wish to retain some of their previous role as class teachers where possible. The dilemma for many is that increased administration and management reduce the amount of time available for working with and being available to children. What options are open to headteachers who want to continue this part of their job for as long as possible?

1 Class teaching

Some headteachers in smaller primary schools have either a full-time or part-time responsibility for a class as a part of their job. For others, teaching classes for a limited period of time during their week, either as a timetabled activity or as an emergency stopgap is both alluring and frustrating. The advantages are:

- it guarantees the headteacher a reasonable amount of non-interference

- it allows some contact with children
- it enables some sort of teaching practice to be maintained.

The disadvantages are:

- the short time span doesn't allow headteachers to work with a class in the way they would like
- it is difficult to get to know many children
- working with one class often means that there isn't time to work with others
- lack of time for preparation.

2 Visiting classrooms

Most headteachers visit classrooms informally and many use classroom visits as a way of analysing the strengths and weaknesses of a part of the organisation. The advantages of regular, informal or semi-formal visits to classrooms by headteachers are:

- it enables all children to see the headteacher each week
- it enables the headteacher to value positive work by children within the class setting
- it enables the headteacher and children to work together within the normal organisation of the class
- it enables the headteacher to communicate important messages about teaching and learning within the flow of a normal day.

The disadvantages are:

- such visits can become so quick and insignificant that many children hardly notice they have happened
- the headteacher concentrates on talking to the teacher or examining poor plumbing
- the headteacher makes comments to children which are not based on a deep understanding of particular circumstances.

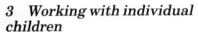

3 Working with individual children

Many headteachers work with individual children in or outside a classroom or within the headteacher's office. Most of these children are either very able or unable. The advantages are:

- good relationships can be built up with a few children
- specific extra help can be given to children who might not otherwise receive it.

The disadvantages are:

- relatively few children are seen each week
- it is time-consuming as a way of involving the headteacher with children
- it may be better for such children to be seen in groups rather than individually
- other children can perceive the visits as favouritism.

4 Receiving visits from children

It is not uncommon for some headteachers to operate an open-door policy which allows children to visit them (or to be 'sent' by teachers) at will. The advantages are:

- the headteacher often sees children who have made particular advances or who have behaved or performed disappointingly
- given the right circumstances, the visits can be motivational for children
- the headteacher provides another opportunity for children to talk confidentially about problems or difficulties.

The disadvantages are:

- sometimes it is inappropriate to see children, who may be disappointed.

A specified time during the week for this sort of visit might help

- the open-door can be manipulated by some children
- it is time-consuming
- headteachers do not always see a full range of children (in terms of abilities, development or motivation).

5 Lunch and mid-morning breaks

Headteachers often share the playground and other rotas with colleagues on the staff. The advantages are:

- the headteacher is able to see a large number of children
- the children are seen in another non-class context by the headteacher
- the headteacher can talk informally to many children
- the headteacher can help to use his/ her position to reinforce good relationships.

The disadvantage is:

- the headteacher might not always be able to guarantee regular rota-time.

6 Clubs and extra-curricular activities

Clubs and extra-curricular activities provide a good way of getting to know some children in greater depth. Apart from the specific focus of the activity this is often the reason class teachers find them appealing (although, of course, pressures of time and the debate about teachers' professionalism have curtailed many extra-curricular activities). The advantages which apply to class teachers also apply to headteachers. At the present time, though, many headteachers find it difficult to commit themselves to a regular extra-curricular involvement with children.

7 Walking about

There is a well-respected theory of management called 'management by walking about'. For headteachers thinking about their involvement with children, it means taking every opportunity, however slight, to work with children somewhere in the school, formally or informally. The advantage is:

- it enables the headteacher to develop a high profile amongst children.

The disadvantages are:

- the randomness doesn't guarantee that the headteacher works with or meets different children

- at various times during the term the opportunities for walkabout may be more limited than others.

Like most things in this book, no one approach is likely to be wholly satisfactory and headteachers will have to choose a number of approaches which compensate for each other and which fit in with the general context of the school.

Notwithstanding the increased administrative and managerial load of headteachers we remain committed to the view that a headteacher who is isolated is no longer one in any understandable use of the term. Contact with children is not only fundamentally important to many headteachers as individuals but it should also remain a necessary part of the job, until such time as schools are run by managing directors.

4.6 Collegial Schools

Since the 1978 Primary Survey by HM Inspectors, teachers have been urged to ensure that the curriculum is coordinated, continuous and coherent. To achieve this staff have been encouraged to take on curriculum coordinating roles. At the same time the school-as-an-organisation should enable healthy communication, consultation and collaboration. Consequently there are two interdependent and simultaneous management tasks. When both tasks are effectively managed and accomplished it is claimed that the school will not only develop but also become a *collegial school*.

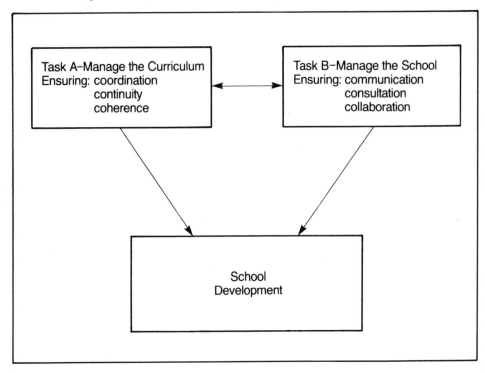

The contemporary image of good practice has been promoted by the Inspectorate since 1978 . . . It is of the 'collegial' primary school, predicated on the two values of *teacher collaboration* and *subject expertise* . . . The image itself . . . shows small working groups of teachers reporting back recommendations for school-wide change to the collectivity of the whole staff meeting for decision-taking. These groups are led and organised by the curriculum postholders, who draw upon expertise from outside school as well as upon their own professional knowledge, in order to enable the staff to develop the curriculum as authoritatively as possible. Occasionally the postholder works alongside class teachers to illustrate ideas in practice, and to become aware of progress throughout the school. The skills involved in these processes are not only academic; considerable sensitivity, personal enthusiasm and charm are required in order to maintain good working relationships in schools where professional practice is being subjected to the scrutiny of colleagues. The teachers involved become used to tolerating uncertainty and working under pressure of time and conflicting demands. Supporting this collaborative effort is the headteacher who has committed himself or herself to devolving responsibility to the staff group; servicing their activities by putting appropriate school facilities, and where possible his or her time, at their disposal.

The image also shows an atmosphere, ethos or climate distinctive to collegiality. The teachers exist in a school in which constructive and critical scrutiny of each other's practice and ideas is the normal expectation. There is a continuing commitment to professional development through in-service activities both within the school and outside it. Although the teachers are not insensitive to the implications of such involvement for their own career prospects, the major focus of in-service training is the whole school, and there is an open understanding that teachers will feed back into school implications they see for their colleagues of off-site in-service courses. The ethos is not created simply by encouraging teachers to feel solidarity with one another, but by deliberate strategies that make role expectations explicit to all staff, and by the head's involvement in school-based development in practical and supportive ways that do not undermine the authority of teachers with special expertise. The overt commitment to evaluate their initiative collectively accustoms the teachers to giving accounts to each other of the reasons and justifications for particular approaches to the curriculum, and so helps them to anticipate representing

their subject or subject area to people outside the school . . . The school thus becomes collectively accountable for its curruculum. The teachers committed to collegiality see the atmosphere in the school as the element most critical to its maintenance, and derive strong personal and professional satisfactions from their involvement in, and contribution to, its continuance. They see the creation and maintenance of such an atmosphere as the responsibility not just of the headteacher, but of the whole staff group. Collegiality will survive the departure of the head.

(Campbell, 1985, pp. 152–53)

In each school the head and staff have agreed aims relating to the academic work and the children's personal and social development. A shared sense of purpose was most evident . . . the schools had curricular guidelines . . . and these had been written after staff discussions at meetings led by one teacher or a small group of teachers able to offer informed advice on the particular aspect of the curriculum. . . . A number of the schools were exploring ways of deploying the staff so that more effective use was made of their abilities and curricular strengths. Their aim was to ensure in all classes that the responsibility for coordinating the work of the class would remain with the class teacher . . . (whilst at the same time) some teachers in these schools were acting effectively as consultants by helping to plan the work and prepare teaching materials . . . In this way the schools were making positive efforts to strike the delicate balance which is involved in making the best use of the curricular expertise of a primary school as a combined teaching unit.

(HM Inspectors, 1987, pp. 31–32)

Collegial schools need a number of key ingredients:

- a general and widespread agreement on aims and purposes
- a headteacher willing to devolve much decision-making to the staff group
- specialist expertise whereby teachers, in turn, can act as adviser and advised
- reasonably harmonious relationships so that discussion and differences can be handled without acrimony and alienation
- a school culture which supports professional and social collaboration.

Where one or more of these ingredients is lacking a school may not be ready for collegiality.

Some advantages of collegial schools are as follows:

- more people make more of the decisions; consequently staff feel more involved and more committed to making the decisions work
- people feel they know more (rather than less) about what is going on; the best practice of each teacher can spread and influence the work of others

- opportunities for teacher development can be increased
- teachers feel less isolated and more supported
- the headteacher's role is enhanced and enriched through the contributions of others.

Some of the disadvantages of collegial schools are:

- headteachers often feel they still need to hold the right of veto over staff decisions
- meetings can be very time-consuming
- small schools may not have sufficient expertise to cater for the whole curriculum
- generating staff cohesion in respect of aims, practice and philosophy can take a long time.

Collegiality is also useful because it demonstrates how primary school management is intertwined with curriculum management and development. Maybe whether a school is collegial or not is relatively unimportant compared to the fundamental question, 'How is the school and curriculum managed so that *everyone* feels involved, challenged and developed?'

4.7 Collaboration and Consensus

Notions of collegiality and effective school management require high levels of staff collaboration, but collaboration neither guarantees consensus nor is it necessarily a 'good thing'. We have highlighted four points which need to be considered when staff collaborate and when consensus is sought.

1 Collaboration takes time

Collaboration is not simply a matter of putting staff together and hoping they will 'get on with it'. Recent work into primary school staff relationships suggests that in order for staff to work together there needs to be a culture of collaboration; that is, a culture in the school which facilitates openness, and a sense of security. This culture takes time to develop.

Also, staff collaboration implicitly means working together in groups and Handy (1981) has shown that groups take time to develop:

Groups mature and develop. Like individuals they have a fairly clearly defined growth cycle. This has been categorised as having four successive stages:

1 Forming. The group is not yet a group but a set of individuals. This stage is characterised by talk about the purpose of the group. The definition and the title of the group, its composition, leadership pattern, and life span. At this stage, too, each individual tends to want to establish his personal identity within the group, make some individual impression.

2 Storming. Most groups go through a conflict stage when the preliminary, and often false, consensus on purposes, on leadership and other roles, on norms of work and behaviour, is challenged and re-established. At this stage a lot of personal agendas are revealed and a certain amount of interpersonal hostility is generated. If successfully handled this period of storming leads to a new and more realistic setting of objectives, procedures and norms. This stage is particularly important for testing the norms of trust in the group.

3 Norming. The group needs to establish norms and practices: when and how it should work, how it should take decisions, what type of behaviour, what level of work, what degree of openness, trust and confidence is appropriate. At this stage there will be a lot of tentative experimentation by individuals to test the temperature of the group and to measure the appropriate level of commitment.

4 Performing. Only when the three previous stages have been successfully completed will the group be at full maturity and be able to be fully and sensibly productive. Some kind of performance will be achieved at all stages of development but it is likely to be impeded by the other processes of growth and by individual agendas. In many periodic committees the leadership issue, or the objective and purpose of the group, are recurring topics that crop up in every meeting in some form or other, seriously hindering the true work of the group.

(Handy, 1981, pp. 160–161)

Clearly, collaboration involves a lengthy process of development. It is not a way of operating which, from the outset, is necessarily 'productive' or 'efficient'.

2 Collaboration relies upon effective group work

'Productivity' and 'efficiency' can be greatly enhanced by groups being well managed and led. Some of the ways of managing groups are outlined in the section covering meetings (see pp. 130–139). One way of beginning to improve group dynamics is to attempt to rate how effective groups are in one's own school or workplace. There are two obvious ways forward.

First, one might canvas staff opinion about meetings. This should be done face-to-face and informally. It is not difficult to suggest some of the questions to address:

- Do our meetings go on too long?
- Is our cycle or pattern of meetings appropriate (for example, weekly, monthly)?
- Is the group size appropriate?
- How might we improve our meetings?
- Do we say what we really think?

Secondly, one could use a systematic approach (see the chart opposite).

3   *Differences need to be faced*

Consensus does not occur because staff collaborate. Talking collectively about what you do and would like to do means that differences (in aims, methods and approach) will be identified. Collaboration can lead to conflict just as easily as consensus. As Handy's stages of group development show, it is important that differences are worked through and worked out. Whilst not always comfortable, done well it is usually constructive.

If differences are not worked out they don't go away, they go underground – creating more long-term difficulties than will ever occur in the working-out stage.

One way of avoiding the negative excesses of both concealed differences and unfettered frankness is to ensure that the social and informal aspects of school life are well tended. For example, the state of the staffroom matters. Comfortable chairs, decent coffee- and tea-making facilities, a sense of order and attention do contribute not only to making the room pleasant but also to staff feeling they actually want to spend time in there and thus with each other. No one wants to stay long in a room which is untidy, where the coffee cups are chipped and where the furniture is uncomfortable. It may seem trivial to spotlight such things as food, drink and chairs but research shows that these things are actually very important. These are practical ways of improving the climate in which staff collaborate. Moreover, the more staff talk about their personal lives, the easier it often is to talk about professional concerns (see Nias, Southworth & Yeoman, 1989).

4   *Consensus or consent?*

Let us suppose, then, that the staff as a group are:

- well formed and mature, at Handy's performing stage
- formally and informally cohesive, spending time with each other
- well led, being effectively managed and economical with time
- sharing and airing differences in a constructive, creative way
- working in a school where there is a culture of collaboration.

Even in such schools (and some do exist! see Nias et al. 1989) *consensus* is not always present. Consensus means full agreement, something close to unanimity. We have stressed throughout the book that unanimity amongst teachers is going to be impossible; a staffroom comprises different human beings concerned at different personal and professional levels about a range of uncertain educational and non-educational issues.

To wait for consensus in such a

Rating group effectiveness

A: Goals

poor		good
confused; diverse; conflicting; indifferent; little interest	1 2 3 4 5 6 7 8 9 10	clear to all; shared by all; all care about the goals; feel involved

B: Participation

poor		good
few dominate; some passive; some not listened to; several talk at once or interrupt	1 2 3 4 5 6 7 8 9 10	all get in; all are really listened to

C: Feelings

poor		good
unexpected; ignored or criticised	1 2 3 4 5 6 7 8 9 10	freely expressed; emphatic responses

D: Diagnosis of group problems

poor		good
jump directly to remedial proposals; treat symptoms rather than basic causes	1 2 3 4 5 6 7 8 9 10	when problems arise the situation is carefully diagnosed before action is proposed; remedies attack basic causes

E: Leadership

poor		good
group needs for leadership not met; group depends too much on single person or on a few persons	1 2 3 4 5 6 7 8 9 10	as needs for leadership arise various members meet them ('distributed leadership'); anyone feels free to volunteer as they see a group need

F: Decisions

poor		good
needed decisions don't get made; decision made by part of group; others uncommitted	1 2 3 4 5 6 7 8 9 10	consensus sought and tested; deviates appreciated and used to improve decision; decisions when made are fully supported

G: Trust

poor		good
members distrust one another; are polite, careful, closed, guarded; they listen superficially but inwardly reject what others say; are afraid to criticise or to be criticised	1 2 3 4 5 6 7 8 9 10	members trust one another; they reveal to group what they would be reluctant to expose to others; they respect and use the responses they get; they can freely express negative reactions without fearing reprisal

H: Creativity and growth

poor		good
members and group in a rut; operate routinely; persons stereotyped and rigid in in their roles; no progress	1 2 3 4 5 6 7 8 9 10	group flexible; seeks new and better ways; individuals changing and growing; creative; individually supported

From Schein, *Process Consultation*, 1969

situation could mean waiting forever; we might never make any changes at all. What is needed is consent. The cohesion we aim for in a school should be aimed at developing the willingness to go along with a proposal, to give it a good try as openly as possible.

Management, remember, is often concerned with being 'as good as possible' rather than ideally perfect.

Work towards consensus but accept consent. Consensus is idealism; consent is realism.

4.8 *The Development Cycle*

Whilst the phrase 'school development' sounds simple, it in fact labels a complex set of activities involving many key processes (see Holly & Southworth, 1989):

- leadership
- self-evaluation
- teaching and learning
- curriculum development
- INSET
- management development
- school culture and climate
- school development plans

Another way of thinking about school development is to conceive of it as *learning*. A developing school is a *learning school*; it is a school which learns by looking inward and by encouraging others, usually outside the school, to help. Yet, this learning needs to occur at different levels:

- the children's learning
- teacher development, i.e. their individual learning
- staff development, the learning of the staff as a group
- the school, all who constitute 'the school'
- the headteacher, his/her learning.

It is possible for learning at all of these levels to occur simultaneously as this diagram shows:

THE CYCLE OF SCHOOL-BASED IMPROVEMENT THROUGH SELF-EVALUATION

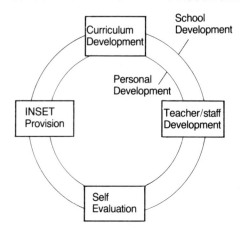

The inside line represents an individual's learning, the outside line represents the school's development. The two need to 'track' each other, first because there can be no school development without individual teacher development, and second because there can be no school development unless the teacher's individual development is coordinated with the school's development plans.

However, although it is useful to conceive of development in terms of levels, tracks and key processes, we also need to remember the complexity. Complexity occurs because of two things:

- *scale*: developing a school involves many aspects of a school, as the notions of level and key processes show
- *interrelationships*: development is not only to do with ensuring that learning occurs at different levels or that a series of individual processes are performed well; development needs *all* of these levels and processes to interrelate

so that they interpenetrate and mutually reinforce each other.

Hence development begins to look like this diagram:

THE DEVELOPING SCHOOL

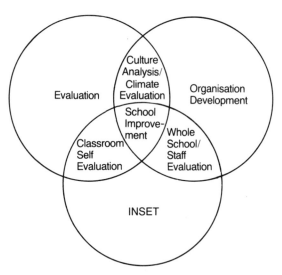

This diagram groups the key processes into three major but overlapping areas: *evaluation, INSET* and *organisation development.*

Evaluation is concerned with reviewing, monitoring, questioning, problem-seeking activities which teachers and others need to undertake to begin to learn about

- the school's culture
- the school's climate
- teaching and learning
- classrooms
- teacher development

Organisation development occurs when answers are sought to some of the problems revealed through evaluation. Hence the school as an organisation might seek to improve the culture, the climate, staff development and curriculum plans. Consequently organisation development includes

- curriculum development
- management development
- leadership
- development plans
- teacher appraisal

INSET concerns all the practical activities, workshops, courses, discussions and reflections which facilitate teacher, headteacher and staff development.

The diagram also demonstrates that school improvement only occurs when all of these processes are arranged in such a way that they not only interrelate but interpenetrate. They support and construct the conditions which will nourish development of the school. By inference the diagram suggests that while it is possible for all of these activities to be taking place in schools (and we would say that they do take place), it is not only the presence of the processes that matters; it is that they are also managed and coordinated in order that the *configuration of these processes* enables the school as a unit to develop.

4.9 Principles of Change

Everything in this book is relevant to the change process. The following principles have been selected because they are the major issues to focus on. We have chosen to highlight six principles.

Principle 1: Assess the situation; identify the change

The key questions are:

- How are we doing?
- Where are we?
- Where do we want to be?
- How do we get there?

Asking these questions individually and collectively can unlock many perspectives (see pp. 23–31), generate calls for change and, crucially, provide a mandate for change. Assessing and identifying change needs to boost motivation:

- staff need to perceive the need for change and feel a responsibility for implementing and sharing in change
- cooperation of staff needs to be gained; a sense of consent (see pp. 63–65) is needed
- communications need to be two-way and on-going
- there is a need for those involved to see benefits for themselves as well as for the school.

(adapted from Day, Johnston & Whitaker, 1985)

Principle 2: Expect and accept resistance

Despite every effort being made to enlist support for the change and for staff to be motivated to make changes one must always expect resistance.

Resistance can come in many forms, not all of them being hostile; inertia, passivity and tokenism are just three kinds of 'resistance'. Another is 'innovation without change'.

> Organisations are dynamically conservative: that is to say, they fight like mad to remain the same. Only when an organisation cannot repel, ignore, contain or transform the threat, it responds to it. But the characteristic is that of least change: nominal or token change.
>
> (Schon, 1971, Reith Lecture)

Principle 3: Change must be managed

Although change can be unplanned and accidental, for whole school change to occur it must be managed. 'It is a prime management task to plan, support and monitor the innovation process, but not necessarily to initiate it.' (Day, Johnston & Whitaker, 1985, p. 109).

The management of change is rather too often seen as the sole task of headteachers; we would dissent from this. Headteachers have a role to play in planning, supporting and monitoring change. They can also initiate change. But they should also involve others and enable others to initiate change. Otherwise, the first principle becomes, over time, progressively more difficult.

Managing change is really a series of procedures:

Procedures in the management of change

1 Assess the situation (people, resources, constraints). For example, you may approach or be approached informally by individuals, or 'hear' a need voiced during a staff meeting, or initiate a staff meeting yourself.

2 Identify an area of concern (general or specific). The realisation that there is a need for change may come through listening to staff and being aware of their thoughts, needs and relationships. If not, the ground has to be prepared for change. This will include planning how and when to implement change.

3 Communicate the concern informally to:
   (a) Headteacher/deputy headteacher.
   (b) Staff colleagues.
   (c) Other involved people e.g. parents/ancillaries.

4 Meet formally with colleagues to:
   (a) Identify the specifics of the problem(s).
   (b) Clarify issues.
   (c) Generate discussion of new ideas.
   (d) Decide on group aims and specific strategies: consensus-seeking; joint formulation of valid alternative strategies, leading to establishment of priorities and agreed deadlines.
   (e) Decide on ways of monitoring the implementation of the plan.

   } Negotiation of meanings

5 Implementation of the plan (with back-up provided, e.g. time, resources).

6 Revision of plan in the light of experience (a recognition that the logic of planning and the logic of action may not match).

7 Reflective appraisal of the effectiveness and new planning if appropriate.

   } Flexibility as a criterion of action

8 Consolidation of new pattern/plan.

9 Long-term evaluation.

Principle 4: Leadership is crucial

At times of change leadership is much more visible than at times of stability. Whoever leads the change needs to be aware that their role is crucial to the success of the innovation.

The leader needs to

- act as manager of the change and follow steps one to nine in the diagram above

- provide adequate levels of support – both psychological and material
- offer (or be able to draw on) practical help
- keep the implementation plan going and on schedule

- apply pressure if complacency, inertia or avoidance begin to surface
- recognise small, incremental changes as the building blocks of major change and praise and advertise these changes to those who have made them and to all other involved parties.

Principle 5: Relationships change

Changing things changes things! We must expect

- people to experience frustration, worry, doubt, perplexity, confusion, uncertainty, achievement, success, clarity
- relationships to alter as different colleagues individually experience different feelings.
- to deal with colleagues' feelings

The leader must be prepared to respond to these, although not always. While support is essential it has also been argued that in order for change to be successfully implemented there is a need for pressure (M Fullan 'Change Processes and Strategies at the Local Level' *The Elementary School Journal* 1985, Vol. 85, No. 3, pp. 391–421). What one wants to avoid is both too much pressure (that is, stress) and too little (that is, no need to change!)

Principle 6: Change is small and modest

Too often change is perceived as sweeping, wholesale and overwhelming. Far too much curriculum change has been seen as grandiose and spectacular. As such, what has been overlooked is the fact that most people only make long journeys in short steps: that major change is really the by-product of lots of little changes.

In order for any change to be successful it needs to be broken down into smaller, component parts which are more modest, more manageable and *doable*.

> . . . innovations have nothing to do with some grand design. They have to do with a thousand tiny things done a little bit better.
>
> (Peters and Austin, 1985, p. 201)

4.10 *Implementation*

Over the last 20 years staff in school have become used to formally meeting together and talking. Staff meetings, working parties, conferences and workshops have multiplied as staff have listed their aims, undertaken school self-evaluation and reviews and made plans to change things.

However, a principal characteristic of an effective school is that staff do not only consult and collaborate when planning, they also go on to do something in the light of their deliberations and plans. In short, *talking is not enough: things need to happen.*

How do we make our plans happen?

Making our plans happen is a matter of implementation. So what are the factors which affect implementation? Michael Fullan (1982) has conducted some valuable work in this area and he suggests the following:

> **A Characteristics of the change**
> 1 Need and relevance of the change
> 2 Clarity
> 3 Complexity
> 4 Quality and practicality of the programme
>
> **B Characteristics at LEA level**
> 5 The history of innovative attempts
> 6 The adoption process
> 7 Support and involvement
> 8 Staff development (in-service)
> 9 Evaluation
> 10 Community involvement
>
> **C Characteristics at the school level**
> 11 The headteacher
> 12 Teacher-teacher relations
> 13 Teacher characteristics orientations
>
> **D Characteristics external to the local system**
> 14 Role of Government (eg DES)
> 15 External assistance

Fullan devotes more space to discussing these than we can. However, we will focus on the ones which appear to impinge directly on school-based change.

Need
Unless staff recognise and appreciate the need for the change, implementation will be severely hampered.

Clarity
Clarity about what teachers should do differently should be developed. All too often teachers are not clear as to what the change means in practice.

In agreeing to make classroom changes teachers need to know what the change will look like in classroom terms. Unless this is understood staff have no real means of knowing whether they have successfully introduced the change or not!

Complexity
Many changes involve lots of smaller or supporting changes. Parental involvement in classrooms means: training for parents; prior explanations of curriculum intentions, approaches and processes; follow-up tasks to see how the parents feel; arrangements at playtimes for parents to enjoy the comforts of the staffroom; discussions about confidentiality etc.

Any change should 'be examined in regard to the difficulty, skill required, and extent of alterations in beliefs, teaching strategies and use of materials' (Fullan, 1982, p. 58)

Quality and practicality of the programme

When the change involves the introduction of a new scheme (for example, science materials, reading schemes, maths materials, art activities, etc.) the materials should be

- provided in good time so that staff are familiar with them
- available in sufficient quantities
- of such a quality that they survive the rigours of use with children and are credible to staff.

Obvious as it may seem, lots of changes have foundered because of such basic problems.

Support and involvement

LEA support and involvement can be a major boost to implementation. The interest and advice of LEA staff can be a stimulus and confers status on the change.

Staff development

With the advent of the LEA training grant scheme this characteristic could also be school based. Nevertheless, if change is seen as a learning experience for the adults involved, then staff development will be

necessary. Anticipating both the nature of staff development and its timing and sequencing will be vital to the success of the change.

The headteacher

The headteacher strongly influences the likelihood of change. Projects *actively* supported by the headteacher are likely to do well. Headteachers and staff need to plan *how* the headteacher will be actively involved.

Headteachers need to: join in; help out; offer praise; support at times of setback; release staff; ask questions such as "How are we doing?" and so on.

It is important to note that it is what headteachers *do* that matters, not what they say they will do!

Teacher-teacher relations

Peer support and learning is important. Isolated teachers with no access to colleagues cannot find out from others how to do the change, nor can they talk about the change. Collegiality, trust, open communication, advice, help and morale all affect implementation.

Teacher characteristics and orientations

When staff feel and believe they make a difference to children's performance, changes are more likely to work well. When staff have low expectations of children and/or of the change, these tend to be self-fulfilling prophecies.

Plan implementation; implement the plan

In the light of these characteristics and context-specific variables, staff should work at how to implement the

change. The following diagram suggests a cycle of questions an implementation plan needs to address:

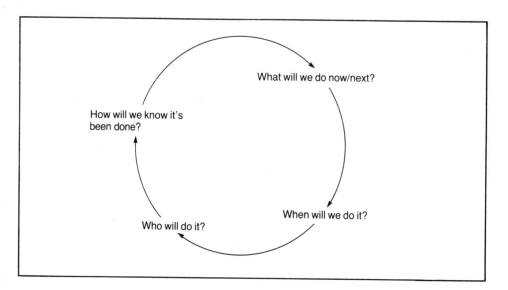

The plan should

- be thorough and careful
- be realistic, especially about time schedules
- include reviews

and then the plan should be put into operation. Once the plan has started, implementation then needs: persistence, energy, a sense of success and direction, and a feeling of getting there. The person leading the change needs to be *visible*, working with their 'sleeves rolled up', touring, talking, making practical adjustments, listening and leading on-the-job reports. Implementation needs energy and is hard work: but when done well it is very rewarding.

4.11 Coordination

Primary class teaching is a difficult and demanding job. Teachers have to

- cater for individual needs
- ensure that class work coheres
- respond to external initiatives
- manage, plan and evaluate the day-to-day work of a class
- be aware of and respond to public perceptions and pressures

among many other things. It is hardly surprising that primary teachers are not omnicompetent and not experts in each area of their professional lives. Given the sheer scale of the task, occasional difficulties are more likely to be natural rather than a sign of incompetence.

Because difficulty is natural, coordinators are needed to offer particular help in designated curriculum or organisational areas. We like the word coordinator. As the House of Commons Select Committee on Primary Education (para 9, 11) said in 1986:

'Coordinator' ... cannot be confused with 'specialist' in the secondary schools sense. It suggests that the person carrying out the role has a positive role to play and does not wait to be asked, as a consultant might. It implies that one works with others rather than on them.

What should coordinators do?

As we have already said, it is too much to expect every teacher to keep up with changes in knowledge and methodology in every field. Each would be helped by having a colleague nearby to turn to for information and help from time to time, and especially so if the roles of adviser and advised could be exchanged on other occasions, i.e. that there was no question of hierarchy.

We envisage that the colleagues giving help should do so in two main ways: by taking the lead in the formulation of a scheme of work; and by helping teachers individually to translate the scheme into classroom practice either through discussion or by helping in the teaching of the children. Much the most frequent method would be discussion. Direct teaching might often take place with the class teacher present, not least so that the class teacher can manage on his or her own next time. But sometimes it might be better to teach the children away from their own teacher because that is easier for the coordinator to manage, or because to do so makes it possible to avoid distraction, or because the class teacher could use the time to do something else. If the teaching is done separately, the class teacher should be responsible for ensuring that the work done fits with the rest of the child's programmes. Linkage with the rest of the programme is what matters, not where the teaching takes place. Children near the end of the primary stage are more likely to need access to additional teachers than those near the beginning.

All of these arrangements occur in primary schools and some have done so for many years ...

Exchanges between class teachers

As we saw in schools, specialist teaching for music and physical education are often arranged by the simple practice of teachers exchanging classes. The critical factor is whether the 'other' teacher can take the music or the PE; what the non-musician or the unfit teachers can do is regarded as less important. They do whatever they can that fits into the time available.

The specialist's class is obviously likely to suffer, particularly if the specialist is required to take every other class in the school, which may amount to more than a quarter of a week for music in an eight class school. This practice cannot be regarded as satisfactory, though it may be unavoidable if every teacher has responsibility for a class. Remedial teaching, work with enrichment groups and the teaching of English as a second language depend on the availability of a teacher not in charge of a class, working either part time or full time. Provisions for these groups or for other children with special educational needs were, we were told, likely to be threatened if the education budget is cut.

The least developed practice is the one that so many witnesses argued for: the coordinator working alongside the class teacher. This practice also requires more teachers than there are registration classes. We accept the arguments that have been put to us for extending the practice and for four reasons: first, it provides an opportunity for in-service training of the class teacher; second, it offers the opportunity to concentrate available teaching skill on the group of children who for the time being require it; third and fourth, because the coordinator will acquire knowledge of what is happening in other classes than his/her own, it should be easier to develop continuity from class to class and to adopt the programme more nearly to the needs of the children and the capacities of the staff.

(House of Commons Select Committee Report, 1986, paras 9.20–9.29)

In short, if class teachers are the weft of curriculum management, coordinators are the warp. Together they weave the fabric of a coherent curriculum (see Holly and Southworth, 1989).

Implications of coordinators

Having sketched the outlines of coordination, it is necessary to note some implications of such an approach. We can see at least four:

1 Coordination is a key task in curriculum management. As such it relies upon teacher collaboration (see pp. 63–65) and may help develop a collegial school (see pp. 60–62).

2 Coordination while aiding the creation of a coherent curriculum will not, by itself, develop a whole school. For whole schools to occur there is a need for further coordination. A key question arises in respect of *who coordinates the coordinators?* We think deputy heads could play a significant part in answering this question.

3 The role of the headteacher is also crucial. There are numerous implications for headteachers in respect of curriculum coordination and the coordinator's role:
   - How much authority and responsibility will the head-teacher delegate?
   - How much support will the headteacher offer coordinators?

- Critically, how much relief will the headteacher offer coordinators in order for them to visit colleagues?
- How much external support (e.g. advisory teachers) INSET time and GRIST funds will the headteacher channel towards coordinators?
- Will the headteacher enable coordinators to *lead* (meetings, workshops, INSET activities)?

4 How will schools utilise *time* to maximise the work of coordinators? LMS, GRIST (the LEA training grant scheme), INSET days, ancillary help, secretarial support, non-contact time, and development plans should all be husbanded and synchronised so that small amounts of time are used to their best effect. Although primary schools do not have lavish staffing levels and thus time is always at a premium, there is no excuse for wasting the precious and very limited amounts that are available.

4.12 Primary Schools and the National Curriculum

The advent of a National Curriculum in 1988–9 heralded many changes. The National Curriculum introduced

- a different way of talking about the curriculum since a new 'language' was devised
- new ways of assessing children, and an emphasis on assessment at certain ages

- a different role for central government and new relationships between schools, the LEA, the DES.

Each of these changes has triggered a number of consequences which are briefly outlined in the next three sections.

A new language

A whole new set of terms was created by the National Curriculum Council (NCC) and the Schools Examination and Assessment Council (SEAC). While teachers were made aware of this language, schools will also have to help others, such as ancillary staff, supply teachers, parents and governors, to become aware of the terms.

New ways of assessing children

Much could be highlighted here but it seems likely that schools will need to look carefully at how they

- informally and formally assess children
- monitor and record children's

progress
- deal with children who enter and/or leave during the school year (especially Travellers' children, and children whose parents are in the armed services).

Different relationships between schools, the LEA and central government

Although LEAs will continue to play a role in the curriculum, schools have rapidly adjusted to the recent arrival of the NCC and SEAC and have begun to become accustomed to the policy statements and advice that these two agencies offer. It is likely that the NCC and SEAC will continue to contact schools directly, informing them of examples of good practice, resources, ways of timetabling and so on. Each school needs to take advantage of this advice while also utilising the help and support of the LEA.

In addition to these consequences there are six others which need to be given serious consideration.

1 Translating and implementing the national curriculum in classrooms

Teachers and headteachers in England and Wales (since a National Curriculum does not affect Scotland at the present time) will have to ensure that the advice of the National Curriculum subject working parties, as finally agreed and recommended by the Secretaries of State, is put into practice. This means

- appraising existing practice to recognise what is already happening in each individual school and whether this practice is in line with the recommendations of successive working parties
- making adjustments, where necessary, to bring practice into congruence with the recommendations of the NCC
- *translating* the recommendations so as to take into account the needs of individual children and the school's individual circumstances.

This applies to the core and foundation subjects plus Religious Education.

2 Time

Each school will need, over the coming years, to monitor how time is devoted to the core and foundation subjects. Where schools work in a cross-curricular, thematic and/or integrated way, schools will need to audit the proportions of time devoted to curricular areas.

Although time accounting will not involve the logging of minutes, individual schools will need to work out

- how to apportion time to curricular activities
- whether timetables are appropriate and to what degree of specificity

- over what periods time should be audited – weekly, fortnightly, monthly, half-termly, termly?

3 New roles

The National Curriculum affects teachers' work to such an extent that headteachers, deputies, and coordinators should spend time thinking about their respective responsibilities. Here are just a few questions which staff ought to address and resolve:

- who will coordinate the school's development plan?
- who will offer advice on implementing subject working party reports?
- who will keep parents and governors informed and involved?
- who will organise school-based in-service work?
- who will lead staff discussions, evaluations, and reviews?
- who will record the school's policies and practices following discussion and decision?
- who will monitor translation and implementation of the NCC's advice?

4 Communication

At times of change communication is vital. Moreover communications should flow in all directions. Each school needs

- to keep alert to information coming from the NCC, SEAC, DES and LEA
- to build a staff library of pertinent leaflets, booklets, materials, videos, policy decisions
- to foster and encourage staff to use the materials and update them
- to ensure that governors are kept informed and involved
- to provide information for parents

- through INSET clusters, pyramids and meetings, to remain alert to what other schools are doing.

5   Children with special educational needs

Each school needs to distinguish how each child with identified special needs should be supported. Also, what allowance, if any, needs to be made in respect of each child's programme of study? In the light of these two questions headteachers will also need to consider how the parents of children with special needs will be kept informed and involved.

6   Children whose first language is not English

These children could be disadvantaged by some aspects of the National Curriculum, particularly during key stage one (but not entirely so). How will schools and LEAs respond to this particular challenge?

A strong emphasis in these points is how each individual school will deal with each of these matters. This is because the National Curriculum affects each and every school, and each school must, to some degree, find its own solutions. Yet, so saying, schools should not feel isolated by this emphasis. Each school should also avail itself of the advice of the LEAs, and their support agencies. Furthermore, much will be learned from schools working together and sharing ideas, responses and solutions. While each school might be responding to the findings of the technology working group, it should not mean that each school is simultaneously reinventing the National Curriculum wheel!

4.13 Special Educational Needs

Definition

The 1981 Education Act tells us:

> A child has special educational needs if he has a learning difficulty which calls for special educational provision to be made for him ... and a child has a learning difficulty if ... he has a significantly greater difficulty in learning than the majority of children of his age.

Who falls into the category

The Warnock Report talked about 20 per cent of pupils coming into the special needs category at any one time. Obviously such definitive statements must be treated cautiously (as the Warnock Report pointed out) but it does highlight the broad nature of special educational needs.

If one in five children may need special educational provision during the course of their school career, we must create at least adequate provision to prevent the problems of this large number of pupils being 'compounded by continuing experiences of failure'.

So the answer to the question is *anyone*. For the majority of children

the help will be temporary and they will receive support relevant to their particular need and then return to mainstream teaching.

For some – Warnock suggested about two per cent – continuing special needs provision will be needed, possibly throughout their school life. For these children the procedure of *statementing* was introduced and is now a familiar part of the management of special educational needs (see below for a detailed explanation).

But before we can begin to try and solve the problems we must identify the child's needs.

Needs identification

Behind the processes used for identification lie *four basic principles:*

1 The approach to identification is essentially optimistic in the sense that where pupils do not learn, there is assumed to be a flaw in what's being offered, not necessarily in the child.
2 A need can only be identified in terms of outcome. Processes of

identification must be formative (including a strategy for future action) as well as summative.
3 The process of identification must take place as early as possible.
4 Identification and appraisal must be a continuous affair, 'so that the child is seen as a changing person for whom there is a continuous monitoring system'.

REFERRAL PROCEDURE

Each school should have its own procedure for referring children so the one set out here is only a model for your consideration. It's based on a large primary school where there is a special area provision which means that children from quite a wide area can be statemented to attend the school and receive specialist help from special needs teachers.

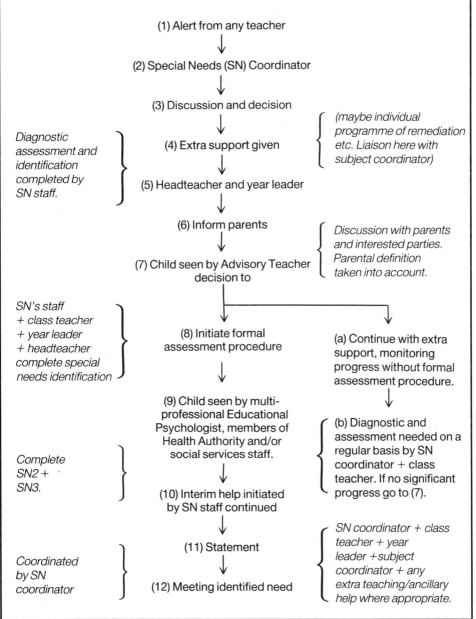

(1) Alert from any teacher

(2) Special Needs (SN) Coordinator

(3) Discussion and decision

Diagnostic assessment and identification completed by SN staff.

(4) Extra support given — *(maybe individual programme of remediation etc. Liaison here with subject coordinator)*

(5) Headteacher and year leader

(6) Inform parents — *Discussion with parents and interested parties. Parental definition taken into account.*

(7) Child seen by Advisory Teacher decision to

SN's staff + class teacher + year leader + headteacher complete special needs identification

(8) Initiate formal assessment procedure

(a) Continue with extra support, monitoring progress without formal assessment procedure.

(9) Child seen by multi-professional Educational Psychologist, members of Health Authority and/or social services staff.

(b) Diagnostic and assessment needed on a regular basis by SN coordinator + class teacher. If no significant progress go to (7).

Complete SN2 + SN3.

(10) Interim help initiated by SN staff continued

(11) Statement

SN coordinator + class teacher + year leader + subject coordinator + any extra teaching/ancillary help where appropriate.

Coordinated by SN coordinator

(12) Meeting identified need

A procedure for assessing and aiding a child with special needs

The following procedures offer a strategy for the identification of a pupil with special needs.

a) Close liaison with other staff who have taught the child.
b) Advice from class teachers. Using the class teacher's professional judgement, and informal testing.
c) Standardised group tests – a screening procedure to be used as a safety net.
d) Assessment materials used by the class teachers. These are the normal curriculum-based resources which should aim at helping the class teacher to design and implement teaching programmes that are matched to each child's special needs. All such assessment should be criterion-referenced with task-analysis including precisely stated objectives.
e) Formal Testing such as:
   i) Miscue Analysis – useful for literacy/reading problems as it is diagnostic and can be used to formulate a strategy for improving certain skills.
   ii) Published Reading Tests – the best are useful both diagnostically and when formal test results are required.
   iii) Published Mathematics Tests – again, those that are diagnostic are the most useful.
   iv) LEA Tests – some have their own testing procedures.

What do you do after assessment?

It is important to realise that the strategies for good practice after assessment must have been described in the assessment. Further strategies should be included as they are an integral part of the testing.

The whole curriculum and educational practice of the school should be flexible enough to cater for individual needs. However, there are three basic procedures which need to be modified and adapted to suit individual needs.

1 If the evaluation of the child's progress indicates they are falling behind their peers in basic academic skills, for example areas of literacy and numeracy, in order to bridge the gap learning should be accelerated. A variety of problem-solving strategies and general skills and concepts should be taught and used in different contexts and situations. This may be done by short-term withdrawal related to the class-year curriculum plus support and extension work in the classroom.

2 The child should be placed 'on the curriculum', identifying skills already learnt and mastered, and so realising skills which still need to be taught. Again the logistics of the teaching should be as above.

3 There should be selection of suitable teaching methods and materials and the correct and appropriate classroom environment must be available for the particular child.

It should be noted that the organisation and teaching strategies for any ancillary help should be coordinated by the special needs staff in collaboration with the class teacher.

What about record keeping?

1 The records and monitoring of progress will be a continuous process throughout the child's school life.

2 The 'records' of children with special educational needs must be kept where both special needs staff and class teachers have access as they will both be contributors to the records.

3 Children with special needs should not have separate records but will require additional information to be added to the standard school record. This information is to be basically the monitoring and mastering of different skills. It will also include the results of any of the formal, informal, and group tests used (see pp. 189–194).

4 Whether or not National Curriculum Attainment targets are appropriate will depend on the child's statement. It is possible for pupils to be exempted on the grounds of special educational needs but this has to be reviewed every six months.

5 Use of checklists and test results to be included in records – but it is useful to remember the limitations of locating pupils on a predetermined ranked checklist of skills. Also, as with any can do/can't do testing, the context-dependent nature of the child's performance must be taken into account when examining results.

6 The video camera is an invaluable tool in record-keeping, particularly as a record of behavioural objectives.

Who is responsible?

'*All teachers* are teachers of children with special needs.'
(Warnock Committee Report)

From this we take it that primary responsibility for the pupils is in the hands of the class teacher. As shown on the referral flow chart the next stage is the *special needs coordinator* whose role includes the following:

1 To provide information and dissemination of any information about special needs children to all staff and to other outside agencies involved, for example parents, support agencies.

2 To provide materials and resources for special needs children throughout the school.

3 To coordinate the curriculum for individual work and general curriculum work with special needs in mind.

4 To coordinate and modify curriculum and curriculum design methodology and teaching materials.

5 To organise school-based in-service work.

6 To liaise with schools, outside agencies, families, etc.

7 To integrate the special needs children into the full life of the school and to provide support and teaching to ensure this comes about.

Also, the *headteacher* has a crucial role in managing special educational needs – particularly in the smaller primary school. It should not be forgotten that an effective special needs policy benefits *all* children in the school. The concern and adequate resourcing provided by the headteacher can make a vital contribution to the success of special educational needs policy in any school.

In the final analysis it is the *governors* who have the ultimate responsibility – this is clearly set out in the 1981 Act. Invariably this is exercised through the headteacher but it is worth remembering that governors should be kept closely informed of special needs policy and the procedures necessary for statementing.

How do special needs fit into the curriculum as a whole?

The following principles are worthy of serious consideration regarding the curriculum and special needs:

1 *Collaboration* towards achieving shared goals. When designing the curriculum, collaboration between special needs staff, subject coordinators and class teachers is essential.

2 The sharing of a *common purpose* between adult and child in curriculum terms usually enables the child to become a much more competent communicator.

3 The *curriculum* for special needs *is the same* as for the rest of the school, not a 'watered-down' version. It should be flexible enough so that it may be adapted or emphasised in areas but essentially it remains a curriculum with real purpose and context.

4 The curriculum is so designed that its real *purpose is obvious to the child* as well as the teacher and it deploys the child's existing strategies as well as introducing new ones.

5 The curriculum is designed so that it deals with conceptual difficulties children encounter. The curriculum for the special needs child should not just try to 'bridge the gap' in certain basic skill areas but should try to *deal with fundamental conceptual difficulties*.

Underpinning all of this is the essential child/parent/teacher relationship. This, combined with other support from outside agencies such as educational psychologists, makes special needs management difficult but very rewarding when we get it right!

Although individual LEAs will place different emphases upon their support agencies in terms of staff and scale of operation, all LEAs offer some kind of support personnel who focus on

- special educational needs
- disruptive pupils
- welfare
- health
- curriculum development
- buildings and maintenance
- non-teaching staff
- school meals
- in-service education and training
- staffing
- early years education
- libraries
- galleries and museums

This list is not exhaustive since the listing of support personnel relies upon some definition of support. We have chosen to take a relatively wide definition at this point because it is important to alert staff and governors of schools to the *range* of support which should be available to them.

So the headteacher and other staff might be involved with

- schools' medical services
- schools' psychological service
- educational welfare officer
- advisory teachers/teams
- teachers' professional development/ curriculum development centres, wardens
- advisers/inspectors
- meals supervisors
- schools' library service
- caretaking and cleaning supervisors
- officers of the LEA's architects' department
- play group/nursery advisers.

You may find it useful to make your own list of support agents.

The first issue which arises from LEA support agencies is one of communication. Staff in school need to develop and sustain positive links with each and all of these agents and with others. It is possible to depict this as a diagram (see next page).

The main purpose of this diagram is to illustrate the size of the communication task. However, before looking further at size, the diagram also shows the changing nature of support work. Although only published in 1982, this diagram is already out of date. Absent from it are educational support grant teams, that is teams of (usually) seconded teachers who offer support in specific curricular or organisational areas. You might like to compare this diagram with your own.

The size of communicating with all these tasks implies that more than one person should be involved. We would prefer, for example, to see both headteacher and deputy head in the centre spot. We would also suggest that many of these agencies deal direct with designated staff. Although custom and practice (and courtesy) dictates that anyone entering a school informs the headteacher of their presence, the scale of such greetings can be dysfunctional (at times) for the headteacher and/or secretary! Once the headteacher and visiting agent have met and become known to each other it is not always necessary for them to keep meeting.

Managing communications can be made easier and more effective if names, 'phone numbers (including extensions) and best times and days of contact are recorded and available to all who are responsible for liaising with the support agency.

MODEL OF RELATIONSHIPS FOR THE PRIMARY HEAD
N.B. Similar models could be constructed for other members of staff.

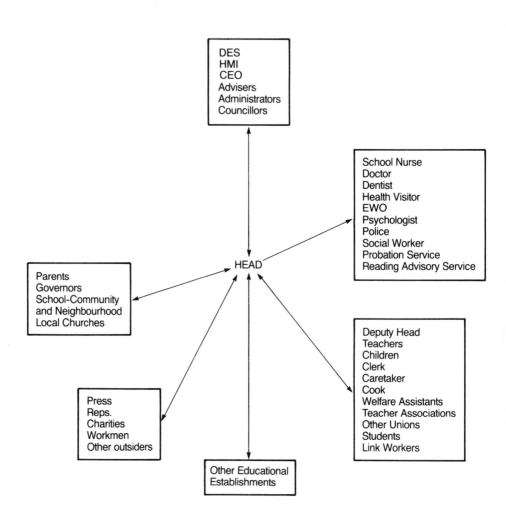

(from *Profile '82*; Salford LEA, 1982)

If size is a potential problem, we would also ask schools to think about the nature of support and involvement. This can best be shown through a series of questions:

- With which of the LEA's support agencies do we have most frequent contact, and why?
- When did we last have contact with each of these agencies, and why?

- Couldn't we make better use of some of these agencies?
- Have we ever invited any of these agents into school for *informational* purposes (as opposed to *action* or *crisis* reasons)?
- Which of these agents might contribute to the development of the school's life?
- Might any of these agents need to be better linked with parent meetings, governors, staff?
- How do we welcome them as visitors?
- How do they know our routines and times when they can see us?

Support agencies are, potentially, a marvellous resource. Unless schools make full demands upon them they will not only be under-used but may disappear if financial 'savings' have to be made to balance budgets. There is also the risk that when LEAs hand over their budgets to schools (and retain only seven per cent for themselves) support agencies may disappear or that schools will have to 'buy into' them.

Supporting curriculum development

Another way of thinking about LEA support agencies is to regard them as offering direct support for curricular activities and innovations.

During the 1980s many LEAs have expanded their advisory and support teams in respect of early years, multicultural education, science, technology, arts and humanities, and computers. Where such teams or individuals exist they can be a tremendous resource to schools –

particularly smaller schools.

Sometimes these teams will come and work in the school, alongside teachers, for a period of time. Sometimes they can be used for in-service days, workshops and conferences, as well as attending curriculum staff meetings where they might offer advice or information. Used in any of these ways they can prove a valuable supplement to a school's development programme.

4.15 *Documentation*

The 1980 Education Act obliged schools to publish information about their curriculum, organisation, discipline and examination results (although the latter was intended only for secondary schools). Of course many schools were already doing much of this before the Act made it mandatory. Nevertheless, the Act gave a new impetus to information and documentation and many schools reviewed, revised and redesigned their approach.

As this extract from Sallis (1988) shows, the rationale for the Act was consumerist rather than aiming to develop partnerships between home and school:

Information for Parents
Apart from the rights given to parents in the 1980 Act itself to information affecting their choice of schools and to consultation about proposed changes in local schools, parents were given important new rights to information from individual schools by regulations (4) made in 1981 under Section 8 of the Act. Individual schools are required to publish specified details about their staff, organisation, curriculum, rules and sanctions, and, in the case of secondary schools, examination results.

I would be the first to complain that these requirements have a strongly consumerist flavour, and are related more or less directly to the support of choice, rather than to the concept of parents in partnership with schools. For instance, schools are not required to tell parents what arrangements they made to involve them in the school, inform them of their children's progress, enlist their help. They are not required to tell them whether there is a parents' association or give them the names of their parent representatives on the governing body – just the chairman. This seems extraordinary when the information rights form part of the same legal package that gives parents for the first time statutory representation on governing boards. The strong implication is that parents need to know more about schools in order to *compare* them, not so that they may through their understanding play a more supportive role in their own. It is precisely this element of comparison of schools which made many people so fearful of the requirement to publish examination results.

The motivation underlying this whole process of opening up to public scrutiny what the schools offer and how they perform is undoubtedly that of the market place. Yet I cannot accept that it has been a bad development, so far as it goes, or that we should try to reverse it. What we must try to do instead is to move forward to better and more complete information services, join up the dots, flesh out the bones. No one in a public service should be allowed to withhold information about its performance from those who have a legitimate interest, and the fact that the information, because it is incomplete, may be used to make misleading judgements is not a reason for denying people the means to make those judgements, but rather an urgent reason to assist them to make better and more rounded judgements. It is essentially the same issue as I raised . . . about the bad press schools get. There is no means of suppressing criticism based on misinformation. One can only build up knowledge and experience to counteract it. To do violence to Gresham's Law once more, I do believe that good information drives out bad.

J. Sallis, 1988, pp. 30–31

Information for partnership

Where schools want to provide information which enables parents to feel part of the school then these schools need

- to provide information about the life and work of the school – and not just the school's rules and preferences
- to provide specific information about the curriculum – what children do and why
- to organise opportunities to see the school at work as well as opportunities to see the work of one's own children
- to strive to find out what the parents want to know, as well as tell the parents what the school thinks is appropriate

Sample page from a school's Humanities document, available to parents

---

How the teacher can make use of the key concepts:

TOPIC: *'Our Community Past and Present'*

Objectives: Intellectual skills 1, 2, 3
Social skills 1, 3.

Key concepts: Power, Values and Beliefs
Similarity/Difference
Continuity/Change

Key questions: The topic will raise key questions for both teachers and children. There is a close relationship between these key questions, the objectives and the key concepts

Key Questions for teachers	Key Questions for children	Skills
POWER		
Who makes decisions?	Where does the money come from?	
How do they make them?	Why do we have to come to school?	Intellectual Skill 1
	Why do we have to have rules?	Social Skill 3
VALUES AND BELIEFS		
What values guide the residents?	How do we live in our community?	Intellectual Skill 1
	Why do we live in this way?	
	Why do people decide to live where they do?	Social Skill 3

- to ensure that the information for parents is jargon-free but not patronising
- to ensure that information about the school is, if necessary, translated into the language of the children's homes
- to provide information on the ways in which parents could help or encourage their children (being mindful of the two previous points)
- to provide information about how parents might participate in the life and work of the school.

These eight points are not exhaustive.

It is all very well listing principles, but how does a school put them into operation? Here are a few suggestions based on wide experience of helping schools create imaginative packs of documents for parents.

- Look at how other schools organise and publish information about themselves.
- Do not just think about booklets. Also use regular newsheets, newsletters, children's work and magazines.
- Why not encourage governors (especially parent governors) to write a termly newsletter?
- Parents' meetings, open evenings, curriculum workshops, open afternoons, etc. are valuable occasions.
- Induction events are essential – but try to provide crèche facilities.
- Do not just think paper or face-to-face information: many schools make use of slide photograph sequences to show aspects of the school's work; many schools have made videos of themselves; many schools have sets of photographs (the school's photographer will often oblige) showing children at work.
- Curricular documents should be available to parents – especially the National Curriculum Council documents.
- Headteachers should foster and facilitate the involvement of other staff in many of the above. Governors, too, should play their part.
- Parent governors and visiting governors might like to contribute to or write a news-sheet.
- Word processing now means that rewriting/updating information from year to year should be easier.

Perhaps more than anything schools should remember a maxim of Joan Sallis's that "an ounce of access is worth a pound of information".

4.16 Management and the Law

The Head's Legal Guide (Croner Publications Ltd) contains about 1000 pages concerning the law in relation to education; it is an invaluable reference work which is updated at frequent intervals and we recommend it to you.

Our section here is not detailed – what we do hope to do is set out the broad legal framework within which schools must operate and highlight areas where further research could be useful.

Acts of Parliament

The regulation of the British education system is set out in a number of Acts of Parliament. Some of these apply only to Scotland, some to England and Wales and some to Northern Ireland. In general, the legal framework in Scotland is different in a number of significant ways. The Acts which affect education are listed below in chronological order:

- Education Act 1944
- National Health Service Act 1946
- Education Act 1948
- Education (Miscellaneous Provisions) Act 1953
- Education Act 1959
- Education Act 1962
- The Local Government Act 1963
- Education Act 1964
- Education Act 1968
- Local Government Act 1972
- Local Government (Scotland) Act 1973
- Education Act 1975
- Sex Discrimination Act 1975
- Education Act 1976
- Education (School-leaving Dates) Act 1976

- Race Relations Act 1976
- Education (Northern Ireland) Act 1978
- Education Act 1979
- Education (Scotland) Act 1980
- Education Act 1980
- Education Act 1981
- Local Government (Miscellaneous Provisions) Act 1982
- Local Government Act 1985
- Education (No. 2) Act 1986
- Teachers' Pay and Conditions Act 1987
- Education Reform Act 1988

As if this was not enough there are also a number of *statutory instruments* which carry the force of law!

The legal basis for the educational system in England and Wales is the 1944 Act which has been amended over the years by a whole series of acts and *statutory instruments*. New provisions have also been brought into effect by some of the new acts. Scotland and Northern Ireland have had their own legislation (see page 93).

Government circulars

Although all the acts mentioned above have a legal bearing on the management of schools, we can cheerfully take much of what they say for granted. For example, the age of transfer for pupils is defined by law

but most headteachers don't need to refer to an Act of Parliament to find out what it is for their school. Most of the legal framework stemming from the 1944 Act is familiar. Where new and complex legislation has been introduced the major sources of definitive information are *government circulars*.

These are issued by the Department of Education and Science, the Welsh Office or the Scottish Education Office and give clarification and guidance on legislation. Many of these circulars require a response from LEAs and so there can be a further stage where new information is given as a result of the LEA response.

Department of Education and Science

Elizabeth House
York Road
London SE1 7PH

Circular No 3/89
20 January 1989

To: Local Education Authorities

The Chief Executives of Inner London Boroughs and the Remembrancer

Heads and Governing Bodies of Maintained Schools

Teacher Training Institutions

Diocesan Bodies

Other Bodies

THE EDUCATION REFORM ACT 1988: RELIGIOUS EDUCATION AND COLLECTIVE WORSHIP.

CONTENTS

1.

Scotland

The Scottish educational system is regulated by the Scottish Education Service (SED) under the control of the Secretary of State for Scotland. The Education (Scotland) Act 1980 is the act which set up the legislative framework although a new education act for Scotland is likely. The day-to-day running of schools is administered by 12 education authorities usually known as EAs.

Northern Ireland

Northern Ireland has its own Department of Education which oversees all aspects of the province's education except for universities. There are also five area education and library boards which work at the local level.

Wales

Apart from the teaching of Welsh the legal framework for Wales is almost identical to that of England. The biggest difference is that the minister responsible is the Secretary of State for Wales rather than the Secretary of State for Education and Science. There is a separate Education Department in the Welsh Office with special responsibilities.

Education Reform Act 1988

This is the most significant piece of legislation to affect education since the 1944 Act. Reference is made to this act in other parts of this book, for example in The School and its Governors pp. 215–219, and as the Act warrants a book on its own we simply list the main areas which affect schools' management; fuller details are contained in other sections of the book.

Major areas affected by the Education Act 1988

- The Curriculum – the setting up of a National Curriculum
- Religious Education and worship
- Pupil Admissions – a policy of open enrolment
- Local Management of Schools – in particular the shifting of financial and budgetary control from LEAs to schools
- Grant Maintained Schools – the 'opting out' of LEA control by a school and transfer of funding to central government.

The Education Act 1988 is having, and will continue to have, a profound effect on the legal aspects of educational management – how far-reaching the change will be in terms of curriculum delivery and the attainment of individual pupils remains to be seen.

The 1981 Education Act brought about a radical change in the ways in which schools deal with special educational needs. The most crucial change was the introduction of *statementing* which set down a legally defined procedure for identifying and resourcing individual pupil's special educational need.

Evaluation is not a single, simple activity. It can take many forms and occur for several reasons and purposes. For example, evaluation can be conducted at different levels (individual, team or department, school, school clusters, LEA). It can be internal to the school (for example, conducted only by the staff) or external (carried out by people outside the school such as LEA inspectors or consultants) or some mixture of the two (for example staff and consultant; staff and governors). Lastly, evaluation can focus on different things – from the 'whole' school to some highly specific part of school (for example what do four year olds do in the reception class?). In this unit we will consider evaluation as internal to the school: what has been called self-review or *school self-evaluation*.

> When a school is reflecting upon and assessing its own work then it is engaging in self-review or self-evaluation. The underlying purpose of such activity invariably is to improve the teaching and learning process in the school. A self-review can have many positive outcomes and may result not only in changes and improvements in the curriculum or organisation of the school but also in the professional development of the staff.
>
> (McMahon et al., 1984)

Many LEAs have produced guidelines for self evaluation (in 1981 40 per cent of LEAs had produced guidelines) but such documents tended to have some disadvantages:

> The majority of the British guideline papers and documents for teachers about school self-review consist of lengthy checklists of questions, many of them value-laden, about the organisation and curriculum of the school. These checklists can be very daunting, not only because of their length but also because they seem to assume that a review should cover every aspect of the school. Few, if any, suggestions are included about how the review process might be tackled.
>
> (ibid.)

Taking up this last question, evaluation is not just about *what* we shall evaluate, it is also about *how*. To *do* evaluation you need to be able to know both *what* to and *how* to evaluate. Hence McMahon et al. (1984) sought to achieve both in order to develop the school (see School Development Plans pp. 143–148):

The GRIDS method

The materials in this handbook are designed to help teachers review and develop their curriculum and organisation. The title 'GRIDS', or 'guidelines for review and internal development in schools' has been carefully chosen. First, the materials are guidelines: they contain structured step-by-step advice about how to conduct a school review and development exercise; schools are not expected to follow these suggestions slavishly but rather to adapt and amend them as required. Second, the focus is on review leading to development for improvement and not on something that stops short at the review stage. Third, the word internal indicates that the review is not for external accountability purposes. Finally, the word school emphasises that the GRIDS process is directed at the whole school rather than at individual teachers or small groups.

The ideas in the title are reinforced and extended in the list of key principles that underpin the materials and which are central to the GRIDS method. These are that:

a) the aim is to achieve internal school development and not to produce a report for formal accountability purposes;

b) the main purpose is to move beyond the review stage into development for school improvement;

c) the staff of the school should be consulted and involved in the review and development process as much as possible;

d) decisions about what happens to any information or reports produced should rest with the teachers and others concerned;

e) the head and teachers should decide whether and how to involve the other groups in the school, e.g. pupils, parents, advisers, governors;

f) outsiders (for example, external consultants) should be invited to provide help and advice when this seems appropriate;

g) the demands made on key resources like time, money and skilled personnel should be realistic and feasible for schools and LEAs.

(ibid.)

In order to enable an evaluation to take place the GRIDS team mapped out five stages of review and development. These are set out in the diagram on page 96.

GRIDS is now a well-tried and tested approach; it is also sufficiently widely available for schools to obtain and utilise (for example, it can be found in university and colleges of higher education libraries, teachers' and curriculum development centres, LEA resource centres, LEA adviser/ inspectorial teams). We believe that, despite some problems, the five stages of review and development still offer a useful model.

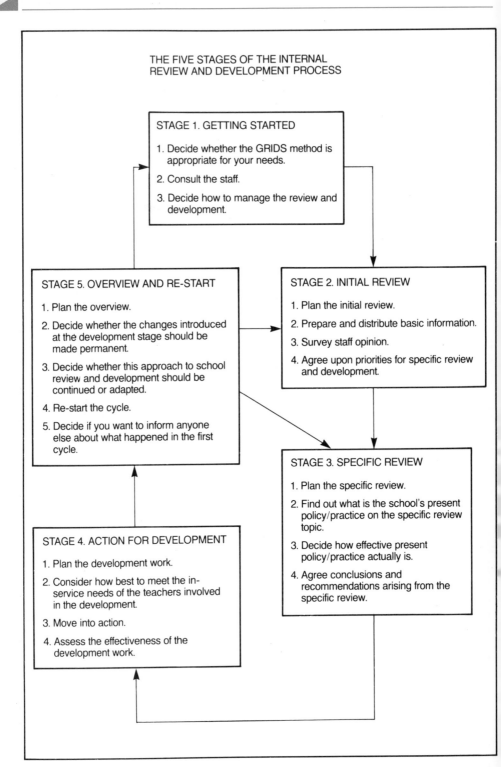

THE FIVE STAGES OF THE INTERNAL
REVIEW AND DEVELOPMENT PROCESS

STAGE 1. GETTING STARTED

1. Decide whether the GRIDS method is appropriate for your needs.
2. Consult the staff.
3. Decide how to manage the review and development.

STAGE 5. OVERVIEW AND RE-START

1. Plan the overview.
2. Decide whether the changes introduced at the development stage should be made permanent.
3. Decide whether this approach to school review and development should be continued or adapted.
4. Re-start the cycle.
5. Decide if you want to inform anyone else about what happened in the first cycle.

STAGE 2. INITIAL REVIEW

1. Plan the initial review.
2. Prepare and distribute basic information.
3. Survey staff opinion.
4. Agree upon priorities for specific review and development.

STAGE 3. SPECIFIC REVIEW

1. Plan the specific review.
2. Find out what is the school's present policy/practice on the specific review topic.
3. Decide how effective present policy/practice actually is.
4. Agree conclusions and recommendations arising from the specific review.

STAGE 4. ACTION FOR DEVELOPMENT

1. Plan the development work.
2. Consider how best to meet the in-service needs of the teachers involved in the development.
3. Move into action.
4. Assess the effectiveness of the development work.

If the GRIDS approach suggested in Evaluation –1 (see pp. 94–96) still offers a useful approach, this is not to preclude other approaches. Peter Holly was a member of the GRIDS team, and he has taken some of the ideas further. For one thing he has simplified the evaluation process into five basic, but fundamental questions:

- What do we need to look at?
- Where are we now?
- Where do we want to be?
- How do we get there?
- How are we doing?

These are simple but *powerful* questions.

Furthermore, he has also arranged them alongside possible techniques which could be selected for each question. The result is a matrix (see below).

This matrix shows that evaluation is a blend of processes and techniques. GRIDS and Holly's five questions are useful ways of structuring the process of evaluation. However, the techniques of ways of evaluation are manifold.

Key Techniques / *Key Processes*	GRIDS Review Sheet	Structured Staff Discussion	Staff Interviews Work Shadowing	Paired Observation	Interest Group Feedback Session	Snowball Session	Formulation of Performance Indicators
What do we need to look at? Identification of Development Needs							
Where are we now? Stock-taking; gathering evidence of present situation							
Where do we want to be? Target-setting							
How do we get there? Strategic Planning; identification of INSET needs							

Examples of evaluation techniques and activities

Evaluations will focus on many things. For example, staff might individually, in pairs or trios talk about and report on:

The quality of interpersonal relationships How well do members of the school relate to each other? Do they mix informally? Is cooperation a factor of the school?

Cohesiveness To what extent is there agreement on the aims of the school and of the methods to be used in achieving them? Do all members understand the roles they are to perform in order to help achieve these aims?

Levels of morale Are members of the school happy to be there, or are there factors which produce restlessness and discontent?

Decision-making patterns How are decisions arrived at? Does everyone understand the nature of the process? Does everyone have as much involvement as they want? Are some vital decisions not taken?

Leadership styles How does the head perform that role? Is there consistency in the style of leadership adopted? Who are the informal leaders in the staffroom? Do individuals have an opportunity to exercise leadership qualities? Are the children encouraged to show initiative?

Levels of commitment Are all the members of the school fully committed to it? Do some teachers feel a conflict between their loyalty to the school and their career aspirations? Is the school adequately supported by the parents? Do the parents feel that the school is adequately meeting their requirements?

Motivational features How are members of the school motivated? Is it by intrinsic or extrinsic means? Are these recognised, understood and appreciated?

(Rodger & Richardson, 1985, pp. 49–50)

Another area of investigation might be to observe how much time was actually spent on curricular tasks in the classroom. It has been shown by research (Mortimore et al., 1988) that in effective schools maximum amounts of time in classrooms are spent on task; or expressed another way as much time as possible is given over to teaching and learning rather than to administration (for example registers, messages, interruptions, classroom organisation). How might teachers investigate use of time? Here is one suggestion:

PRACTICAL ACTIVITY 7.3

Aim: To record the time available for curricular activity.

Method: The time available for curricular activities is the time remaining in each teaching/learning session, once it has properly started, excluding interruptions and up to 'tidying-up' time. All that is necessary here is to use a notebook and a watch to record the actual time available for activities throughout a school-day.

Follow-up: Assuming that a fairly representative day has been chosen, it

---

---

may provide a salutary experience to multiply the total for the day by the total number of school-days in the year, excluding holidays, 'occasional days' and election days if the school will be closed, etc. Similarly, it may prove interesting to analyse the proportion of time spent on each area of the curriculum.

(Pollard & Tann, 1988, p. 108)

Lastly, how might a school manage the introduction of parents working in classrooms? Here is one way:

PRACTICAL ACTIVITY 7.2

Aim: To prepare for having parents or ancillary assistants working in the class-room.

Method: A pro forma, such as the one below, could be used to prepare for a session with parental involvement, to monitor it and to get the parents' feedback.

Initial discussion with parent about involvement ☐

Parent's feeling about involvement ....
Parent's strengths ....
Interests ....
Availability ....
Any possible problems ....

Educational activities and objectives for sessions
1 ....
2 ....
3 ....

Best contribution for parent ....

Specific discussion about parent's contribution with parent ☐

The aim, and parent's degree of responsibility, is agreed ☐

Comments ....

The sessions in action ☐

Comments on how it went ....

Follow-up discussion with parent ☐

Notes on feedback ....

Follow-up: It is unlikely that this activity would be carried out for every session involving parents, but it is very valuable when starting off a new partnership for classroom work with a parent. It is also useful on an occasional basis to heighten awareness and to check that benefits are being maximised.

(Pollard & Tann, 1988, p. 107)

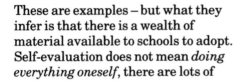

These are examples – but what they infer is that there is a wealth of material available to schools to adopt. Self-evaluation does not mean *doing everything oneself,* there are lots of ways of making both the task more realistic and the process more effective. We would encourage schools to look at, even obtain for their staff libraries some or all of the following.

Suggested further reading

P J Holly & G W Southworth, *The Developing School* (Falmer Press, Lewes, 1989)

A McMahon, R Bolam, R Abbot & P Holly, *Guidelines for Review and Internal Development in Schools: Primary School Handbook* Schools Council Programme 1: Purpose and Planning in Schools (Longman/ Schools Council, York, 1984)

A Pollard & S Tann, *Reflective Teaching in the Primary School: A handbook for the classroom* (Cassell, London, 1988)

I Rodger & J Richardson, *Self evaluation for Primary Schools* (Hodder & Stoughton, London, 1985)

5 ISSUES INTO PRACTICE
5.1 ANALYSING THE ORGANISATION

5.1.1 *The Benefits and Constraints*

Primary schools are particularly busy places. If those who work in them are not involved in producing curriculum policies then they are responding to the demands of the National Curriculum; if they are not thinking about what resources they need and can afford, they are concerned about where to store those they already have; if they are not working with children in classrooms then they are dealing with them during lunch breaks; if they are not setting up a stall at the annual jumble sale then they are concerned with reporting financial management to governors; if they are not desperately trying to find a new member of staff two weeks before the Christmas break then they are trying to decide how best to help a colleague with personal or professional difficulties.

And none of this, of course, takes into account the lavatory which won't work, the leaking roof, the broken window, the new parents who have just walked in the door, the established parents concerned that their child's reading is not good enough, the visit from the education committee, the INSET session after school or the two children who have bloodied each other's noses ten minutes ago in the playground.

It is only too easy to see why recommendations to sit still or slow down, to think about and analyse the classroom or school in which we are working should be met occasionally with hoots of derision. "When have I time?" seems an only too reasonable response.

'Seeming to be reasonable' doesn't make it right, though, and all our personal and organisational experience suggests that an overview of where we are, an understanding of our situation and that of those around us and an inventory of our strengths and weaknesses can bring benefits which help to reduce rather than increase the pressures upon us.

Analysing our classroom and school isn't time wasted; it is time well spent.

The Benefits

1 *We have a clearer view of what is happening*
Much of this book tries to explain the complexity of schools. Because schools are complex the truth is that it is unlikely that anyone will fully understand the range of views held by staff, children and parents about one school or classroom or totally comprehend all of the strengths and weaknesses which exist within it. Not being able to understand everything fully is no excuse, though, for not trying to understand at all. We need to have a clear view of the shape of the wood as well as an intimate knowledge of every single tree it contains.

2 We have a better chance of taking appropriate action

There are a variety of responses we can make to any situation, including doing nothing at all. Whether we always choose the most appropriate is doubtful and some fine tuning of our decisions is usually required. Understanding the organisation we work in is more likely, however, to help us resist making inappropriate responses to situations which occur.

3 We develop a set of reference points for future judgements

Most of our judgements are relative ones; they depend upon comparison with other judgements we hold about similar activities, people, situations.

Increasingly staffs of schools are being asked to report on what they are doing, why they are doing it and how it is going. Without a reference point developed through analysis these questions are almost impossible to answer; with such reference points they become much easier. Analysing classrooms and schools is a fundamental part of running an effective organisation. What we choose to analyse given the limited time that is available is equally important and we will suggest certain key features of schooling and one or two ways in which the analysis can be carried out in the next few pages.

Before we get there, though, there are also constraints upon analysis about which we need to be aware.

The Constraints

1 Our own personal perspectives

Perhaps we need to analyse these first; they will certainly form an important part of everything which goes on around us. If, for example, our principal aim is to create a 'happy school' we may be unaware of, or unwilling to analyse, the academic performance of the children we teach. (The opposite is, of course, also true!)

If we don't know much about modern primary science practice it is going to be difficult for us to analyse the strengths and weaknesses of our colleagues in that area of the curriculum.

Equally, our own perspectives will affect the judgement of what we see. Research of any kind works in two ways:

- researchers have points of view which they use as evidence to confirm or deny (but usually confirm!)
- researchers gather evidence as neutrally as possible and then develop a theory from it.

Both are problematic. The first often ignores much useful evidence so that the researcher can say "This school is just like/completely different from my last school". The second presents difficulties for the researcher in interpreting evidence without allowing it to be coloured by personal views.

The second method is more helpful in organisational analysis, if you can manage it. During the period of your analysis, keep a check on which approach you are taking and how your own perspectives are affecting the judgements you make.

2   Time

Despite the fact that "when have I the time?" is not an excuse for failing to analyse our organisation, it is still true that there is only a limited amount of time available. If we don't use that time effectively by choosing appropriate areas for analysis and appropriate methods then we are hardly likely to reap the benefits of the time we put in.

3   Choice of focus

Precisely because schools are so complex there is an almost limitless range of possibilities for analysis, but some are clearly more appropriate than others. A class teacher concerned about the social relationships of the children in her class shouldn't perhaps spend too much time analysing the colour of everyone's socks; a headteacher could perhaps do a little better when going into classrooms than checking on the quality of the skirting boards. Our choice of focus will affect the quality of our overview which will, in turn, affect the quality of our actions.

4   Methods of analysis

Choosing an appropriate focus doesn't guarantee useful information. We need to think carefully about the methods we use to gather the information too, both in terms of the quality of information they will provide and the time they will take. (The trade-off between these two is one we all have to get used to.)

5   The confidence of others

Because schools are people-dealing places much of the information we will need in our analysis of our school or classroom will have to come personally from those involved in it. Few of us are willing to disclose information to those whom we don't trust or to those who will misuse it.

If our colleagues, parents, governors and children haven't been able to develop confidence in us then we shouldn't be surprised if they are unwilling to reveal attitudes, opinions or practices which are very personal to them. Nor should we be surprised when, consequently, the analysis we make is critically flawed.

We mentioned in the previous pages that the very complexity of schools presents us with a bewildering array of possible areas for analysis. All of them can be interesting and many of them will be important. Within the time available, though, priorities have to be made. Some of those priorities will occur as a result of local demands made upon schools and some as a result of the individual interests of those making the analyses.

There are areas of analysis, though, which seem to us to have importance to almost everyone working in schools. Some of them are obvious, although that won't stop us from at least mentioning them. One or two others may be less obvious but are still, in our view, very important. On these three pages we itemise what these areas might be.

1 The curriculum

a) The usefulness of school policies
   - How clear are they?
   - How do they help colleagues' classroom practice?
   - How up-to-date are they?
   - How are they communicated to different audiences?
   - How many colleagues were involved in their production?
   - How have newer colleagues been introduced to them?
   - How many curriculum areas do they cover?

b) Classroom action
   - How much does classroom action reflect the policy statements?
   - How does each classroom atmosphere add to or detract from children's opportunities to work to their best ability?
   - How much do the relationships in the class between teacher/children and children/children contribute towards non-academic growth in children?
   - Are the classrooms organised effectively?
   - Are children allowed a reasonable degree of independence?

c) Teachers' planning
   - How much of the work which takes place in classrooms is planned?
   - How do the plans help teachers implement what they want to do rather than describe it?
   - How much do the plans take into account not only objectives but also activities, resources, relevance, time and some idea of finished work?
   - How much do the plans build upon that which has gone before?
   - What procedures are there for plans to be shared between teachers throughout the school?

2 The children

a) Attitudes
   - To what extent are children understanding of each other?
   - What level of care do they show towards their environment?
   - Do their attitudes reflect an interest in their work, a bored acceptance or an obvious rejection?
   - How confident do they seem when facing newcomers in the school?
   - How do the children behave when unsupervised?

b) Classroom performance
   - Does the work given to children in each class seem to be pitched at appropriate levels?
   - Are there grounds for concern about the apparent

performance of some children?
- Does the general level of performance seem reasonably appropriate for the ability of the children?
- Are the informal judgements made by teaching staff appropriate or inappropriate?
- Are the formal tests used in the school appropriate? Do the results of those tests give cause for concern?

3 The parents, governors and community

a) Attitude
- Does the feedback from the parents, governors and community seem generally supportive or antagonistic? (Supportive does not rule out critical!)
- Have parents, governors and other members of the community any opportunity to gather real evidence for their opinions and views?
- Are there cliques within each group which appear to present an apparently majority view?
- How much evidence has been gathered by you in order to arrive at these views?
- Are there particular people within or activities of the school towards which these groups hold particular views?

b) Involvement
- Do those parents, governors and others who wish it have an opportunity to be involved in the life of the school?
- How much information does the school provide to parents and others?
- Is this information appropriate?
- Is it presented appropriately?
- Are there established

procedures throughout the school for those parents and others working in classrooms or with children?

4 Administration

a) Areas
- Are there systems in operation for the administration of:

  Admissions to and departures from school
  Financial matters
  Appointing staff
  Stock ordering and control
  Producing reports
  Dealing with parents and visitors
  Sickness and absence
  School visits and journeys
  Handling local authority and DES material?

b) Administrative staff
- Have the administrative staff been given duties beyond their abilities?
- Has so much been 'delegated' that they are doing the jobs of others?
- Do they know what it is they are supposed to do?
- Have they the opportunity to provide input and give feedback?
- Do they work cooperatively on behalf of the school or antagonistically against it?
- Do they work in a pleasantly conducive environment?
- Do they present an acceptable first impression of the school?

5 The teachers

a) Knowledge and understanding
- Do the staff understand what is being asked of them at a local and national level?

- What individual difficulties can be identified within the staff group?
- What use is made of school or centre-based INSET by staff?
- Are professional magazines and journals used in the school (other than to look for new jobs)?
- Does informal professional debate take place?

b) Relationships and influence
  - How professionally do staff handle each other?
  - Are there particular friendship groups on the staff?
  - Do these groups work positively or negatively for the school?
  - Are there individuals with particularly clear positive or negative power in the school?

- Are some staff more hierarchical than others?
- Do some colleagues appear to feel isolated in any way from the rest of the staff?

There are others, too. Even our list of very important areas runs the risk of appearing to be endless. (We would, for example, want to give the same consideration to an analysis of the caretaking, cleaning and school meals staff as we have done to all the others who work in our schools and we would also want to find some way of analysing ourselves in our own roles.)

You may reasonably have a different view of your immediate priorities ; that is all well and good. What we should share in common is our understanding of the importance of both analysis and prioritising.

5.1.3 *Analysis in Practice*

Analysing is an active verb. Everything we have spoken about until now has been preparation for the doing of it; important, but preparation nonetheless.

Let's examine some factors which help to make analysis effective:

1 Focus down

Before you begin gaining evidence be sure you are clear what you are gaining evidence about and why. You won't be able to analyse all of the issues at the same time even though some may conveniently overlap. Knowing what you are looking at and why will help to determine the strategies you use, who or what you use them upon, which evidence can be temporarily discarded and which is likely to be immediately useful.

2 Gaining evidence

There are a whole range of formal and informal strategies for gathering evidence about schools. Some of them are very sophisticated and require the specific understandings of trained researchers. This shouldn't prevent you from considering them. Sometimes the introduction of external researchers or consultants into a school can reveal things which would not otherwise have come to light.

Many of them are less sophisticated and can be carried out within the normal life of the school. The problem with less sophisticated approaches, such as talking conversationally with colleagues, children or parents, is that we have to be aware of the interpretations all the parties are placing on the conversation. Generally, the less sophisticated the analytical technique the more evidence is required to support any conclusions which might be drawn from it.

Strategies which might be used include:

Formal strategies
a) standardised tests
b) questionnaires
c) annual exams
d) record cards
e) written profiles
f) comparisons involving national or local statistics
g) inventories

Informal strategies

a) observation of
   i)   lessons and class activities
   ii)   parental responses
   iii) staffroom atmosphere
   iv)   children around the school
   v)   governor involvement
   vi)   administrative staff

b) talking with (individually and grouped)
   i)   parents
   ii)   teachers
   iii) children
   iv)   governors
   v)   ancillary staff

c) comparing with
   i)   other schools
   ii)   other points of view
   iii) previous experiences
   iv)   HMI reports

d) general impressions of as much as possible

e) using
   i)   outside consultants
   ii)   inspectors

Each of these strategies has its strengths and weaknesses; each is more or less appropriate in a given setting. It is important that we choose strategies which are best suited to the information we are trying to find out.

Comparing the reading ages of three different class groups of children is not best done by discussing with each child their views about the test they have just taken. A well-designed chart, a pencil and a little statistical understanding will see you through.

On the other hand, finding out about children's attitudes to reading will not be successfully achieved by handing each of them a piece of paper on which is written 'Do you like reading? Answer YES/NO'.

Analysing your school or classroom should, for the most part, be a shared activity. Sharing the analysis

- relieves the load
- can help to create a group identity
- challenges individual · interpretations of the evidence
- enables a range of strategies to be used more easily.

3   Has enough evidence been obtained?

You will never know whether you have all the evidence it is possible to gather but you should be aware when you might not have enough. Rushing to judgement is very tempting; the time constraints and sheer volume of work in schools can cause those making the analysis to shorten the evidence gathering period to such an extent that any decisions resulting from it are counter-productive.

This doesn't mean that you should go on gathering evidence interminably. You have to decide when to stop. However, determining parental reaction to the school (or an aspect of it) is unlikely to be successful if all you have done is stand at the gate and talk to three parents. Determining the interest and understanding of your colleagues towards the teaching of history will be similarly doomed if you only ask "Do you think we ought to teach it?"

Think about the amount of evidence

you have obtained, its quality and the breadth of strategies you have used. Extra care is required because you haven't the time to behave as full-time researchers.

4   Recording your evidence

The process of gathering evidence and formulating decisions is both a circular and a cumulative one. It is circular because you will gather evidence and form temporary decisions which are subsequently affected by the next batch of evidence. It is cumulative because the evidence, and the decisions, keep on growing.

Even where the analysis has been well-focused it will be difficult to retain everything you have seen or heard. (Formal analysis is less of a problem since there will be written evidence available.)

The evidence you have gained is vital. You will use it not only to make decisions about the direction of the school but also to support and defend those decisions, too.

Where possible, keep notes of important evidence you gather, particularly that which refers to remarks made in conversation, to things seen in and around school and so on. Jot down summaries every two or three days. Then, if your decisions are challenged by parents, colleagues or governors, for example, you will have some of the support you need.

5   Does the evidence you have gained enable you to make a decision?

There are two important decisions which result from an analysis of your school or classroom:

- What is it like?
- What action needs to be taken?

In the first instance you should be concerned with answering only the first of those questions. Deciding about action is important but only when you have a clear idea of why action needs to be taken. In analysing your organisation you are trying, first, to describe it as accurately as possible.

The 'decision' you need to take first, then, is "Are we able to describe our organisation?" and not "What are we going to do?". Sometimes, the answer to that question will be negative. You will have to decide to carry on gaining more information.

When you feel you can describe the organisation with reasonable accuracy test the description you have made. By making it with others it has a greater chance of accuracy. Nevertheless, test it against the evidence you have accumulated and against some of those to whom it refers. Your analysis of your school or classroom is going to underpin almost every significant action you take in the future.

5.2 STAFF

5.2.1 *Staff Selection*

Selection is really a *process*. Selection is much more than advert, application, interview and decision. It should be a *systematic process* which seeks two goals:

- to attract candidates suitable to do the job
- to achieve a match between person and post which eliminates, or reduces as far as possible, the risk of mismatch in the eyes of either party.

Thus, selection is not just about the headteachers and governors wanting candidate K to do the job, it is also about candidate K wanting to do the job on offer. *Selection is a two-way process.*

Selection involves thinking about four questions:

- Do you know what you want?
- How do you get the right person in front of you?
- How do you recognise the right person when you see them?
- How do you know you have got it right?

(from Barry & Tye, 1972)

1 *Do you know what you want?*
This question needs to be asked before any action is taken. The selectors need with some precision to *decide the nature of the vacancy*. To decide the nature of the vacancy there is a need to

- assess the present situation
- look at the opportunities this post may afford

- ask the person who is leaving to write down all the jobs they do
- talk with staff
- talk with governors
- look at the school's development plan.

In the light of this kind of diagnosis of need the headteacher and others should then *define the post*. To begin with, you need a job description, even though the final working version will be negotiated between you and the successful candidate. You cannot select without knowing something about the job on offer, thus the writing of a job description is central to the whole process. From the job description flows the advert and supplementary details.

Asking the question, "Do we know what we want?" means

- describing the job to be done
- describing the situation where the job will be (for example, school context, policies)
- specifying the person to do it.

Specifying the person sounds mechanical and de-human. Yet, unless we know the professional qualities we are looking for, how can we appoint? In truth, most people *do* know but are not prepared to tell others. This can mean

- it is difficult for applicants and candidates to work out how they are being judged
- it is difficult for the selection panel to work together. Unless the panel know and agree what they are looking for they could each be looking for very different people!

In thinking about the person we need to focus purely on *professional* issues. Let's look at the following example.

In seeking a teacher to accept an Incentive Allowance B post for Language Development in a medium sized 5–11 primary school we would look, perhaps, for a person who:

i) possesses a clear philosophy and interest in the teaching of language skills and arts throughout the primary years;

ii) is able to design and revise school policies and programmes of study in consultation with the headteacher, deputy head, teaching colleagues and ancillary staff;

iii) has a working knowledge of the requirements of the National Curriculum and Schools Examination and Assessment Council programmes;

(iv) is experienced in curriculum implementation;

v) is able to offer help and advice to colleagues;

vi) is willing to inform and advise governors and parents.

Hence, the desirable *qualities* might be:

- to involve others in the language work of the school (for example, staff, parents, governors)
- to be able to consult
- to be able to secure the maximum cooperation of others
- to be aware of developments beyond the school
- to be able to write policies and reports
- to read relevant reports, documents.

"Do you know what you want?" is the fundamental question, and knowing the answer (as far as possible) provides the key to unlocking answers to the other three questions and to enabling the full and enriching involvements of all other parties to the selection.

2 How do you get the right person in front of you?
Here we need to think about

- the advert
- the job particulars
- any specific questions/issues we might want applicants to write about
- preliminary visits of applicants
- references
- short listing

Increasingly, applicants are being guided to address and write about specific issues in their application. This is useful, but do ensure that the issues you ask them to address are pertinent to your particular school and the vacancy.

Visits are useful for the applicants to get 'the feel of the school'.

References are needed but they can be misleading. It is easier to write a reference when the referee

- knows about the post on offer
- is guided to write about specific issues
- knows whether the reference is open or confidential
- knows how long they've got before the deadline.

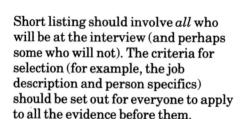

Short listing should involve *all* who will be at the interview (and perhaps some who will not). The criteria for selection (for example, the job description and person specifics) should be set out for everyone to apply to all the evidence before them.

Candidates should be short listed according to the criteria for selection.

3 How do you recognise the right person when you see them?

Here, we are thinking about short listed candidates, the final four, five or six who will be interviewed.

The successful candidate should be recognised by

- being invited to visit the school and meet the selectors
- being interviewed 'informally' by the headteacher and/or chairperson of governors and perhaps one or two other selectors
- being interviewed formally by the panel of selectors.

However, each of these approaches should serve only to provide more information about the candidate.

Then, in the light of *all* the information, for example

- letter of application
- application form
- references
- data from visit
- data from informal interviews
- data from panel interview

a selection is made on the basis of the best match between person and post.

The criteria established in answer to the first question should provide the basis for the selection and thus be the means by which a group of selectors recognise the person they perceive to be the most suitable.

4 How do you know you have got it right?

In truth it will be some time before you can answer this. Selection is really a matter of making a prediction, and only when the person is actually in post, settled in, and doing the full range of tasks described in the job details can you really say whether they are the right person for the post or not.

The formal selection interview is a well-established, traditional part of the selection process. Unfortunately it is all too often regarded as the only part of the process. Staff selection should entail far more than a single 30 minute interview (see pp. 110–112). Indeed, the interview is only *one* part of the selection process and in many ways it should be the least important.

The panel interview is notoriously unreliable. All too often selectors

- make hasty and subjective judgements
- fail to ask appropriate questions
- take small pieces of evidence and expand them to create negative impressions of a candidate
- spend too long thinking about the next question and fail to listen to the answer
- have not studied in depth the documentation on each candidate.

We undoubtedly need to make an interview as good as we can. This means we need to *plan*, and *prepare*.

Planning means

- reading each candidate's papers
- analysing the evidence
- thinking about what else we wish to know
- determining the areas we will focus on and pursue in our questions.

Preparing means

- choosing the interview room with care

- thinking about appropriate furniture and layout
- providing a timetable for candidates so they know when they will be interviewed
- ensuring candidates wait in a suitable room
- providing selectors with summary sheets on each candidate (but also having sufficient full copies on each candidate to hand)
- letting candidates know if they need to stay afterwards or not
- giving each candidate a list of names and titles of each selector on the panel.

Such preparation is little more than courtesy.

Interviewing rests on

- planning the entrance and settling in of the candidate
- controlling the interview so that the candidate is telling you things you need to know
- letting the candidate speak for the greater portion of the time (they ought to talk for around 70% of the time)
- listening actively
- asking appropriate questions
- avoiding stress methods
- avoiding showing the candidates they are wrong – the panel should remain neutral.

That being so, at the heart of the process lie *questions*.

Asking questions

Asking questions is not as easy as it sounds. A good question is straightforward and shows the candidate what they are to talk about in their answer.

Open questions

The conventional view is that one should ask open questions but not too open! For instance, "Tell me about yourself" is too open, but "Tell me about your classroom this week" is better balanced – the candidate has a subject to talk about but is not confined to talk about a specific detail which might be irrelevant or inappropriate.

Closed questions

They should be used sparingly but they can be used to check some facts, for example, "Have you taught in open plan schools?"

Questions to avoid!

1 **Mazy questions** such as:

"What are your views on handwriting? Should it be taught or caught? When and how should it be taught and do you favour a single style for every child or a more pluralistic approach? Importantly, what about handwriting and the slow learner and children with special educational needs?"

2 **Leading questions** such as

"You will want to continue as the previous postholder did, in supervising the environmental area?"

3 **Questions which show a judgement** such as

"I'm sure you'll agree with us that the National Curriculum has been a useful development?"

4 **Fantasy questions** such as

"Let's imagine you've got the job. It is the first day of term, the head's just 'phoned to say she's had a car crash, the heating isn't working and the building is cold, the cook's unable to prepare a lunchtime meal, it's snowing and two staff think the school should close, another believes in trying to stay open and the caretaker's just broken his leg. What would you do?"

Listening

Listening is not easy but it is absolutely vital if an interview is to be effective. Good listeners work out, in advance, the main questions they intend to ask each candidate. They resist imposing their own views on what the candidate is saying. They listen to the nuances of meaning – the words emphasised, the hesitations and inconsistencies in answers. They talk as little as possible, concentrate as much as possible and show the candidate, by nods and eye contact, that they are interested in what is being said. They have the patience to allow the candidate to complete the answers and they can tolerate silence. They are also sympathetic to candidates who struggle to articulate an answer by allowing them time to gather their thoughts. Listening can be made more productive if the questioners use what they have heard to ask *supplementary questions*.

If fairly open questions are used as a starter then they should be followed up with a series of supplementaries so that you probe candidates, and pursue things they have said. That way you will find out about the candidates' attitudes, understandings, and experience.

Keep some brief notes

If you are interviewing several candidates it is hard to remember what each has said. Therefore, after each candidate has left the room spend two or three minutes writing down your impression of them – both strengths and weaknesses.

Obviously, these ideas are merely introductory. Interviewing is a great skill. If you want to improve your skill

as an interviewer we recommend you look at:

C Roberts, *The Interview Game and How It's Played* (BBC Publications, London, 1985)
J Gratue *Successful Interviewing* (Penguin Books, Business & Management Seminar, London, 1988)

5.2.3 *Staff Development*

It is widely accepted that both school and curriculum development rely upon staff development. Unless teachers develop – either in terms of improved skills or new skills – nothing will really develop.

Staff development means the development of everyone on the school's staff: it is an all-embracing term – no member of staff should be excluded from developing. Secretaries need 'developing' in order to enhance the school's communications and image. Ancillary staff should be included since they have important conversations with children. Headteachers need developing as managers, as leading professionals and as enablers. Teachers need to develop in order to keep abreast of new developments in knowledge and in research.

Staff development can occur in many ways, for example through

- award bearing courses at universities and colleges
- non-award bearing courses at universities, colleges, teachers' centres
- conferences
- professional association and union activities
- local support/interest groups
- visits to other schools

- school-based workshops and activities
- experience of working in a number and range of schools
- teachers learning from colleagues in school
- increasing awareness through discussion and reading
- critical friendships, paired observations, peer appraisal.

Not all of these need to be planned, since a lot of staff development can occur informally and almost casually. Nor are any of these listed examples mutually exclusive; many teachers, over the course of a year, are involved in a number of these activities, sometimes occurring simultaneously or overlapping.

It can be seen from this introduction that staff development

- does not mean only *career* development
- is not only for the lethargic and weak
- is for everyone including the able and 'gifted' members of staff
- includes appraisal as one component part
- can be a by-product of other developmental processes
- is not achieved simply by attending courses.

Individuals or institutions?

One important feature of staff development is the need to strike a balance between developing individuals and the institution in which they work. Until recently many teachers attended in-service events and activities, and acquired numerous

skills and insights. Yet all too often these skills were gained opportunistically, randomly acquired and/or served the interests and needs of the individual teachers, as this in-service record suggests:

Northstone Education Authority Schools' In-Service Record; Academic Year 199_ – 199_ School: St. Nowhere School		
Activity	*No. of staff involved*	*Length*
Investigational Maths Workshop	1	1 day
Pottery for Beginners	1	6 evening sessions
Parental Involvement in Reading	2	10 evening sessions
Evaluating Computer Software	1	3 evening sessions
Deputy Heads Management Course	1	2 days (weekend)
Classroom Observation	2	1 day (Saturday) conference
Diploma in Geographical Education	1	1 evening per week for 6 terms
Special Needs in the Ordinary Classroom	2	3 day conference

Now such a record of in-service could be both useful and creditable. But suppose that no school-based in-service activities took place and that throughout this particular year the school was seeking to develop its work in science? Plainly, insufficient in-service time, of the kind recorded here, would have been devoted to supporting the *school's* emphasis on science. In short, the issue of individual/institutional development is not one of either/or, rather it is one of *synchronisation*. Unless staff are involved, in some way or other, in teacher developmental activities which correspond to the school's emphases, then the development of both the curriculum and the teacher is likely to be inhibited simply because the two are not coordinated or even congruent.

This view is supported by several research investigations into curriculum change and into teacher development. However, let us also make it clear what we are not saying. We are not saying there is no room for individual teachers to pursue their individual needs, interests or aspirations. We are simply saying that the individual's and the institution's development should be linked and school development plans (see pp. 143–148) are one way in which they can be linked and coordinated.

In-service days

The introduction of in-service days also facilitates school-based development. Now all the staff can meet together, during the daytime, and focus on some particular issue of concern. What will be important for schools – especially those with stable staff groups – is to record how, over a two or three year period, the in-service days are adding to the school's development. In-service days might need to be conceived as offering a spiral curriculum of school development. This is stressed because just as St. Nowhere's staff were devoting too much time to individual interests, so too might in-service days become an unconnected series of 'one-offs'.

The introduction of teacher appraisal will obviously contribute to the diagnosis of individual teachers' needs. In-service arrangements will need to respond to whatever the appraisal highlights. Moreover, appraisal should reveal things about the school as an organisation. Some of the 'weaknesses' of teachers may turn out to be 'weaknesses' in the school. In-service, and staff development schemes will need to be alert to this.

One powerful method of developing staff is for each teacher to act as host to all other staff. Thus the staff will assemble in their colleague's classroom and the host teacher might then

- explain why the classroom is organised as it is
- explain the reasons for and purposes of the displays
- focus on a particular curriculum area/activity
- talk about the work of the class in general.

These are only suggestions and lots more could be generated. Variations on this might be to visit pairs of classrooms, or departments or teams.

Visits to other schools is another idea.

Use trigger questions or sentence stems to develop discussion. Day, Johnston & Whitaker (1985) have many examples, as do Pollard & Tann (1988). Schools might also find Patrick Easen's book *Making School-centred INSET Work* (1985) useful.

The staffroom should have a staff library. Perhaps part of the INSET funds could be given over to this. The library might contain:

- weekly – the *Times Educational Supplement*
- monthly – a selection of professional journals
- termly – a new book or two. These could be practical or more theoretical.

Where schools do have a staff library (or shelf!) the materials should be utilised from time to time. Articles and extracts might be seen as topics for formal staff discussion.

Each teacher should keep a record of their in-service work and contributions to school-based INSET activities. The headteacher should draw upon the records when co-ordinating the school's development plan. The school's INSET coordinator should also have access to them. The headteacher should make use of them when writing a teacher's reference.

> For new teachers, the first months in a school have too often in the past been more of a test of survival than a time of professional growth and development. What can be done to smooth their path into the profession so that their early experience can be a secure foundation on which they can build their teaching careers?
>
> *Making Induction Work*,
> DES, HMSO, 1978

The pattern of local authority provision for probationer teachers across the country is very patchy. Some probationers receive very little input, others a hastily thrown-together few sessions, others well-planned meetings after school and some – a lucky some – a full induction programme including numerous day-releases throughout the year. Probationers have said

"No one has said anything to me since I arrived and no one has been into my classroom. I'm really floundering and don't know what to do."

"I get regular visits but nothing much seems to happen afterwards. No one discusses them with me or gives me any advice."

"My headteacher has been really good. Every time I come into school he says 'Hello' and he always says 'Goodbye' in the evening. He's very nice."

"As soon as I arrived at the school I was given lots of information and a full programme of what was going to happen. They have stuck to it, as well. It's been good."

The induction of probationer teachers into the profession ought to be a right which they come to expect rather than a luxury they hope to receive. However good the local authority's central induction programme is, each school has a key role in introducing new colleagues into the profession.

Why the school-based induction of new teachers should be so patchy is not clear. It may be, although unlikely, that induction hasn't been identified as a priority by many schools. Whatever the reasons, successful induction programmes have revealed some interesting similarities.

The components of successful induction

1   *A supportive atmosphere*
Such atmospheres are common in most good schools. Where probationers had particularly good induction years, though, the staff had made a professional commitment to be as available as the probationer needed them to be. The support wasn't defined by luck or any one individual's personal qualities.

2   *A 'professional friend'*
A professional friend is one who takes on the role of guaranteeing personal and professional support throughout the induction year. That support is usually confidential between the 'friend' and the probationer.

An important feature of the success of the professional friend is that they are not chosen because of any hierarchical position in the school. Indeed, the use of someone in a senior position can often cut across the beneficial confidentiality. Given that someone with experience is required, good 'friends' are chosen to meet the needs of each probationer; probationers are not asked to fit in with the school's designated and permanent 'friend'.

3   *Good documentation*
Probationers like to feel they are a part of the school as soon as possible and documentation which helps them to learn about and fit into routines quickly is welcomed. Staff handbooks usually fulfil this role admirably.

Schools which are well documented with good policies, parents' booklets, staff handbooks, newsletters and so on can confuse probationers by issuing them all at one time. There is a need for both the planned introduction to the full range of documentation a school possesses and also some digest versions of policy and other important documents which provide probationers with a flavour of what is happening.

4   *Identification of key areas*
It is impossible for a probationer to focus on everything during their first year and difficult for them, without help, to know what to focus on. Identifying key areas within which to work with probationers seems to help. Areas of importance include

- *Planning*: what to plan, ways of going about it, the problems of over-planning, breadth, relevance, first-hand experience
- *Classroom organisation*: how to physically organise classrooms to contribute to the good working conditions
- *Classroom management*: how children are spoken to, giving them independence, dealing with queries, staying one step ahead
- *Display*: a variety of effective and efficient ways of displaying children's work
- *Assessment*: formal methods used by the school and the strengths and weaknesses of informal methods used by teachers
- *Record-keeping*: the records kept as part of the school's own system and those which might be usefully kept by teachers in addition
- *School organisation*: how the school works, channels of communication, using the structure effectively, finding out what is there
- *LEA organisation*: putting the school in the broader context of the LEA, its decision-making processes and its demands.

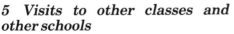

5 Visits to other classes and other schools

Most probationers understandably want to concentrate on their own classrooms in their first few months in school. Once reference points of what it is like to be a class teacher have been established, then planned visits to other classes within their own school and subsequent visits to other schools can be very useful.

6 A structure for the year

Even the most experienced teacher would be unable to take all of this on board simultaneously. Schools need to identify a structure which introduces all of the elements gradually and appropriately throughout the year. For one school the structure looked like this:

Autumn term Planning, classroom organisation and classroom management

Spring term As above but concentrating on display, assessment, record-keeping and in-school visits to other classes

Summer term As above but concentrating on school and LEA organisation plus release time to other schools.

7 Regular visits to the probationer's classroom

If probationers are to be advised throughout their induction year then such advice needs to be based on the probationer's own practice. Probationers should be visited each week, if possible, by someone who works alongside the probationer rather than sits back and 'inspects'.

8 Opportunities for discussion

Most discussion in schools takes place informally. Probationers need more than that, particularly as they may not be confident enough to take part in informal discussions at the beginning of their time in school. One school

- guaranteed a follow-up meeting to every visit to the probationer's classroom. Where possible, this took place on the same day as the visit, provided feedback and gave the probationer opportunity to raise any immediate points
- organised fortnightly after-school meetings between the probationer and the headteacher or deputy head at which the probationer could raise any matters of concern. These meetings were put into the school diary at the beginning of the school year.

5.2.5 *Motivating Staff*

Headteachers, deputy heads, curriculum coordinators, departmental coordinators, and others all perform leadership tasks. Being a leader is all very well and good, but how does one motivate staff?

Well, first, it is important to rephrase the question. It is clear from the research into motivation that if someone tries to 'motivate' others then that person is slightly 'off-key'. Rather, work should be approached and organised in such a way that the work itself will be sufficiently motivating. Therefore, planning and organising the work is a basic task in itself. Do staff want to teach their allocated classes, in their chosen spaces and with their nominated levels of ancillary help? Motivation and de-motivation have their roots in such questions. Rather than ask "how do I motivate you", which in any case implies you need to be motivated, it is better and necessary to review the prevailing working conditions and climate, and see if things might be organised differently.

Motivation is not really external; it is generated by our own 'internal' needs. Our needs cause us to act as we do. There seems to be widespread agreement that there are four needs common to us all, although they occur in different strengths and alter at different times. Hence each person will have a unique 'profile of needs'.

Needs common to us all

Day, Johnston & Whitaker (1985, p. 98) identify the following common needs:

1 Affiliation: the need for a sense of belonging. Do all staff feel that they belong in the school and are regarded as part of the team? The headteacher's skills as a communicator are of great importance in meeting this need.

2 Achievement: the need for a sense of 'getting somewhere' in what is done. Do the staff feel that they are achieving things in the tasks they undertake? An ability to ensure that roles and responsibilities are clearly defined and understood will help people meet this need.

3 Appreciation: the need for a sense of being appreciated for the efforts one makes. This relates very closely to achievement – are the staff shown appreciation for both effort and achievement? People thrive on praise and it is probably one of the highest motivational factors – when did the headteacher last offer praise to someone on the staff? Has the headteacher praised all the teachers during the last term?

4 Influence: the need for a sense of having some influence over what happens within the work setting. The ability of the headteacher to delegate effectively has considerable bearing on this issue. Staff do not wish or expect to have complete control over everything that happens in school but there are specific areas where they are able to use their expertise and have some influence. Teachers are most highly motivated when they feel that they can contribute significantly to the shape of the curriculum.

Given these four common needs it is not difficult to compile lists of 'things to do' and 'things not to do' when considering the motivation of staff. Day, Johnston & Whitaker (1985) have done such a task when running in-service courses on primary school management. They suggest the following considerations.

First, teachers are most likely to be well motivated in regard to changes when:

- they are involved in the formulation of the new approaches
- there is a feeling of 'solidarity'/community among the staff
- there is a demonstrable need for change
- staff are confident of their own abilities to deal with an activity
- skills for dealing with an activity have been fostered within teachers, or will clearly be developed in the future
- the headteacher recognises the extra time/effort put in by staff
- the headteacher provides positive support and involvement
- the teacher feels generally secure within the school
- there is a sense that what is being done is also laying a foundation for future success
- as a venture, it is easy to join in at any time
- clear educational and social goals are obvious
- there are regular discussions for the interchange of ideas, information and experience
- the previous experience of staff in comparable situations is utilised
- there is an open and friendly atmosphere generally within the school
- teachers are sure of support if difficulty is experienced
- the staff have confidence in the headteacher based upon their credibility and reputation for success
- the staff concerned have specific and clearly defined responsibilities

- a provision of time in 'working hours' is made
- the senior staff are actively involved in the work.

Teachers are least likely to be well motivated when

- they are simply told that they must . . .
- they are put into a threatened position
- the activity is not well planned
- it is felt by teachers that the plan is a 'gimmick' promoted by a senior member of staff to further their own ends
- the teachers feel that the plan is being carried out merely to satisfy higher authority
- a lot of hard work is involved without any apparent or obvious results
- initial moves are badly organised, with consequent initial negative feedback
- the teachers feel alienated from the school or from whoever is responsible for the plan
- the headteacher assumes the role of the 'expert', and there is a lack of opportunity for teachers to develop, or to exercise responsibility
- there is group pressure from colleagues to 'opt out'.

The practical steps that a headteacher might take to increase the likelihood of the staff being well motivated include:

- facilitating early initial discussion within the staff
- keeping overall control of the programme
- developing staff, especially their skills, understanding and self-confidence
- making available as much time as possible (and letting it be seen that they are doing so)

- leading by example
- involving all staff and not just teachers
- providing aid, back-up and support, especially when there are particular difficulties
- utilising the skills and expertise of particular staff
- making a very careful appraisal of the status quo, prior to committing the school to change
- encouraging staff to suggest developments and modifications once the change process is under way
- building up a system of steady, reliable support for teachers who are attempting to innovate in their own work
- building upon success and not failure
- delegating carefully; and delegating authority as well as responsibility
- appreciating work already done, however trivial; not alienating those who are committed to the system which the headteacher may wish to change
- not personalising opposition – keeping it on a professional level.

Work in America also suggests that when leaders provide a purposeful context for teachers increased motivation occurs. Some of the practical ways of setting such a context are:

- leaders avoid, or keep to the absolute minimum, interruptions to the teaching
- teachers are involved in curricular decisions
- staff meetings are useful to teachers since they are targeted at teachers' concerns, are result orientated, stick to the agenda and end on time
- in-service activities match teachers' and the schools' needs
- time is set aside for teachers to exchange ideas
- teachers learn from one another by observing one another's strengths
- leaders display sincere interest in teachers' work
- staff receive ongoing recognition and support.

This last point is significant. Although the list tends to talk about teachers, there is a clear need to consider *all* staff. Ancillaries, secretaries, peripatetic, supply and welfare staff should all be given due recognition, interest and support. After all, one thing must be absolutely clear, ancillary workers can hardly be in the job for the money! What is it that motivates them? And what else might be done to make their work more interesting and motivating?

Perhaps the greatest aid to motivation is simply talking to people about their work, their aspirations and desires to do a good job: *and then doing something alongside them to help.*

Job descriptions can be very useful tools in the management of a school. For the headteacher, good job descriptions

- provide a quick check that important areas of the school's development are being covered
- enable evidence of this to be presented to other interested parties such as the LEA and governing bodies
- help to ensure that appraisal procedures relate to previously agreed, and therefore more neutral, agendas.

For the 'owner' (including the headteacher) they

- establish the boundaries of responsibility over a given period of time
- provide a way of defining work done when applying elsewhere
- give confidence that appraisal procedures should not cover unexpected areas.

Job descriptions also have negative features, too. They can

- create mistrust – 'Are you saying that you don't trust me to do anything without having it written down?'
- create demarcation disputes – 'We agreed that I was responsible for mathematics in this school. I don't want her to have anything to do with it.'
- create friction – 'It's his job. It says so here. Why hasn't he sorted it out then?'
- create distress – 'I know we need someone to look after science but I'm the last person she should have chosen. Fancy not even asking me if I minded. I just can't do it!'

Negotiating and maintaining job descriptions need to be carried out with sensitivity.

The apparent definitive quality of job descriptions can also lead to other misunderstandings about what they can and cannot do.

Job descriptions describe what should be done; they describe a series of activities. What they cannot do is describe how those activities are to be carried out. In schools and other organisations, *how* the post-holder carries out the job is as important as the nature of the job itself.

> "I know that Arthur has the post of responsibility for maths in this school and I know that I am supposed to go and see him if I am in any difficulties, but I just can't. He's so horrible. I don't know what it is but he is so superior. Every time I talk to him I feel as though I'm not his colleague but his worst pupil.
>
> What do I do if I have problems with my maths teaching? I go next door and talk to Liz. I know she has the responsibility for PE but she is so much more understanding. I get so much from her."

> "The fact that Gill has responsibility for the art and craft stock doesn't mean that the only time I should be able to go into the cupboard is when she says so – on a Tuesday lunchtime."

Giving someone a job description, therefore, doesn't also confer the ability to carry out the tasks the job description contains.

Devising, negotiating, allocating and accepting job descriptions: some golden rules.

1   The tasks need to be within the capabilities of the person.
There is little point in presenting people with a list of tasks they cannot do. This is more likely to create tension and breakdown than positive feelings. There is nothing wrong, though, including in a job description the need for preparation, as in the following:

'During the year I will prepare for the introduction of problem-solving into the school by developing it in my own classroom, attending relevant INSET and building up appropriate introductory resources.'

2   The tasks need to be as precisely defined as possible
The introduction of appraisal procedures, greater involvement of governing bodies and more rigorous interviewing procedures all mean that the frequency of judgements upon teachers is becoming greater.

One way of helping both the judge and the judged to meet this situation more equably is to reduce the ambiguity of job descriptions as much as possible. A sentence which reads 'I am responsible for improving resources in PE this year' is open to all sorts of interpretations and misunderstandings. Changed to 'I am responsible for introducing new resources which enable hand–eye coordination to be developed in the first three years' is much better.

3   Job descriptions should be negotiated, not given
Job descriptions which are given rather than negotiated have two major failings.

First, they can only be given on the assumption that the person defining them understands everything there is to know about the organisation. This is unlikely.

Second, most of us work better when we have a sense of ownership of our work. Job descriptions which are given cannot create as strong a sense of ownership as job descriptions in which the recipient has been a creator, too.

Given those two factors and a degree of confidence it seems reasonable, where possible, to ask the recipients to write their own job descriptions and negotiate around those.

4 Job descriptions should be dynamic rather than passive
The tasks in a job description should help to move the school forward in one direction or another. Job descriptions should, therefore, follow on from analysis of where the school is and, if possible, the creation of a school development plan. At the beginning of each negotiation the key sentence is not 'What can I do?' but 'What needs to be done?'

5   Job descriptions should be time specific
It is well known that not everything gets done in the time allocated for it, but it is also often true that if deadlines are not created little gets done at all. If both the school and the 'owner' of the job description are to benefit from what it contains, some time scale is vital.

Often this means that a job description will be re-negotiated each year. It can mean, though, that different activities within the job description can be allocated different deadlines of a term, a few weeks or, occasionally, more than one year.

Nobody can do it all – and those of us who think we can simply make our schools run less effectively. There is just too much to know, too much to understand and too much to do for one person to even pretend they can manage everything.

Hence the need to share or delegate the work we do. Sharing can be carried out between any two or more people but delegation is different. Delegation involves the concepts of hierarchy, power, authority and responsibility.

The person delegating is invariably in a position of power. Delegation involves giving over some of that power to someone else. Delegating the *power* to make things happen doesn't mean, though, that we also delegate the *responsibility*; that stays with whoever is able to delegate.

> "In a large school such as the one we work in – it's a Group 7 primary school – the new INSET arrangements obviously take up a considerable amount of time and I just didn't feel as though I had enough time to do it properly.
>
> When we were sorting out our job descriptions for the year I asked Peter if he would take on the job of arranging our INSET and looking after the INSET budget – and he's made a really good job of it.
>
> Every so often he and I get together and he tells me everything that has happened – partly so that I know what is going on, partly just to check that I think we are heading in the right direction and partly to give Peter the confidence that everything is going well. It's only right that if we should mess it up I should be responsible."

In this school the headteacher has delegated reasonably. She has trusted Peter to carry out the task effectively, rarely interferes in the day-to-day work and yet keeps herself sufficiently involved to be able to take full responsibility should anything go wrong.

Almost everyone in the school will be involved in delegation at some time or another either by having tasks delegated to them or by delegating to others. At whatever level within the school delegation takes place, it is important to remember that the responsibility for the task stays with the person doing the delegating.

Trust and control

The two elements always at the centre of delegation are *trust* and *control*.

Control remains in the hands of those delegating through the responsibility which they retain, but to delegate effectively those in possession of power must have *trust* in the person to whom they are delegating. Trust is usually based upon previous experience; we earn trust as a result of the sum total of our past joint experiences – that is why it is, quite rightly, so difficult to delegate immediately to a new colleague.

Trust, though, is two-way and those to whom we are delegating must have trust in us if they are to carry out the tasks they are set with commitment and enthusiasm. A number of factors can affect the levels of trust given to the person in positions of power. It is reasonable, for example, that

- the delegated tasks are matched to willing individuals
- the tasks are matched to individuals capable of doing them
- the tasks are appropriate to an individual's perceived role in the school

- once delegated, the day-to-day ownership of the tasks is given to those most closely involved
- the tasks should be seen as useful to the school
- the act of delegation is seen as team-building rather than team-destroying
- the task should be clearly defined and the amount of day-to-day control for it clearly established.

"We were worried about the little amount of parental consultation that seemed to take place in our school compared to other experiences we had all had, so the headteacher asked me to chair a working party to see what could be done.

As a deputy, this was one job I really wanted to do and so I brought together some colleagues from across the school. After a couple of months of visiting other schools and discussions with everyone about what was reasonable we produced a policy for the full staff to consider.

At the staff meeting there were obviously some disagreements about our final recommendations – including one or two from the headteacher, I think – but after some discussion our recommendations were accepted.

The headteacher was really good, actually. He had seen our recommendations before they went to the staffing and told us that they were so much along the right lines that he wasn't going to make any fuss about the one or two bits he disagreed with. He was very supportive throughout."

This school seemed to get this particular piece of delegation about right. The task was seen to be important, the person delegated to the task was keen to be involved and had, as far as we can tell, status in the school. She was allowed to organise things in her own way although the headteacher was constantly informed and was able to accept the final recommendations even though they weren't exactly as he might have wished. The deputy and her team, quite rightly, felt as though they had done a good job.

Matching the task to the person is one of the key skills in delegation. To do this it is necessary to have a clear view in your own mind as to exactly what the task is and of the particular qualities and attitudes of those to whom it might be delegated.

Delegation is very much a part of staff development. Selecting the right person to carry out a particular job should be as important as which jobs are given out. Your colleagues, or the children in your class, will have different skills and needs; appropriate delegation can help them to build on existing skills, develop new ones and improve their strengths.

Carefully thought out delegation can have a profound effect upon the self-concept of those to whom we delegate. We have all taught children for whom the delegation of a particular task has been a turning point in their lives; our colleagues are not that much different.

One of us remembers only too well the feeling of being a probationer, struggling to keep a head above water and not too sure about the success of much that we were doing. The moment of being asked to take responsibility for the entrance hall display – "because you have done some smashing things in your classroom" – seems like only yesterday. It was a moment which defined a professional status which was able to grow from that point onward. Without that simple – and appropriate – act of delegation who knows what sort of career might have followed?

The negative power of delegation

As with most of the concepts in this book, delegation has its negative side.

"We had a litter problem at school. I'm not suggesting we didn't – but it was mainly caused by the children being sold snacks to eat at playtime to raise money for the school fund and not enough bins to throw their rubbish into.

We were discussing it at a staff meeting one day when the headteacher suddenly asked me to do something about it. I was so taken aback I hadn't time to say no and anyway, I didn't want to cause a scene in the staff meeting.

When I finally got round to it, it was obvious what the problem was but when I discussed it with the headteacher he said he wasn't going to stop the tuck shop because we needed the money, we weren't going to spend any on new bins and the children couldn't come into school at playtime to throw their rubbish into a classroom bin because it was one of the rules.

The whole thing was a farce and a waste of time. We still haven't sorted out the problem and the other day Mrs ... blamed me for not doing anything about it. It's really made me fed up."

Delegation helps to create atmospheres. It can be a vital and positive force in a school or it can be negative and deadening.

In primary schools meetings take place all the time. Whenever two or more staff get together they are having a meeting. The fact that most of these meetings are informal, may be concerned with personal or professional matters, and are often *ad hoc* and of short duration should not prevent us from calling them meetings. Nor should their informal nature make us underestimate their value. Informal meetings play a vital part in the smooth running of the school's network of communications and they contribute to the life and work of the school.

Informal meetings, though, are only one approach to developing and sustaining healthy communications. Regardless of their size, primary schools also need formal meetings. The current buzz words of HMI, LEA advisers, management pundits and many schools are

- collaboration
- consistency
- continuity

All of these words imply that teachers need to work together. All of these words rely upon effective communication during meetings.

It is no surprise then that virtually every primary school has regular and frequent staff meetings. Many schools also have other kinds of meetings; working parties, year team meetings, departmental meetings, case conferences, and planning meetings for particular events (concerts, visits, sports events, festivals, etc.). Yet having a meeting may not, in itself, be enough. We have all been in staff meetings which were a waste of time, went on for too long, devoted too little time to the important business, and which we did not really need to attend in the first place!

In recent years primary teachers have increasingly noted that there is a lack of time to cater for all the demands they face. Meetings are both important ways of helping teachers work together and a way of using up precious time which could be allocated to any number of other pressing tasks (preparation, marking, planning). Meetings may be necessary but it is not sufficient simply to have meetings; what is needed are effective and efficient meetings.

Organising meetings

If a meeting is to be worthwhile, some thought should be given to its preparation. The questions in the flow chart opposite are designed to help avoid some of the common pitfalls of meetings, such as staff not knowing where the meeting was to take place, whether or not a teacher should or could attend, the aim of the meeting, and so on. Problems like these occur more often than you might expect, and are avoidable.

The questions might also trigger fresh approaches. For example, perhaps the caretaker and/or ancillary staff should attend certain meetings. Maybe the parent governors' views would inform certain decisions. Perhaps some meetings could take place at times other than before and after school, or during a lunchtime? Decisions taken when staff are rested, relaxed and in comfortable surroundings and not interrupted may be more effective.

Many schools proceed from one meeting to another out of habit and custom. These questions should stimulate you to reflect on practices which may need revising.

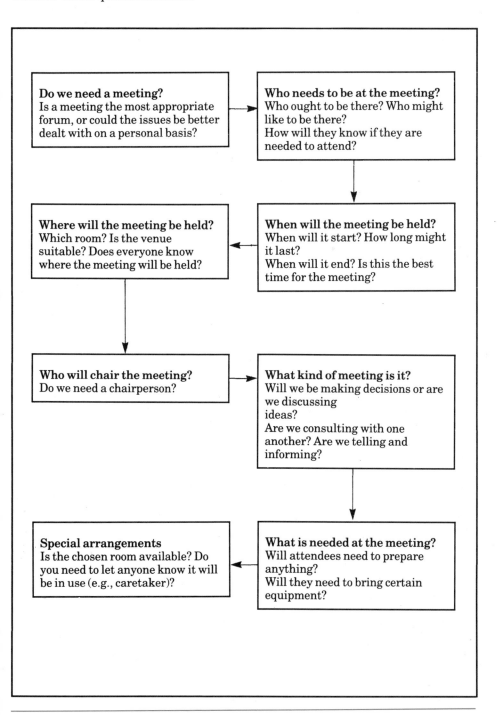

Do we need a meeting?
Is a meeting the most appropriate forum, or could the issues be better dealt with on a personal basis?

Who needs to be at the meeting?
Who ought to be there? Who might like to be there?
How will they know if they are needed to attend?

Where will the meeting be held?
Which room? Is the venue suitable? Does everyone know where the meeting will be held?

When will the meeting be held?
When will it start? How long might it last?
When will it end? Is this the best time for the meeting?

Who will chair the meeting?
Do we need a chairperson?

What kind of meeting is it?
Will we be making decisions or are we discussing ideas?
Are we consulting with one another? Are we telling and informing?

Special arrangements
Is the chosen room available? Do you need to let anyone know it will be in use (e.g., caretaker)?

What is needed at the meeting?
Will attendees need to prepare anything?
Will they need to bring certain equipment?

Agendas

Questions about how to organise a meeting are largely to do with the context of the meeting. The next thing to organise is the content, which is where use of an agenda can prove valuable.

It is worth considering defining some agenda items in detail to avoid any confusions over what is to be discussed. An agenda should be circulated to all those expected to attend. In addition, it may sometimes be useful to display a copy in a prominent place so that all members of staff have access to it.

Priorities

From looking at the advantages and disadvantages of approaches to creating agendas a number of points emerge:

- Priorities for the meeting's agenda should be identified by someone. What is included/excluded? What is urgent/can wait?
- How much time should be allocated to some items? It is wasteful to spend 40 minutes on the colour of

tissue paper for party hats and five minutes on a new paired approach to reading!
- Staff do need to feel involved, consulted and listened to. If they do not then their participation in the meeting may be reduced.

Too much?

Agendas that are too long are frustrating and inefficient. It may be more useful to have two meetings instead of one. Many staff now use one meeting, often each week, to deal with 'housekeeping' matters – things that require little discussion and are invariably concerned with giving information (lost property, list of visitors, tidiness around school, changes in arrangements).

Another option is to suggest that certain items are present under any other business (AOB). This usually works well. However, in large schools there can be another whole meeting's worth of items under AOB and if the meeting has already been lengthy it can go 'an item too far' for some members!

Remember!

If you want your meetings to be successful there's more to it than putting a group of people together and starting them talking. Agenda

creation is one element that will contribute to the effective and efficient management of meetings.

The Role of the Chairperson

The changes initiated in the latter part of the 1980s have increased the number of meetings held in school. You've probably noticed it already. Staff need to look at the implications of the National Curriculum, to discuss the findings of the subject working groups and may have to reconsider their approaches to evaluation and assessment. Moreover, many of these meetings will be in addition to most schools' existing programmes of staff meetings as there will still be a need to consider such things as resources, timetables, budgets and day-to-day 'housekeeping' matters.

Unfortunately, the time available for all of these meetings remains constant, therefore more meetings have to be packed into the same amounts of time. Consequently, the need for efficient meetings is all the more important. One way in which meetings can be improved is by having an effective chairperson.

Who should be the chairperson?

In primary schools, the headteacher commonly chairs meetings. This can have advantages, but there is a danger that too much control rests with one person. For example, such an arrangement usually means that the chair does most of the talking. Chairing is not the privilege of position and meetings in school should not be chaired by just the headteacher and/or deputy. Everyone on the staff should have the chance to chair meetings. This also has advantages when staff are not chairing in that they are likely to have a clearer understanding of the difficulties involved, and are more likely to perform better in meetings generally.

Preparation

The chairperson needs to be well prepared. This includes knowing who is coming to the meeting, and ensuring that an agenda has been circulated to all concerned. The chairperson should decide whether minutes should be taken or not. Copies of minutes of any previous meeting and other relevant notes and papers should be prepared in advance and circulated with the agenda.

The setting for the meeting should be given some thought. If possible, chairs of similar height should be arranged in a circle so that all members of the meeting can see each other and feel included. Tables may be needed, but if so all members should sit around them, rather than just one or two individuals sitting magisterially behind one.

If someone is to make an individual presentation or lead the discussion on some particular agenda item, then that person should be consulted prior to the meeting to check how long is needed or is available.

Preparation is thus fairly obvious and a matter of common sense, yet in the hurly-burly of school life it can easily be forgotten. Preparation by the chairperson will not necessarily ensure a smooth meeting, but it should increase the meeting's chances of being effective.

What kind of meeting?

One of the most important pieces of preparation is to determine what kind of meeting or discussion will take place. This is not a matter of deciding whether the meeting will be friendly or hostile – unfortunately, not even the chairperson can predetermine that! Rather, it is to know whether the whole meeting, or certain agenda items, can be categorised as:

Informational   concerned with the giving out of news and information.
Consultative   finding out what those present think and feel about some specific matter.
Decision-making   making decisions either by the collective meeting or by an individual who is party to the meeting.

Whether it is on an item-by-item or a meeting-by-meeting basis, everyone needs to know the function of the meeting or discussion. The chairperson should preface each discussion by clarifying its objectives.

Process for the meeting

① Starting the meeting

The chairperson should not be late, and should take steps to avoid being called away or interrupted by something outside the meeting's focus. The meeting should start on time. Do not wait for someone who is late – a person who is five minutes late keeps the whole group waiting five minutes per person and will waste a considerable amount of collective potential working time.

At the start the chairperson should make such introductions as are necessary, inform the group of the time the meeting is to end, explain the aims of the meeting or discussion and commence the work of the meeting without further ado. A few simple words, some preface to the first item and such 'rules' and procedures as are necessary should be all that is required. The meeting should not be delayed by a fussy or garrulous chairperson.

② During the meeting

The most obvious rule is *'keep to the agenda'*. This is sometimes easier said than done, but nevertheless the chairperson should try and keep the discussion relevant to the business in hand. If discussion begins to take an inappropriate direction then it is up to the chair to call the group's attention to serious diversions from the agenda.

The chairperson should be *vigilant about time* and warn the group if prearranged schedules are slipping.

When time begins to run out the chairperson may need to rearrange the agenda or appeal to the group for guidance as to which items should be given priority.

Another function of the chairperson is to *help the group establish shared meanings*. For example, if abbreviations, acronyms and jargon are used, the chair may need to intervene and check that everyone understands the terminology. Such checking is fairly straightforward. More difficult is the establishing of shared meanings at the end of a group discussion. Here the chair should try to summarise the discussion and reflect back to the group the positions taken up by the group or individuals. This is not easy but it is very important as otherwise individuals may leave the meeting unclear of what was said, meant or decided.

Of course, it is not always clear what has been said or decided! Talk is often contradictory, inconsistent or imprecise. It may be appropriate at times to ask the person taking the minutes to read back the relevant part, as ultimately this will be the record, and, as such, should be clear to everyone.

Throughout the meeting the chairperson should *constantly listen, and talk only a little*, but this should not be taken as sign of inactivity. It is up to the chair to show that they have heard, remembered and considered what others have said.

The chairperson should *ensure that everyone feels included in the meeting*, through eye-contact and invitations to individuals to speak or comment, and they should try to avoid creating favourites or enemies. On the whole, the chairperson should be relatively neutral since it is the chair's function to enable the group to work. However, if the chairperson has views central to some particular issue, then they may need to consider temporarily handing over to someone else.

Common problems

Overtalkative people
The persistent talker usually adversely affects the progress of the meeting. When it is clear that such a person has exhausted the goodwill or the concentration span of the group, then the chair should intervene. A few diplomatic words may be needed, or a direct question such as, "So you are against this proposal?" The overtalkative use up precious time, so they may need to be reminded of time (and thus controlled), "We've only 10 minutes left, please could we hear another view?"

Sometimes it is not the sheer volume of a single statement that takes the time, but the persistent pressing of opinions. The overtalkative may modify their behaviour if the chair fails to approve of or acknowledge their comments. When 'controlled', an 'offender' should be reinstated into the

group otherwise relationship and communication problems may ensue.

Silence
When gaps occur in the conversation the chairperson could invite those who have not contributed to do so. Eye-contact with a silent member, whilst another is talking, may establish whether a contribution to the discussion is going to be forthcoming.

Sometimes an individual's silence may imply fatigue, anger, boredom, lack of interest or ill-health. Frequently in schools one is aware of such things, but some sensitivity will be needed when directly inviting the quiet members to speak. The chairperson should not insist on an individual contributing.

There are different sorts of silence, the reflective, the anxious, the puzzled, the confused, even the

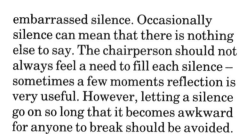
embarrassed silence. Occasionally silence can mean that there is nothing else to say. The chairperson should not always feel a need to fill each silence – sometimes a few moments reflection is very useful. However, letting a silence go on so long that it becomes awkward for anyone to break should be avoided.

Differences of opinion

In most discussions differences will emerge. The chair should try to remain impartial and to see any differences as constructive. Quite often a contrary view stimulates greater thought and awareness, thereby contributing to more sensitive and informed decisions.

There may be outbursts of anger or hostility. Where they are directed at the chairperson, an appeal to the group will usually help to defuse the tension, for example "Is that how you all feel?" or, "Is that a fair summary of what we believe?"

If the anger is directed elsewhere, say outside the group, it may be prudent to encourage the ventilation of pent-up frustrations, fears and disappointments. When a decision has to be made it is easier for the chairperson to be leading a group the members of which agree and like each other. While consensus is a worthy aim in meetings, chairpersons might be better advised to seek consent. Not everyone need agree with the proposals, not all differences need to be resolved; consensus is a bonus rather than a necessity. Perhaps all that needs to be secured is the extent to which the group will go along with a decision.

If consent is limited or difficult to ascertain then it may be useful to defer a decision. Allowing more thinking time often means that people have a chance to get used to the idea.

Ending the meeting

At the close of a meeting the chairperson should recap briefly what has happened, note decisions taken and points which need further action.

Often one meeting leads to another, in which case the date, time, venue and purpose of any subsequent meeting should be mentioned and minuted.

Effective chairperson – effective meetings?

You may feel that the picture presented here is of a chairperson who is some paragon of judicial restraint and diplomacy. That may be, but if the chairperson can contribute to people wanting to meet, looking forward to discussions and sharing different ideas and approaches, and if the chairperson conducts effective

meetings, then the outcome is a healthier climate amongst staff, a greater sense of oneness and thereby the opportunity of working in a more effective school. Chairpersons contribute to effective meetings; effective meetings contribute to effective schools.

5.2.10 Managing Meetings – 3

Minutes

Minutes can play a valuable role in the management of meetings. Unfortunately they are often not used, and when they are they tend to be taken for granted and not used to advantage.

Why take minutes?

The first and most obvious reason is the need to record what happens in a meeting. This is particularly necessary when some staff do not or cannot attend all meetings, or when there are a lot of meetings in the school. Minutes help all members of staff to keep track of what is going on.

However, minutes can do two other things. First, they can act as an *aide-mémoire*. A rapid read of the minutes of the last meeting should remind us who agreed to do something and when they agreed to have it done by. This is very useful if that person turns out to be you! An *action* column helps to highlight those who need to do something as a result of the decision made in the meeting.

Second, minutes should give a consensus of understanding. At the start of a meeting, members should agree the minutes of the previous meeting. In effect, what they are doing is saying

- this is an accurate record of what happened
- this matches my understanding of what was decided.

Minutes are intended to ensure that those things which were agreed in the heat (or the cold) of a meeting are understood and accepted.

Keeping minutes

Whoever keeps the minutes usually has a thankless task. It means

- extra work
- being able to listen
- being able to write quickly and succinctly, and selecting and re-ordering the vital elements from what may have been a discursive and unstructured exchange of views
- often having to take a less directly involved role in the meeting.

It is not necessary for the same person to keep the minutes each time, but it is never a good idea for the chairperson to try to keep the minutes. Neither is it helpful if the minute-taker is someone who is likely to make a major contribution to that particular meeting. However, it is unlikely to be a popular job, so perhaps the most democratic solution is for everyone to take a turn.

Although the person who takes the minutes may be less directly involved in the meeting, it does not mean they should be passive or silent. At certain points, perhaps at the chairperson's invitation, it is a good idea for them to report back their impression of what has been said and decided. In so doing the minute-taker should not feel that their record is being tested for its integrity and accuracy, but to ensure that common understandings are being developed. Thus the *process* of keeping minutes can help create consent and avoid misunderstandings.

What should be included?

Minutes should recall facts:

- date, time, venue
- name of meeting
- who was present
- apologies

They should include agenda items serving as headings, under which should be noted

- main points raised in discussion
- decisions taken
- actions required, by whom and by what date
- future plans
- unresolved matters
- date, time and place of next meeting (if relevant).

Minutes should not record everything that is said, only the main points. However, deciding what the main points are can sometimes be difficult.

The minute-taker should concentrate on identifying the key points a speaker is making. In discussion it is reasonable and normal for speakers to illustrate their points with a variety of anecdotes, explanations and illustrations. It's quite normal, too, in many forms of writing. Minutes, though, are a specialised form of writing and should be as concise as possible.

One advantage of letting members take it in turn to minute meetings is that colleagues can learn from each other's approaches. They can also understand how long-winded speeches or lack of clarity can make the minute-taker's task more difficult and, more importantly, make the speaker's contribution to the meeting less effective.

After the meeting

The person who minutes the meeting should be responsible for ensuring that the minutes are promptly circulated, approved and filed in the appropriate way.

The circulation of minutes is particularly important. If actions are required as a result of a meeting, minutes can be used as a prompt to the person who is responsible for taking that action. Minutes which arrive two weeks after the meeting has taken place may be an accurate and concise record, but may not be helpful in getting things done!

The attitudes of the people who receive your minutes often depend on the way in which those minutes are presented.

Informal meetings can often be represented by quick, handwritten, informal minutes. But the minutes of a meeting at which important decisions have been made should be presented in a way which reflects the status of what has taken place.

The prepared minutes should be shown to the chairperson prior to circulation. Again, this is not to judge the minute-taker's ability, but to agree the recorded impression of the meeting.

Opposite there is an example of some minutes taken at a real meeting. We have added some comments to them which emphasise their strengths and weaknesses.

*List might indicate full
names, if there are
newcomers on the staff*

*Clear heading, main
details clearly
shown*

```
        YEAR TUTORS' MEETING MINUTES
          30th APRIL, 12.15 PM
             A. P.'s OFFICE

Present: AP LC DJ BT LJ PS RD                    ACTION


A.      MEETING FOR SUMMER TERM

The proposed groupings for meetings as set out in
Anne's document were discussed.

Timing of the meetings were discussed, including the
possibility of re-introducing some 8.30 am staff
meetings for points of information only.  LC
suggested that we should try, as a temporary measure,
to reduce the number of full staff meetings so that
people would have more time to give to working parties.

AGREED: Attendance at meeting will be in directed time.

Re-introduction of 8.30 am staff meeting will be put to
next full staff meeting on 7th May.

Dates and timings of working party meetings will be
decided by those opting to join the groups.

B.      ACTIVITY WEEK

AGREED

This will be in the week beginning 8th June.  The
usual option system will operate and planning and
deciding on options will take place at year group
meetings.  Y.G. Tutors will co-ordinate the week.
DJ will design an option form for consideration         DJ
at our next meeting.

C.      A.O.B

RD asked that from 11th May to 15th May we avoid any
activities which might cause distraction to Fourth
Years as Higham Secondary has requested that we arrange
for parents to be present when Fourth year pupils have
their individual interviews with Higham School staff.

D.      DATE OF NEXT MEETING

Tuesday 12th May at 12.15 pm
```

*Effective synopsis
of discussion*

*Clear statement of
agreement*

*Newcomers might
need further
information*

*Clear indication of
responsibility*

*Unclear – this actually meant to say that children moving
from primary to secondary should be available, and on
normal timetable, when secondary staff visit the school.*

5.2.11 *School Policies*

A 'policy', according to *Chambers Concise Dictionary,* 1985, is a 'course of action'. By that definition schools are already full of policies, each of which responds to the hundreds of situations in which teachers, children, parents and others find themselves each day.

The weakness across the whole school is that many of these individually held policies can be contradictory and confusing, reducing the smooth running of the organisation and ensuring that children's education, as they move from class to class, is haphazard and unstructured.

School policies attempt to counter that weakness by creating agreed procedures, methods, approaches and decisions which enable a school to work as an integrated unit, moving and developing in more or less the same direction. School policies are not only about curriculum matters, although they are obviously important. A school might want to create policies about (among others)

- acceptable children's behaviour
- the involvement of parents
- community work
- staff duties

The existence of a policy doesn't mean that it will be followed identically by everyone in the school. One of the common threads running through this book is the inevitability of different perceptions within and about a school and, clearly, each individual will interpret a policy in a slightly different way. What it does mean is that those interpretations should be focused around similar procedures and outcomes.

Why are policies important?

1 Policies provide a measure of agreement
Schools are incredibly busy and demanding places. If they are to run as smoothly as possible then everyone who is connected with them needs to have a framework within which to work. Policies exist to provide this framework.

2 Policies help to provide continuity
Schools, like many other organisations, cannot function effectively without some measure of continuity. If each change of staff were to alter the broad direction in which a school is heading the likely result would be chaos. Policies ensure that the direction of a school, while not resistant to change and development, is also stable enough to withstand certain inevitable pressures.

3 Policies create security
At a time when the pace of educational change is great and the external pressures on teachers and schools so enormous, the existence of policies can help to create security for teachers. A policy document represents an accumulation of professional discussion and the translation of that discussion into recommendations for practical action. Policies explain what a school is doing and why. A good policy document should free teachers from having to make individual defences of their work and provide evidence to others – parents, inspectors, HMIs and so on – that decisions have been clearly thought out by the school.

4 Policies help to ease negotiations about practice

Personalising issues – feeling that a contrary point of view is a personal attack on ourselves – is counter-productive to professional development. Unfortunately, because education is essentially a human activity the opportunities for such personal and interpersonal offence are frequent.

If we are to be able to think through issues in a less personalised way we need a neutral starting point from which to begin discussions. School policies can help by creating such a neutral context. With them, the evaluation of practice can begin with questions such as "How does what you are doing fit in with our agreed policy?" rather than "I disagree with what you are doing."

What should policies contain?

Certain features do seem to be important if policies are to be useful to schools.

First, policies need to provide examples of what should happen as a result of the policy being put into action. In other words, policies need to be practical.

All of us will have either seen or worked on school policies which, in the end, resemble nothing more than a text-book about a subject, often apparently written more for the career prospects of the writer than for the benefit of those who are supposed to use it.

If policies are to coordinate a school then they need to be used. It is unlikely in these busy times that teachers will even give policies a thought if they don't offer strategies which can be used in practice. So the first thing a policy must do is to answer the question "Will people who use it have a good idea of what they are supposed to do?"

Because many of us who read

policies have a range of different abilities it is also important that such practical strategies should be understood by the least informed and able in the school rather than the most. This has implications for the process through which policies are produced.

Second, policies need to provide reasons why the strategies they contain have been recommended. In other words, it isn't enough for a policy to only contain practical strategies. If the policies are to create confidence and security amongst their users then they need to provide reasons for action as well as the action itself.

Third, policies need to be designed in such a way that those who have to use them can gain access to the information they need as quickly as possible. A policy presented as a series of densely written A4 pages is likely to be neglected. Once neglected, the advantages of school policies are lost, however much hard work has been put into the early stages.

How should policies be produced?

Policies should benefit a school long after the process of their initial production has ended, but there is no doubt that we need to think carefully

about that process if the policies are to be as effective as possible. The process of producing policies in a school has a personal and professional effect upon those involved and upon the outcome of the policy itself.

Just occasionally, we can understand that some schools might need hastily written and imposed policies for specific reasons.

In general though, school policies are more effective if as many as possible of those whom they will affect have had a part to play in their formulation. In involving the whole staff and others

- a considerable amount of INSET work takes place
- the range of attitudes and abilities with which the policy has to deal is revealed more clearly
- a fuller range of expertise can be

utilised than resides in one or two individuals
- the presentation and appearance of the policy can be criticised before 'publication'
- the 'ownership' (and, therefore, the effect) of the policy is likely to be greater.

Involving the whole staff is a phrase which sounds simple but which hides complexity. Those involved in producing policies need to understand that it takes time, patience, diplomacy and understanding. On the other hand, if policies are to be long-lasting and effective such involvement is essential.

One final point

Policies, however well prepared and useful, will not continue in a school unless they are supported. The production of a written policy document is only the beginning. Issues contained within each policy need to be regularly brought into focus, reviewed and discussed. Those responsible for school policies need to

make them live rather than remain inert; those who take ultimate responsibility for the school need to ensure that an agreed policy is respected, worked towards and followed. Only then can we hope to maximise the advantages such policies bring.

A school development plan is a policy statement which maps the school's intended and anticipated areas of development. This could be expressed in terms of curriculum:

- to introduce the proposals of the National Curriculum working party report on geography by summer term 1993

or in terms of organisational arrangements:

- to review the way supply teachers are introduced to and supported in the school and the classroom.

A school development plan might embody both of these.

Primary schools need to plan on a broader rather than a narrower front. For example, if a school decided to develop only maths this year and science next year it could be many years before other areas of the curriculum were developed. Moreover, schools need to develop more than the curriculum, which is only one strand, however important, in the organisational life of the school.

The sheer scale of school development creates the need for priorities. Priorities will help staff make sense of the log-jam of issues needing or awaiting development. Thus, making priorities is one characteristic of school development plans. There are others:

- a belief that school development grows best from within
- the plan is a whole school plan
- the plan takes into account LEA and central government policies
- the plan is agreed with the school governors
- time schedules should be provided
- outside help should be identified
- the plan defines responsibilities
- the plan is a contract.

Below, we examine these points in more detail.

1 A belief that school development grows best from within

Although there is benefit to be gained from the kick in the pants from outside an organisation, most *development* does grow from within. In good schools teachers work continuously and actively towards their own and their school's improvement. There are three obvious reasons for this. First, staff feel more in control and committed when relating to their own development. Second, spreading the talents of those who work together facilitates much staff development. Third, internal school development is always necessary. No scheme – national, LEA or local – can work unless each school and teacher is a part of that development.

2 The plan is a whole school plan

All staff should be appropriately consulted and involved in devising the plan. The planning should provide a forum for staff to share and bring together the views of all members of the school's staff. As much as possible, the plan should also be the staff's collective view of how and where the school should be developing.

3 The plan takes into account LEA and central government policies

While development grows from within, teachers and schools work and exist within the context of national and local legislation such as policies for equal opportunities or special needs, Diocesan Agreed RE Syllabuses and the National Curriculum Council. Internal development does not mean ignoring such policies.

4 The plan is agreed with the school governors

The 1986 and 1988 Education Acts make such a characteristic an imperative. Schools clearly need to consider

- involving parent governors in the processes of planning
- involving the chairperson
- presenting and explaining the plan to governors
- securing the governors' support.

5 Time schedules should be provided

Target dates should be agreed and noted on an action sheet. These might vary as in

---

Action Sheet: Academic Year 1990 to 1991

Curricular Developments

1 Handwriting policy and scheme to be adopted and working in all classes by end of Autumn term.
2 Each class to undertake one educational visit within locality, each term for this year.
3 Technology Working Party Report to be discussed in Autumn term; our interpretation and resources analysed in Spring term; implementation to commence in Summer term and following academic year.

---

6 Outside help should be identified

'Growing from within' means that the responsibility for developing the school comes from those who are associated with it. It doesn't mean that outsiders should never be involved.

7 The plan defines responsibilities

Given that the plan is a whole school plan and that the staff are committed to making it work, it is reasonable for it to contain statements of individual responsibility which will enable the plan to happen. These statements of responsibility will be very close, if not identical, to job descriptions.

8 The plan is a contract

Agreement on the plan by the staff, governors and possibly the LEA effectively makes the plan a 'contract'. Having gone through the process of creating a school development plan it would be folly not to see it as 'morally' binding on all.

As new members of staff join a school they will need to be made aware of the school's plan and, crucially, be expected to accept it until such time as it is renewed, when the time for input occurs.

All of these characteristics are important. Each interlocks with the others to give the plan its strength. From these characteristics it can be seen that school development plans are:

- sensitive to issues both internal and external to the school. They should be a judicious blend of inside and outside interests and concerns
- a mix of wide ranging consultations and decisiveness. At some point consultation must pause and decisions be taken
- firm yet flexible. The plan must be sufficiently firmly established so that staff are committed to it and know that it really matters. Yet some flexibility is needed to take account of unexpected events. The plan must not be allowed to evaporate, but neither must it become unalterable.

School development plans will thus offer some clarity and certainty. At a time of change and uncertainty school development plans provide continuity and a way of making sense of the existing and new demands being made of schools. They provide help for everyone to

- know what is to be done
- know why it is to be done
- know when it is to be done
- know what help is available to do it.

The Key Elements and the Main Areas

There are three key areas to school development planning. They are

- review
- action
- evaluation

Review

Before saying where we should go it is necessary to find out where we are. Hence some system of review, school self-evaluation and self-appraisal is needed. At this stage policy documents laid down by national government and local authorities are likely to be particularly important as they provide an opportunity for schools to find out how far their existing practices already reflect the proposals contained in existing documentation.

The review procedure will involve consultation with all interested parties including parents and governors. The results of the review are particularly important as they will be instrumental in determining the first action statements the school makes. Any temptation to rush into 'action' should be resisted until a consensus of agreement has been reached about the school's present position.

Action

'Action' is self-explanatory. The action part of a school development plan describes what the school is going to do within a particular area over a given time span. The use of the word 'action' also implies a commitment to getting it done.

For the 'action' to be more than words on a page, a number of conditions have to be fulfilled.

1 Priorities have to be established

There is only so much a school, and particularly a small school, can achieve and attend to whilst simultaneously continuing with the day-to-day education of children.

2 The priorities have to respond to perceived needs

Priorities have a greater chance of being realised if those involved in delivering them can see the benefits which accrue. There is little point in embarking on a grand scheme to build a swimming pool for the school if teachers, parents and governors are aware that the book provision is both out-dated and of poor quality.

3 The priorities must be achievable within the time span

A school development plan is not an opportunity for grandiose boasting. It is a way of representing honestly the school's strengths and weaknesses and what is to be done. Once priorities have been declared then it is only reasonable for teachers, parents, governors and others to expect them to be achieved. Achievement should be the aim.

It is also true that priorities which are unachievable will very quickly lose the support of those expected to achieve them.

Evaluation

Evaluation represents a very similar stage to 'review' with one important difference. In the review stage the school was judging itself against wholly external criteria; in the evaluation stage the school also judges itself against criteria – the action priorities – which were created in-house. The evaluation stage assesses the school's ability to devise effective action plans as much as it assesses the school's ability to achieve them.

The six key areas

We can identify six key areas around which a school development plan might operate. They are the developing curriculum, the staff, the school constituency, resources, organisational systems, and the school climate.

The developing curriculum

'Curriculum' means here 'all the learning that is planned and guided by the school'. Divisions of this curriculum have always been open to debate although agreement is more likely as the National Curriculum becomes established.

The word 'developing' is important. No one would expect schools to *be* fully developed across all curriculum areas, but they might reasonably be expected to be responsive to changing ideas, perceptions, insights and demands so that their curriculum provision is continually developing.

The staff

The quality of the whole staff in a school is of immense importance. All members of staff are capable of developing as people and as professionals. The notion of school development plans assumes that each will exhibit strengths and weaknesses relevant to their role which can be supported and developed.

The school constituency

Schools are not insular places; they interact with and respond to a variety of outside influences (see pp. 12–14). The way in which a school interacts with those influences and the confidence they return to the school will influence the effectiveness of children's learning.

Resources

Resources can mean those items which directly support curriculum action, such as tape recorders, books, paint-brushes and so on. It can also mean the buildings and the use to which they are put to enhance the way in which children are educated.

Organisational systems

Schools need effective systems for a wide range of activities. Whichever systems are chosen will depend upon the context of each individual school, its size, the age range of its pupils, the nature of the buildings, the levels of support staff and so on. Ineffective systems are both time-wasting and confusing; school development plans should consider them carefully.

The climate

'Climate' is much harder to describe but no less important than the other elements. 'Climate' is something felt, the essence of a school which binds everything else together. It is what you feel as soon as you walk in the door. The fact that it *is* hard to describe shouldn't preclude schools from considering it very carefully.

School development plans are at the organisational heart of this book. Everything it contains affects in some way or another the actions which need to be developed and contained within a development plan.

School development plans are not an aspect of a school's life; they are the guiding force behind it.

5.2.14 *In-service Education and Training (INSET)*

The purpose of INSET is to further develop teacher professionalism and so help the implementation of change. So INSET aims to serve both

- the individual's needs and wishes
- the school's needs

In addition INSET is viewed by central government and LEAs as an agent of change. It is within these three circles of interest that INSET is provided. When analysing and identifying needs this simple model is worth keeping in mind, as there will be occasions when the provision can fall within the area where all three circles intersect; this might help in drawing up priorities.

There are bound to be times when a tension exists between the individual's perception of their own needs and those of the school, LEA or central government. A school may not wish to fund or use up allocated space to allow staff members to attend a course which appears to be for their benefit

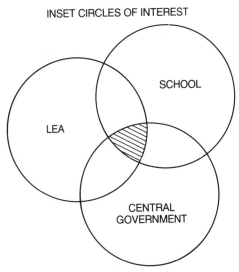

INSET CIRCLES OF INTEREST

LEA

SCHOOL

CENTRAL GOVERNMENT

alone. On the other hand individuals may not see the need to take part in INSET activities on behalf of the school without apparent benefit to themselves. It is, therefore, vital to make sure that the process of identifying INSET needs is as effective as possible.

Identifying needs

Identifying needs is central to the provision and support of INSET. How they are to be identified is often problematical – but there are strategies which can help.

A framework for policy making

The Advisory Committee on the Supply and Education of Teachers (ACSET) made the following recommendations:

1 Every school should have a policy for INSET, based upon a process of identification of the school's needs and those of the individual teachers.

2 LEAs should have coherent policies for INSET.

3 There should be appropriate preparation and follow-up work in schools.

4 There should be a continuation of the identification of national priorities.

At its simplest, needs identification involves looking at *what is actually happening and comparing it to what we want to achieve*. It's also worth remembering that INSET also has the dimension of *what others want from us*.

Weindling (of The National Foundation for Educational Research) suggests the following stages as a method of determining needs:

1 Identification of the problem.
2 Collection of the data.
3 Needs analysis.
4 Specification of objectives based on the priority needs.
5 Development of strategies.
6 Implementation of the programme.
7 Evaluation of the programme.
8 Revision.

Number 1 above sets the tone for the exercise by taking a 'problem-solving' approach in which a definition of INSET requirements emerges as a response to problems the school or individual is likely to face rather than a straightforward external assessment of their needs.

What we must do is move away from the "Jill's going on another maths course", which simply defines what is happening, to "does Jill need to go on another maths course?" and if so, why?

Hopefully the answers to such questions lie in the *school development plan* (discussed in detail on pp. 143–148. This is a means by which the staff of a school contribute to identifying the major thrust of the school's activities over a given period. The plan covers a number of important areas in the life of a school and takes into account both the internal wishes of those who work in it and the external constraints imposed by parents, governors, LEAs and central government's policies.

A needs identification process, starting with a school development plan, might look like this:

LOOKING AT INSET NEEDS

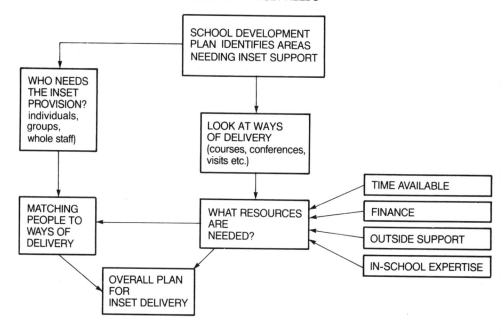

There is a crucial assumption made here which is that the school development plan has been drawn up by a process which involves all members of staff and so everyone has had the chance to make their own concerns known. Of course, this doesn't mean that *all* needs can be met but by focusing INSET around a school development plan the advantages include:

- the direction of the school will have been accepted by most of the staff
- individual teachers will be more able to respond to situations they see arising
- the overall needs of the school can be better assessed within a manageable time scale
- the existence of an agreed or accepted plan helps to de-personalise the sharp edge of decision making.

Making INSET work—a brief guide

Weighty tomes have been written about INSET; from many of these sources (some of which we list in the bibliography) it is possible to distil some key points:

- professional development is more effective when it is part of an overall plan
- 'one-offs' are not usually very useful although they are frequently used
- school-based courses are greatly helped by follow-up support
- teachers tend to prefer practical input rather than theory
- the aims of any INSET provision should be clear to all potential participants
- the best INSET providers listen to and act upon feedback
- there should be an interaction between the demands of school, LEA and central government
- whenever possible individuals should be able to define their own needs while accepting the necessity of overall planning.

Management's task in all this is to set up genuinely consultative processes to identify needs, decide on priorities, plan provision, acquire and allocate resources, set up and respond to evaluation.

Final thought

In times of rapid change the important role of staff development/INSET becomes vital. Without doubt it is one of the key tasks in managing the primary school.

5.2.15 *Time Management*

Time management is about planning your time effectively. If school development plans are a way of responding to the increasing complexity of school life, and term and lesson plans are a way of responding to the increasing complexity of classroom life, then time management is a way of responding to an increasing complexity at a personal level.

Time management, too, begins from the premise that the more complex a situation, the more important planning becomes as a means of dealing with it. Teachers and headteachers need to be

- calm
- well-organised
- thoughtful about educational issues and arguments
- conscious of all aspects of their organisation
- influential
- open to outside influences and not totally school-bound.

A Headteacher's Day

08.00	Arrive at school. Deal with mail, staff absences, phone messages
09.10	Assembly
09.30	Teach a class
10.30	Breaktime. See a parent
10.50	Teach second class
12.00	Lunch duty
12.20	Staff meeting
13.00	Eat sandwich
13.15	Work on governors' report
14.00	Go over School Development Plan for LEA
14.30	Phone LEA and deal with Development Plan, School Finance, Support Services
15.15	See two new families coming to school
15.45	See concerned parent
16.15	See two members of staff
17.00	Arrive (late) at Headteacher's liaison meeting
17.45	Go home and read report on local management of schools for later meeting
18.30	Return to school
19.00	Governors' meeting
22.00	Leave school.

It is impossible to conceive how, within the present context of teaching and headteaching, these attributes can be maintained without an effective time management plan.

Two difficulties

Most people find time management difficult to think about for two reasons. Sit still for a moment and ask yourself the following questions.

1 Do you appreciate the need for managing your time?
Often, time management is seen as something which someone else needs but not ourselves. Consider the list of attributes described above. If you cannot answer yes to all of them then you need some degree of time management help.

2 Do you appreciate how your job has changed?
Primary school teaching and headteaching have changed

"I used to take a club every lunchtime at school and people used to say to me 'You are doing too much' but I really enjoyed it so I carried on. During the teacher action a couple of years ago I stopped doing lunchtime clubs as part of my protest and suddenly found that I was enjoying my afternoon teaching so much more. I've gone back to running one lunchtime club a week now but it took the action to show me that I was using my time badly."

enormously over the past fifteen years and the pace of change and the levels of responsibility and complexity continue to increase.

These changes mean that our approach to the job has to change, too. Unfortunately, some of us find that change harder to make than others. By refusing to assess how the job has altered we try and hang on to an outdated style of teaching or headteaching, with the result that we are always trying to fit a quart into a pint pot.

One of the realities of those changes is that some things may have to be discarded or given lower priorities. If the fundamental shifts in the job are not appreciated those changes will be almost impossible to make.

What can be done

In the first place, as with all planning, it is important to understand the situation now.

Think about the most important functions of your job.

What is your job about as we move into and through the 1990s? You will probably experience some conflict between what you would like it to be and what is being demanded of you but try and develop a list of priorities.

Think about how you spend your time now.

For a week or so, write down a summary of what you did every half hour you were at work. How much of that time was concerned with the priorities of your job you thought about earlier? How often did you manage to build in longer than half an hour for any one task?

Think about yourself

At what time of the day do you work best? Which aspects of your job are you really committed to? Which are you most enthusiastic about? How frustrated about time do you feel? Is lack of time having an effect upon you, your family, your social life and your friends? Does it matter to you?

Taking Action

Second, you need to take appropriate action. No one of the strategies we suggest below works for everybody, but they have all been proven in different situations to be more rather than less effective in helping people control their time.

Prioritise
Be ruthless in the tasks you choose to do. Jettison temporarily or permanently those which are not crucial to your job. Concentrate on the tasks which matter. There is significant research which suggests that 80% of our results come from concentrating on just 20% of our possible tasks. Identify that 20%! It may be the key to your success.

Delegate
Sounds simple, proves difficult. Many of us seem to want to hang on to everything, to be personally responsible, to have everything done to a level of expertise only we can master. We are also concerned that delegation means overloading

someone else, even though one great attribute of delegation is that it also gives people experience. (Much of the worry new headteachers have when taking over their first school is attributable to the lack of responsibility previously delegated to them.) When you delegate:

- delegate authority but not responsibility – that remains yours
- delegate to others' strengths, not to their weaknesses
- don't overload the delegation
- delegate for results rather than method. Accept some ways of working different from your own.

Question

While you are getting used to managing your time, question every activity against your priority list. Don't let too much interfere with it.

Plan time blocks

Some very important tasks need a considerable amount of time. Writing your report to governors is even more important now; planning your talk to parents about the National Curriculum needs very careful preparation.

Plan well ahead for these situations; their success will have an important effect upon your school and your colleagues. Block off enough time in the diary to do them well. Don't try and find time at the last moment.

Fit tasks to suit you

Some times of the day are better for you than others. Do the difficult, more thought-requiring tasks when you are alert. Save the mundane for another time. Try and create congruence between your personal state and the tasks you have to do.

Use time management systems

Filofaxes, and their like, have become a yuppie joke but they were in use long before the middle eighties made them socially acceptable. Their long history and military and religious origins are due to the fact that they are a help. Use the many different pages which are available to help you prioritise your daily, weekly and monthly tasks. Writing it all down and being responsible to your writing does help. It is also wonderful to put a line through tasks achieved!

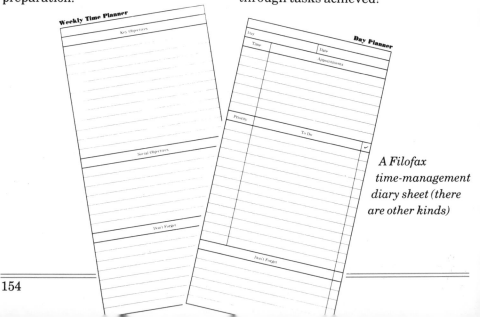

A Filofax time-management diary sheet (there are other kinds)

5.3 CHILDREN AND CLASSROOMS

5.3.1 *Organising the Classroom – 1*

Children and Teachers

Classroom organisation is one of the key management tasks of a teacher. Well-organised classes enable rather than hinder effective learning.

Classroom organisation should respond to the needs of the teacher and the class, to the work they have to do and to the peculiarities of resource provision and classroom or school design. Many attempts to display diagrams of 'effectively organised classrooms' fail because they don't take into account this personal and particular context. Everything you read on the next four pages has to be put into practice in situations only you know.

Whatever decisions are made about classroom organisation will have a major effect on the day-to-day running of the class, the freedom available to both teacher and child (but particularly the teacher) and the quality of the learning which takes place. In many ways the organisation of classrooms is a sure indicator of the degree to which the aims and objectives of a school are being implemented.

Looking at six school brochures at random, all of them contained statements such as:

> "We believe in the importance of developing independent learning"
>
> "We believe that our children should begin to take responsibility for themselves as soon as possible"
>
> "Practical work is important in our school"

The key to translating these beliefs into action is the effective classroom organisation of people and resources.

Children

Organising children in classrooms involves

- basic day-to-day systems which cope with 'low-level' activities
- a format within which most learning can take place.

Basic day-to-day systems
The section about 'Motivating Children' (pp. 180–182) suggests that children enjoy calm and fair classrooms. One of the ways of creating such conditions is through establishing a series of acceptable and workable routines which everyone has to follow. They may include

- what children should do (or can and cannot do) when they come into class first thing in the morning
- what has to happen at the end of each working session
- what the arrangements are for going to the toilet
- who is responsible for the

distribution or care of classroom
equipment

- what freedom children have to move
around the classroom on their own
- what noise levels are acceptable.

The decisions you make about these
and other areas need to take into
account first, your aims. (It is difficult
to justify the development of self-
responsibility if a child is not allowed
to sharpen a pencil unless given
permission.)

Second, they need to take into
account their effect upon the general
atmosphere of the class and the
children's ability to concentrate. (No
one is going to concentrate if everyone
wants to sharpen their pencil at the
same time.)

Third, they need to take into account
the needs of individual children. (Some
children are just not capable of even
sharpening a pencil without
'training'.)

Fourth, they need to take into
account your teaching time. Systems
are necessary but they should be self-
operating. No one is paying a teacher
to monitor systems which control the
sharpening of pencils. The systems are
supposed to free you of that.

A format for learning

Organising effective day-to-day
systems and sticking to them will
create more time and a better
atmosphere in which teaching and
learning can take place.

Those systems add to the learning
situation; they don't define it. What
does that is the general organisational
pattern you choose for your class.

There are three basic models –
whole class, individual or group.
Which you choose should take into
account the same four factors
mentioned earlier. No one pattern of
organisation will suit all learning

situations or all children, and you have
to be prepared to alter your basic
framework when it is right to do so.
Nevertheless, it is difficult for a class
to work effectively with a constantly
changing organisational pattern. A
choice has to be made.

Assuming the kind of aims
suggested above there are advantages
and disadvantages to all three models:

- Whole class teaching

+ More direct teacher control
+ Allows for the teaching of common
topics

– Teacher/child contact time low
– Practical work by children difficult
– Rates of child development vastly
different
– Resource provision is high
– Teacher talking time tends to be
high
– Children's involvement can be low.

- Individual teaching

+ Theoretically, the inverse of almost
all of whole class teaching's
disadvantages

– Repetition of teaching points
throughout the class
– Time defeats good teacher/child
contact
– Resources difficult to look after
– Organisation difficult
– Children tend to visit teacher when
problems occur and not before
– All children need to be well-
organised.

- Group teaching

+ Class can be divided into ability or
other groups
+ Child/child support is possible
+ Allows more discussion between
teacher and children
+ Resource organisation easier
+ Easier to monitor progress

- Different rates of progress can still exist within ability groups
- Other groups need to be well-organised.

Remembering that none of these models is perfect and that all can be used appropriately in every classroom, there are strong arguments for group teaching being the basic model for most classrooms. The major criticism teachers make about both group teaching and individualised teaching is the need to make sure all other children are reasonably well-organised before the teacher can work uninterrupted with a child or a group of children for a reasonable amount of time.

This criticism is fair. It can only be answered by saying

- the alternative (whole class teaching) is wholly inappropriate for mixed-ability classes or for an education which values practical work and first-hand experience
- other factors are important in maintaining order and enthusiasm in a class (see basic systems above and 'Motivating Children' pp. 182–184)
- good planning which provides well-chosen work can alleviate the difficulty.

The Teacher

Usually, teachers respond to the demands of children in the classroom so it seems difficult to imagine how teachers can 'organise' themselves.

In one sense the systems teachers operate with children also define their behaviour and the mix which is decided upon has to take into account a teacher's ability to put it into action. New headteachers who immediately announce that "We are all doing group teaching now" in schools where class teaching has been the norm for the past twenty years risk disaster. It is much better to work with and through people than against them.

The other key element in teacher organisation is the desk. If 'management by walking about' makes sense elsewhere it also makes sense in the classroom. Busy, active classrooms need teachers who are on the move – checking, reassuring, intervening. Teachers who operate their classrooms by remote control from their desk will either encounter inevitable behaviour problems amongst their children or fail to be a part of either the children's learning process or their lives.

Examine the part your desk plays in your classroom. Is it the central focus of the room? How often do you leave it?

5.3.2 Organising the Classroom – 2

Resources

'Resources' here means everything in your classroom except the people – desks, chairs, tables, cupboards, equipment, books, etc.

The same four principles apply to resource organisation which applied to people organisation. You need to take into account

- your educational aims
- the effect on the atmosphere of the class

- your needs and the needs of individual children
- your teaching time

and, of course, the particular nature of the classroom and the resources you have. The suggestions on these pages take into account some of the basic issues, but they are not tablets of stone. Each teacher will have to interpret them in the light of their own situation.

Tables and chairs

Tables (or desks) and chairs obviously take up most space in classrooms. Organising and arranging them carefully is vital. Don't be nervous of taking advice from other colleagues about this; some people have the knack of 'seeing' how furniture can best be arranged. Others, including the writer of these pages, always seem to have problems!

To decide on group learning as the basic structure for your class means that your tables or desks will have to be organised in groups. The way in which tables are grouped will be defined by

- the academic or social mix of your class
- the need for space
- the decrease in teacher/child interaction once groups become larger than six
- the needs of individual children
- the wish to create certain 'areas' in your class for, say, mathematics, science, language or art.

Most of these are self-explanatory but one or two reinforce the idea that no one single method of organisation will be wholly satisfactory. The social mix of your class may mean, for example, that for a time certain children should not work together however evenly they may be matched academically.

This doesn't mean that such children should be separated for ever. The aim should always be to work with those children in order that they should be able to work alongside each other; continuing opportunities should be given for them to succeed in doing so. The reality of classroom life tells us, though, that this isn't always possible.

Similarly, you may want to create one or two work areas in your class to which individual children can go as the need arises.

Space is another controlling influence. There is little point in having all the table arrangements you need academically if no one can move or, in doing so, they interfere with the working conditions of others.

Equipment

Even the worst-equipped classroom carries more equipment than anyone realises. Well-equipped classrooms often seem like warehouses.

Before considering the organisation of the equipment two questions should be asked:

- Has this room the basic equipment it needs?
- Do we need all of the equipment this room contains?

Definitions of 'basic equipment' can differ from teacher to teacher and school to school. It is a good idea to define as part of the internal school policy exactly what equipment should be in rooms used for teaching children of different ages. This enables each teacher to check what is required, makes stock-ordering simpler and 'manages' away a potential source of conflict or aggravation between colleagues.

Many classrooms – even those which are short of agreed 'basic' equipment – are over-equipped with other resources. Many of those resources are justifiable within individual classrooms but some are not. Having an over-equipped classroom

- makes the management of equipment more complex
- denies the use of some equipment by other colleagues
- often damages otherwise unused equipment
- causes over-ordering through unawareness of existing stock (and, therefore, wastes money)
- takes up valuable space.

The first step in managing equipment in the classroom is to look at what you have and discard everything which is unlikely to be useful in the forthcoming year.

What is left can be divided into two categories:

1 Usable by children.
2 Dangerous or unusable by children for other reasons (e.g. size).

As a basic principle everything which is usable by children should be arranged so that children can use it on demand. This means that such equipment needs to be

- stored at child height
- clearly and understandably labelled
- easily able to be returned after use.

It is at this point that the organisation of people and the organisation of equipment meet. Most teachers accept the importance of developing independence and self-reliance in the children they teach. To do so means giving children the opportunity to practise. To do that means arranging the classroom so that children are able to carry out tasks independently of the teacher. To help them do that the teacher needs to organise 'low-level' people systems (see page 155) which increase the probability of children being successful.

The organisation of people and the organisation of resources are inter-dependent. What can nullify them is a lack of confidence in teachers that young children are capable of obtaining necessary paper, sorting out paints, sharpening pencils, using mathematics equipment or using reading corners without the consistent supervision of adults. Some children are not, that is true, but the evidence from classrooms in a range of socially and academically different primary schools is that, given the kind of organisation we have discussed here, children are more capable than many would imagine.

Dangerous equipment should be obviously identified ("If you need to use anything with a red label on it then you must see me first") and stored in areas that will minimise even accidental injury. This is more than common sense; it is career protection.

Other issues

Many of the other issues about the organisation of equipment in classrooms are common sense. Difficulties can often be resolved not by reading books about it but by wandering into colleagues' classrooms and testing one's own methods of organisation against theirs.

Two issues are worth mentioning briefly. Many classrooms only provide opportunity for the display of two-dimensional art work and it is this lack of display which helps to limit the potential of primary art and craft. Creating the availability of three-dimensional display space can increase the amount of work which takes place.

Finally, all primary classrooms pay respect to the need to display fiction and non-fiction books but occasionally the displays are not as stimulating to children as they might be. As a general rule

- display fewer books but rotate the displays frequently
- display books cover out rather than spine out
- arrange the books in theme clusters
- organise an effective 'low-level' system of book care.

Organising the teaching of 30 mixed-ability children across six or seven different 'subject' areas (and, often, integrating two or three of those subjects under one theme) is a complex task and, like all complex tasks, it requires a measure of planning to make it work.

The time taken to produce effective plans should benefit the teacher who has written them and, consequently, the children in that teacher's class. Good plans should enable teachers to answer these questions:

- What are the purposes of my teaching?
- What activities will the children do to achieve those purposes?
- What resources do I need to allow those activities to happen?
- What finished work will emerge as a result of those activities?
- How can I assess the success of my teaching?
- Will my planned work fit into the time I have available?

Good planning does not guarantee good teaching but it is rare to find good teaching which has not been well planned. Let's look at the five key questions good plans should answer.

1 What are the purposes of my teaching?

Teaching has purposes. Teachers work in classrooms to achieve certain objectives with and on behalf of the children they teach. If teaching is to be most effective those purposes need to be made as clear as possible.

Defining 'objectives' needs to be precise because the way in which objectives are written will help to define the answers to many of the other questions about planning. Nevertheless, writing effective objectives often causes problems.

Objectives can refer to 'facts', 'skills' and/or 'concepts'.

'Facts' are true statements which children can be expected to learn and recall. 'Henry VIII had six wives' is a fact.

'Skills' are accomplishments which children learn through doing. It is impossible to 'do' a fact but almost impossible not to 'do' a skill. 'Riding a bike' is a skill which is learnt by doing. In the classroom, 'observation', 'hypothesising', 'using evidence' and so on are all skills which children need to 'do'.

'Concepts' are general notions of things which are arrived at after exposure to a range of facts, skills and experiences. 'Power' is a concept. We cannot 'know' power like we know 'Henry VIII had six wives' and we cannot 'do' power as we do 'observation'.

Much of the documentation arising from the National Curriculum contains objectives against which teachers are expected to plan. One of the principal benefits of a well thought-out National Curriculum should be to free teachers from deciding 'what' has to be taught and allowing them to concentrate on 'how'.

2 What activities will the children do to achieve those purposes?

To achieve these objectives children have to do things in classrooms. The objectives themselves don't define those activities although they should make it easier for them to be defined.

Activities need to be appropriate in three different ways. First, they need to be *applicable to different kinds of objectives*. An objective which is essentially factual requires a different level of activity from an objective which is skills-based. Equally, while a factual objective may require only one activity for it to be successfully achieved, a skills-based objective, in which children have to learn to 'do' things, is likely to require a greater number of activities.

Second, the activities need to be *applicable to the different ability levels of children in a class*. Accurate 'matching' of activities to children will continue to be one of the most difficult tasks teachers have to face as children's responses to the activities they are asked to do depend so much on immediate contextual matters such as mood, relationship with the teacher, attitude and so on. Nevertheless, it is important that 'matching' is seen as an important aspect in the definition of classroom activities.

Third, the activities need to be *relevant to the children*. If we accept that we learn by assimilating new material in the light of our past experiences, the activities we plan must enable our children to handle them from within the experiences those children have already had. If we don't do that children are unlikely to learn effectively.

3   What resources do I need to allow those activities to happen?

There is little point in thinking carefully about objectives and learning activities if the resources are not available to activate them. Being clear about our resource needs in our planning helps to

- check that activities we want to happen can happen
- provide information on new resources which are required by a class or a school
- ensure that teachers are properly prepared for each series of lessons. (Who wants to rush around frantically at lunch-time unless they have to?)

4   What finished work will emerge as a result of those activities?

There is nothing wrong with having a reasonable idea at the beginning of a term or half-term of the kinds of work children will be expected to produce at the end. Indeed in some ways it is crucial that this happens.

If we support the view, for example, that language is a cross-curricular subject then we need to know what particular aspects of writing, reading, listening and talking will be covered by any other work we are planning. Only then can we look at the breadth of our language provision for our children and devise compensatory or supplementary activities where they are necessary.

5   How can I assess the success of my teaching?

Good plans, and particularly carefully defined objectives, help in the assessment of both teaching and learning. Assessment is important. Well-formed objectives often contain within them the evidence that is required about children's achievement. There is little doubt about what children have to do to prove that they know that Henry VIII had six wives; simply answer the question "How many wives did Henry VIII have?"

The problems occur when the objectives are either ill-defined or inappropriate for conventional assessment techniques. Eliot Eisner has drawn an important distinction between 'Instructional' objectives and 'Expressive' objectives.

'Instructional' objectives are those in which what is to be learnt is specified; 'expressive' objectives are those in which the learning which occurs is individual and unpredictable.

So to know that Henry VIII had six wives is an 'instructional' objective; to experience the moods created by Holst in *The Planet Suite* is an 'expressive' objective.

Assessing 'expressive' objectives is less a matter of defining clear tasks and more one of judging the appropriateness of response, discriminating, in Stenhouse's words, 'understanding from misunderstanding'.

6   Will my planned work fit into the time I have available?
Teaching takes place within limited time scales. As we write this, the calendar for next term shows that it is only nine and a half teaching weeks long. Planned, purposeful work needs to be completed; work which is left 'hanging' with primary children can rarely be successfully picked up again.

Once you have defined objectives and organised learning activities and resources, it is important to ensure that the planned work fits into the time you have available for it. Given the naturally hectic life of primary schools this suggests that planned work should not fill every available space which appears to be free at the beginning of a term; something unexpected, and time-consuming, always happens!

5.3.4 *Planning Classroom Work – 2*

You may wonder whether there are any curriculum areas which shouldn't be planned. The answer is no: all areas need planning. It is important to understand the difference between 'instructional' and 'expressive' objectives described on the previous page and the implications of choosing one or the other. Defining the work you are planning in wholly instructional terms can destroy much of what some subjects are really about; defining work in wholly expressive terms can deny children access to important information and skills.

It is not a case of planning some curriculum areas and not others. All curriculum areas should be planned. What is important is to understand the nature of the work being planned within a curriculum area. 'Instructional' and 'expressive' objectives help to do that.

Theme work

Much of the evidence from HMI Reports suggests that thematic work is attempted in most primary classrooms and poorly executed in many. Much of the reason for that can be found in the quality of the planning behind the theme. Organising work thematically has a number of advantages for young children but it also presents much the most difficult planning activity for the teacher. When planning themes you need to be sure

- of the balance between the various 'subject' components (for example, science, history, geography)

- that the content of each 'subject' is appropriate to the theme
- that the balance of work between the 'subjects' is maintained throughout the year
- that the required objectives can be covered (particularly important with the National Curriculum)
- of the cross-curricular work in other subjects (language, mathematics, art, technology, physical education, music, RE and so on) which your theme is facilitating. This will affect your planning needs in those subject areas and suggests that themes should be planned first.

What time span should plans cover?

The answer to this question is dependent upon a number of factors including the range of subject matter covered, the age-group of the children and the time of year.

Plans which cover a shorter time span are more appropriate for younger children or for situations in which the teacher's knowledge of the children is relatively poor.

In general, it seems ineffective to devise plans which work for less than half a term or longer than a whole term.

What should be in my plans?

Your plans should contain information which enables you to answer the key questions of planning:

- What objectives do I want the children to achieve?
- What activities will the children need to do to achieve them?
- What resources do I need, to allow those activities to happen?
- What finished work will emerge as a result of those activities?
- Will my planned work fit into the time I have available?

What do plans look like?

There are numerous ways of devising plans which contain answers to the questions above. Whatever your plans look like, they should

- be easily accessible. Information should be obtainable from them very quickly
- enable other teachers who might take your class during the year or later to see what you have done
- allow the answers to the key questions to be recorded clearly.

There are arguments which suggest that teachers should each be responsible for their own plans and what they look like, but the need to coordinate children's learning as they move through a school is a strong reason for staff to think carefully about the presentation of plans and their completion. Effective and similar planning by every teacher in a school can reduce misunderstanding and increase effective information flow about the children and the work they have been doing.

The sample page illustrated on page 166 is part of one school's attempt to produce just such a coordinated package which answers the key questions. It is not the only way of presenting plans and, we hope, might stimulate others to improve or change radically these designs.

There are nevertheless some criticisms of effective planning. Some staff will be unhappy at having their 'freedom' to plan in their own way (or, to be honest, not to plan at all) taken away from them.

This presents a staff management issue which has to be handled carefully. You might want to look at 'Dealing with Differences' (pp. 32–34) about this. The benefits for the children of effective planning undoubtedly outweigh the disturbance to some colleagues.

Sometimes plans are criticised because they "never work out like that in real life". This is very true. Nothing succeeds as planned and no one would argue that the plans you create will succeed in their entirety. Sometimes time will run out and sometimes your plans won't have been as appropriate or relevant as you thought. Changes will have to be made.

What plans are about is reducing the degree of uncertainty to a reasonable level and increasing the probability of children being provided with an appropriate education.

Sometimes plans are criticised because "they take a long time to do".

CONTENT	ACTIVITIES	RESOURCES	FINISHED WORK
1. Some plants can be grown from their own seed	A) Explore a range of plants to look for seeds. Look for • number of seeds • pattern of distribution • shape	Tomatoes, Apples, Pears, Chestnut, Water Cress	Drawings, paintings, wax-resist of inside of fruits + particular seeds
	B) Gather a range of seeds from children's homes. Display/discuss Look for • shape • texture • colour Classify	Seeds brought from home Plants/fruit they came from Illustrations of "	Discussion about appearance Drawing + writing comparing two seeds
	C) Discuss conditions required for growth		'How to grow a plant from seed' chart – written and drawn
	D) Plant variety of seeds Look for • growth rate • pattern of growth	Seeds for each group Plant pots, water, John Innes, plastic bags, trays, information books	Measurement of plant growth Close observation Drawing Modelling Written work – 'what happened' Poems + story

A sample page from a school planning document

Good planning can (and should) take up some of what has previously been seen as 'holiday' time and/or INSET days. The advantage of planning before the beginning of a term is that it saves considerable time (and tension) as the term progresses.

5.3.5 Record-keeping

There are times when record-keeping is the bane of teachers' lives. There seems too much, too often, and no one is quite sure what happens to it all anyway.

There are other times when it seems absolutely vital; nothing is more frustrating than the absence of information when trying to organise and plan for a new class.

As the curriculum becomes more complex and demanding both of these views will strengthen. Time to complete records will decrease; the importance of having them will increase.

The problem is simply expressed – how to devote minimum time to maximum effect and do full justice to each of thirty or so very different individuals.

Who needs records anyway?

Various groups require records of one sort or another.

The LEA will require certain records to be kept on an authority-wide basis. In some local authorities these will be restricted to mathematics and language and may often take the form of the results of standard assessments.

The government, through the guise of the National Curriculum, will want similar information on a national scale, again as an end-product of a series of nationally organised continuous and formal assessments.

Secondary schools require information from primary schools about the children joining them at the beginning of the new academic year. Just occasionally, secondary schools mistrust the quality of information they are given; equally occasionally, primary schools wonder whether the effort of producing it was at all worthwhile.

Parents require information which will help them understand their children's attitudes and abilities. There is a growing feeling that many parents are dissatisfied with bland, generalised comments at open evenings and parents' meetings and that, while unpleasant information is difficult to take, a spread of honest information given consistently throughout a child's school career helps parents to see their child in a more realistic context.

Teachers, most importantly of all, require effective records. Sometimes these may be very specific and linked to learning problems; at other times they may be very general. Some may be a way of responding to national and LEA demands; others may be to help plan on a week-to-week basis which children should be doing what. Without them, teaching becomes impossible.

Which records need to be kept?

If records have to respond to the variety of audiences outlined above and time is short, it is important to be clear about those which need to be kept. Some of these needs will be statutory; others will be personal to each teacher. There is no definite

answer to this question and the list produced on page 168 can be amended or added to depending upon your situation. Nevertheless, it seems important for the following to be kept by, or be accessible to, each teacher.

'Subject'	Need to Record
Mathematics	Facts, skills and concepts understood Progress made in scheme (if used) Comments which reveal weaknesses Attitudes
Reading	Reading level Reading progression Attitudes to books and reading Specific weaknesses
Written/Oral (Language)	Level of communication and listening abilities Ability in factual and 'creative' writing Spelling or phonic weaknesses Attitude to talking and writing
Theme work (History, Geography and Science)	Skills practised Level of content learnt and concepts understood Confidence in practical work Social skills in peer group
Creative Arts (Music and PE)	Special abilities Serious difficulties Progression through scheme (if appropriate)
General Profile	Summary of academic ability Attitudes and application Personality and social development
Parents' evenings	Summary of comments to parents Parents' attitudes, queries or concerns Action taken or reference made
Medical records	Any condition affecting school performance or child's development
Special needs	Full records and reports of case conferences, statementing procedures, psychologists' reports etc.

What formats should the records have?

Some of the formats for record-keeping will already be pre-determined. Those developing other formats should bear in mind 'minimum effort for maximum effect'. Record-keeping is time consuming enough anyway. The trick is to devise formats which

- contain all the information you need
- are easy to complete
- are easy to read.

Record sheets often suffer through being ill-designed. Schools which have taken care to consider in detail the record-keeping they require would find it worthwhile, if there is no in-school expertise, to take advice (voluntary or otherwise) about record sheet design.

While most teachers accept the need for comprehensive records, disillusion sets in when the completion process becomes unnecessarily arduous.

Children's names	Content/skill						Content/skill						Content/skill						Content/skill					
	Activity						Activity						Activity						Activity					
	A	B	C	D	E	F	A	B	C	D	E	F	A	B	C	D	E	F	A	B	C	D	E	F

<u>Above</u> This planning sheet records particular activities.

<u>Below</u> This sheet shows teacher and parent responses to a Home-shared Reading System.

TEACHER			PARENT									
Book	Date	Message	Was the book enjoyed?			Was it understood			Did your child seem confident?			Message
			☺	☻	☹	easily☺	☺with help		△	⬦	⬦	
Sniff Sniff	14.9.87	Please read this to Ann	✓			✓			✓			Much enjoyed
Mog's Mumps	16.9.87	To share + enjoy	✓			✓			✓			We like this series
Our dog	21.9.87	Ann will read to you today	✓			✓			✓			She read it lots of times

Below This sheet records children's attitudes towards and ability in problem-solving activities.

Below This sheet shows teachers' comments to parents at an Open Evening and parents' responses.

NAME:
James Thomas

Graphicary Skills:-

Excellent - Map of London - Hungerford Bridge area accurate. Loves this work   Made several 'own maps'
Mazes - Puzzles, games - original ideas
                 still untidy

Investigation of local environment

Knows Road Names   Gd.   Shares knowledge gained.
       Knows simple routes   home/school

Observation (Hist + Geog)

V. interested in family background   Close Obs drawing
Gd. ability   Questions ✓   excellent
                    uses colour ✓

Social Studies

Sexual stereotypes - but argues convincingly + persuasively!!
Wants to check numbers of male/female drivers in Croydon Rd!
   (arrange this)

Any other Comments / quotes etc.

Some difficulty in a group of 4 - changed to 2 x 2
Likes to lead + can dominate ✓✓
Original ideas - independent work
   Interesting family background (France) leads to other interests.
Followed these up well with good support from parents
(+ later grandparents)
Very untidy recorded work - not improving. (Handwriting
v. poor - discuss with parents too.)

N.B See sep. Sheets for activities completed for each skill.

[Theme - Family History + routes from home to school.]
Date . Summer Term 1987

NAME: HISTORY/GEOGRAPHY + SOCIAL STUDIES
James Thomas   SKILLS + CONCEPTS (see plans)

Discover 1st hand evidence thro'senses + a variety of sources:-

Photos ✓ older photos   Questionnaire - v. gd interpret.
Visit to France well used + discussed   + use   Gd.
     class museum. contributions money ✓

Discuss + question what we see around us :-

Above av. ability - many excellent questions. - uses answers to
         gd. use of visits   develop thinking etc ✓

Record in relevant ways + use correct vocab:-

Block graphs - accurate (untidy!) ✓✓   Picture story
Written reports careless - informative   sequencing accurate

Group + compare (from observation + experience):-

Used old newspapers - individual research then rated with Nicola
Excellent work here. gd accurate comparisons. Enjoyed school
           comparisons - gd. list.

Finding Information:-

Interested in ref. bks. Understands contents/index ✓✓
Old newspapers. Letters from grandparents with inf..

Any evidence of empathy imaginative re-construction etc:-

Yes.

Name : Adam Marley   Open Evening
                            July 87

1   Academic Abilities

Maths (Gmm Level II Stage - 34)
Gd steady progress but should contribute more to group discussion.
Problem solving - interested + works for long periods   av. abil for class

Language   Reading 123 +   Test Score :- 104
          bk 10 - average ability - reads widely + well
Area of strength - Creative
Written - Creative ability v. gd. Poems. Can   Presentation weak -
                          handwriting
Oral - Use of lang gd. - excellent vocab. Enjoys drama
History) skills. A good topic bk. gd. skills. Gd use of questionnaires etc
Geography) Graphicary skills weak. Encourage spatial awareness etc.
Science) Not this term (but v. able here)   suggest to parents
Art/Music/ P.E.   Recorder player - encourage at home please

2   Attitudes + Application - works well + concentrates for very
long periods now. (This is an improvement - parents please praise)

3   Personality + Social development.
Outgoing + popular with peers. Needs to share ability in some areas
in group work - can become isolated + forget group!

4   A.O.B.   Check holiday date - school time ?) ask
        Reaction to sister starting school ?)

Parents Comments / Concerns etc :-
    Agreed with above.
    Asked about instrumental tuition next year - (see R.G.)
    Sister starting school - no problems noticed
    Holiday in school time next term - (mention to GT.)

What does it mean?

Although there are many differences in detail concerning definitions of profiling, the broad features invariably include

- *recording* achievement
- *reporting* on progress
- *monitoring* progress
- *involving* the child
- *involving* the parents.

What profiling attempts to offer is an all-round balanced view of children and their academic and social development. Many schools will have record-keeping systems, reports for parents, LEA record cards, etc. What a pupil profile sets out to do is bring together all the bits and pieces about the child into one document which will grow as the child moves through the educational system.

Profiling is a formative record of achievement and attainment which can be seen as integral to the child's learning.

Why profile?

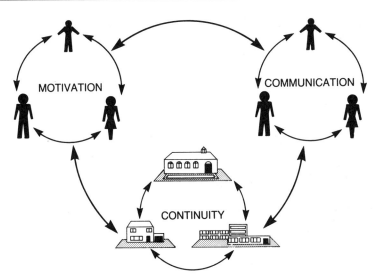

We profile in order to . . .

Motivate children by involving them in their own goal setting.

Enable the child's experiences, attainments and competencies to be valued and to help the child develop as an individual and encourage a positive self image.

Provide the child, parent and teacher with an expanding source of information which is accessible, available and to which all parties have the opportunities to contribute.

Ensure development of learning and foster effective teaching by providing the school with a record of the child's personal achievements as a way of maintaining continuity/compatibility between and within primary and secondary education.

Brief of account of a person

What does the profile contain?

PORTFOLIO OF ACHIEVEMENT

Evidence of achievement in the form of cross curricular samples of best school work selected by the pupil, together with their teacher. Items may be part of normal course work or produced especially for the portfolio. The portfolio contents to be reviewed and updated on a regular basis.

PERSONAL BIOGRAPHY

A record of interests, activities and achievements beyond the main curriculum from both home and school. It also provides an opportunity for the child to set personal targets in the broadest of contexts, be it to improve spelling, gain the next gymnastics club badge, or keep their bedroom tidy.

ATTAINMENT RECORD

A formative and summative record of attainment in core and foundation curriculum areas including:

Record of National Curriculum Attainment Target progress and the school's record of the child's progress through the various curriculum areas.

Results of school, LEA and national standardised testing and assessment.

Summative records of attainment including those required by the LEA.

The following are examples of one approach to profiling development in Devon by a group of headteachers. We were impressed by the clear aims and objectives and attention to practical detail. This is management in the sense of setting attainable targets for teachers and supporting them by giving useful, realistic advice.

1 Achievement

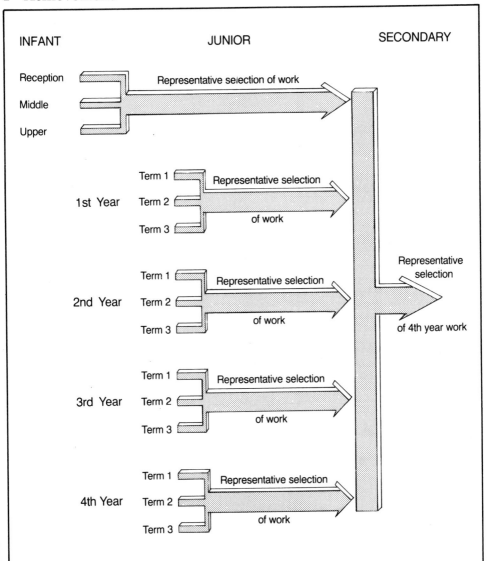

As the child progresses through the primary school, representative work from all the stages is selected, reviewed and retained as appropriate, termly and annually, to provide a formative record of achievement. A final selection of fourth year items providing evidence of achievement would then form the nucleus of secondary transfer documentation.

2   Biography

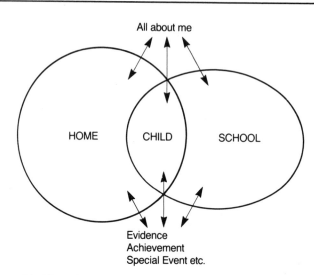

All about me

HOME   CHILD   SCHOOL

Evidence
Achievement
Special Event etc.

The key focus of the biography is on the child's world of experience and achievement beyond the classroom. The main contributors would be the child and/or parents. The school's science/health programme may contribute to the biography as an ongoing record of the child's development. Extra curricular activities could also form part of the school's contribution.

The biography recognises that personal development is an ongoing process which continues outside the main curriculum of the school and that education is a partnership between parent, teacher and pupil. It provides for achievement and experience beyond the classroom to be recognised and valued and for children to set their own goals and to develop a positive self image.

Essential components of the child's biography can be seen as a record of:

        — physical growth

        — developing abilities

        — interests and enthusiasms

        — personal targets and ambitions

        — additional contributions by parent and child

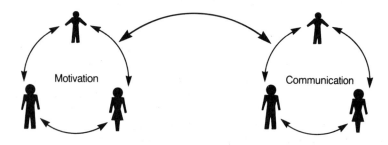

Motivation   Communication

3 Attainment

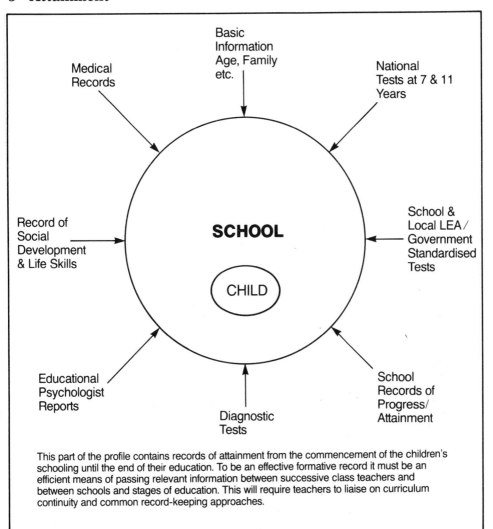

This part of the profile contains records of attainment from the commencement of the children's schooling until the end of their education. To be an effective formative record it must be an efficient means of passing relevant information between successive class teachers and between schools and stages of education. This will require teachers to liaise on curriculum continuity and common record-keeping approaches.

Profiling and the National Curriculum

With the increased accountability brought about by the legal requirements of recent education legislation the profile offers a very practical way forward for primary teachers. Many schools already have effective and well thought-out record-keeping and reporting procedures, but many don't! Managing the important areas defined by profiling not only helps record progress but is formative – helping define future action. The National Curriculum has made at least one aspect of record-keeping essential; profiling can help give the balance and breadth needed to provide a rounded view of our pupils.

Schools are essentially about educating children, about the processes which take place within the classroom. Everything we do in schools is supposed to be geared towards that end, even if increased devolution of responsibility and the consequent increase in administration sometimes makes it harder than it ought to be to keep that in mind.

For 'managers' in schools – headteachers, deputy heads, post-holders – visiting classrooms remains a crucial part of what ought to be done each week in school.

Six good reasons for visiting classrooms

1 To contribute to an overall picture of the life of the school

If classroom life is so central to schooling then it is important for 'managers' to have a view of a school which takes into account the day-to-day practice of teachers and children in classrooms. At this level the impressions one gains are not intended to be judgemental but to contribute to the sum total of the knowledge carried around.

2 To assess and evaluate the quality of the work taking place

In addition to a generalised 'feel' about teachers and children in classrooms there is also a need to make assessments. Such assessments might be about

- the implementation of agreed school policies
- the atmosphere within classrooms
- the level of independent working shown by the children
- the physical organisation of the classroom
- the management of the children by the teacher
- the use of available resources
- the effect of certain children upon each other.

Assessment and evaluation of classrooms are important if those who work in a school are to plan for the future as effectively as possible.

Equally importantly, the introduction of appraisal procedures over the next few years means that classroom visiting becomes a necessary part of any 'management' orientated activity. Without it, appraisal procedures will be still-born.

3 To keep a hand in (and to make mistakes!)

Headteachers, in particular, have less opportunity to visit classrooms than they used to have. Even when opportunities were more frequent, one of the justifiable criticisms of headteachers was that they had 'lost touch' with the reality of classroom life.

As the demands upon teachers have grown, as the curriculum has broadened in its scope and as there have been inevitable changes in attitudes towards schooling, it is easy to see why some teachers feel that headteachers just 'don't know what it is like any more'.

Because the headteacher's job is different from that of a class teacher some of this is unavoidable. (Interestingly, it may be that the increased administrative role of the headteacher may soon result in the deputy head being accepted as the senior teacher in the school).

For now, though, it remains important that headteachers should experience the range of pressures class teachers are under and open themselves to making the same range of small day-by-day 'mistakes' which are a feature of classroom life. The management of change in schools is made easier if those responsible for the change are aware of the context within which new behaviours are expected to operate.

4   To pass on messages of good practice

The risk of declining awareness of classroom life is one which grows the longer headteachers stay as headteachers. It doesn't mean, though, that headteachers never have expertise which they can pass on to other colleagues. One of the reasons many teachers, including headteachers, have been promoted has not been their fitness for the job into which they are being promoted but their excellence in the job they are leaving. Headteachers are likely to have been very reasonable teachers.

Headteachers are not the only members of staff with expertise, either. We hope that teachers with specific responsibilities will have some expertise in the areas for which they were appointed.

If it remains true that 'actions speak louder than words' then a classroom visit could be more beneficial to a colleague than an hour-long meeting after school. It almost certainly means, especially given the practical orientation of most primary teachers, that any discussion about practice should, where possible, be supported by practice in action.

5   To look at individual children

Individual children have needs which require assessment and action. Some assessment has to take place out of the classroom but all assessment should involve in-classroom work as well. What matters about a child's performance is both the raw data of a child's abilities and how that ability is reflected in the reality of day-to-day classroom life.

Looking at children in classrooms may reveal that a problem which seemed to be one of ability was actually one of attitude; it may tell us that some children are not being allowed the conditions under which they can develop certain attributes. It will certainly enhance understanding.

6   To provide particular help to a class teacher

Class teaching is a much busier, more intense activity than it used to be. Class teachers welcome specific help from time to time. It is as simple as that.

Getting the right balance

If time is limited for both headteachers and post-holders then achieving an acceptable balance between the reasons for classroom visits is important. The weight you attach to each reason will be directly related to the particular conditions within your own school. Beware of certain pitfalls, though.

"As soon as I went to the school as headteacher I offered to help my colleagues in their classrooms as much as I could. All they had to do was ask.

Well, they did. In no time at all my time was taken up with regular, fixed visits to each member of staff. They felt good about this and so did I.

It was only when a parent came to complain about a teacher that I realised I had never been in that colleague's classroom other than on a timetabled basis. They knew I was coming and I really ran the lesson. So I had never seen that class – or any class, I suddenly realised – working normally, without me being in control."

"I think she had the best of intentions, so I'm not grumbling about that, but what happened in practice was that she ended up going into just one or two classrooms a lot and leaving the rest of us alone. I know they asked for help and had one or two difficult children but we were never, and I mean never, visited. It made us feel as though we weren't a real part of the school any more".

All of the reasons for visiting classrooms have their own importance; you have to achieve a balance between them. In doing so, of course, you create a set of messages to your colleagues which can be supportive but can also be counter-productive.

Don't hide the reasons for classroom visiting. Declare them. Let everyone know they exist. Talk about the difficulties of balance but be seen to be trying to get it 'right'. In this way you will minimise any difficulties which might occur.

Doing It

In the previous section we suggested a number of reasons why visiting classrooms is important. As with much of what we talk about in this book, though, theory and action don't always sit well with each other. Knowing that classes should be visited is no guarantee that the visits will be productive. There are important factors at play.

Atmosphere and trust

Teaching is a stressful occupation. Dealing with 30 mixed-ability immature children across seven or eight different subject areas and trying to devise, organise and coordinate successful learning experiences for them all is not a job for the faint-hearted. Teachers talking in staffrooms seem to mention three failures for every success. It is hardly surprising that many are not keen at first to be observed as well.

Maximising the advantages of classroom visiting means seeing the classroom operating as normally as possible. Seeing the classroom operate as normally as possible means creating an atmosphere of collaboration and trust. (Of course there will be times when classrooms cannot be observed in this way, such as disciplinary procedures, responding to the complaint of a parent or the report of an inspector. But it is to be hoped that these occasions don't represent the everyday life of a school.)

How you do this is inevitably bound up with your own personality and the relationships you develop. Ideas which have worked in our own experiences and those of others include

- beginning by asking others to assess and evaluate your own work first. In other words, lead from the front
- making it clear why visits are essential to your job
- not rushing to judgements too soon
- identifying and discussing mistakes in your own teaching first
- declaring your own curriculum strengths and weaknesses
- taking advice from other members of staff
- allowing teachers to start from where they are
- not expecting all teachers to respond equally enthusiastically
- concentrating first on the areas of teaching in which each teacher feels most confident
- staying calm.

Some of the reasons for class visiting are less threatening to class teachers than others. If you are genuinely visiting classrooms to keep your hand in, work with individual children or provide general help then the way in which you carry out those visits will contribute to the atmosphere and confidence you create.

Assessment and evaluation

It is clear that assessment and evaluation of work in classrooms presents the biggest threat to teachers and that there are understandable reasons for this. Yet assessment and evaluation also present the best

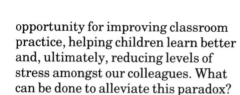

opportunity for improving classroom practice, helping children learn better and, ultimately, reducing levels of stress amongst our colleagues. What can be done to alleviate this paradox?

1 Be clear about the purpose of the visit

Any visit to a classroom provides evidence of some form, however subjective. If the purpose of the visit is to make a deliberate assessment or evaluation of what is taking place, however, then this should be declared openly. There can be little more undermining than knowing that the person who has just 'come in to help' is watching every move you make.

2 Focus down onto something particular

The 'feel' of a classroom *is* important and develops over days, weeks and months. Visits which are made specifically for assessment and evaluation need to be more focused; the person making the visit (and the person(s) being assessed) need a clear idea of the purpose of their visit.

This doesn't mean that the purpose has to be defined so tightly as to be a straitjacket. Discovering a class who are all capable of forming the letter 'u' correctly might hide the fact that none of them can form the other 25 at all.

3 Understand the teacher's and/or children's intentions

If it is a colleague's or child's performance we are assessing then we need to know what that colleague or child is trying to do and why. This information should help us to make our judgements more effective by raising two questions:

- Is the colleague/child trying to do something reasonable?
- Is it being achieved?

If the answer to the first question is "No, I don't think so" then the discussion which follows will be much different than if the answer is "Yes".

4 Gather sufficient and appropriate evidence

Assessing and evaluating classrooms has the same difficulties as all other assessment and evaluation.

A 'rush to judgement' is dangerous. Make sure that you have sufficient evidence before any judgements are made.

'Sufficient' refers to quantity. Equally important is to gather evidence of quality. This will partly be touched on below. What it also means is that the evidence we obtain of the often subjective, messy reality of classroom life needs validating before it can be used. Don't rely on one point of view.

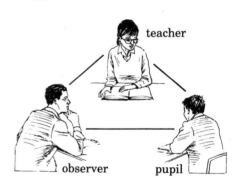

5 Choose appropriate strategies

There are a range of strategies through which information can be gained – anecdotes, interviews, observation schedules, questionnaires, video and audio recording, photographs, records. Each of them has strengths and weaknesses as both a means of getting information in the classroom (video may be off-putting) or of revealing appropriate information (interviews may not be the best way of finding out about andwriting). Choosing the appropriate strategy is important.

5 Provide feedback

Most people prefer feedback of one form or another following assessment or evaluation and teachers are no different. What is important is that feedback should

- be presented constructively at all possible times
- be given in a manner which respects the receiver
- be clear
- contain examples which refer to the points made
- not be judgemental until it is possible to be
- when negative, contain positive suggestions for improvement
- be followed up.

The last point we want to make is this. The most effective form of professional and personal development is that which occurs from within, which we 'own'. One of the purposes of providing feedback on assessment and evaluation of classroom visits is to find areas which colleagues will want to consider for themselves and to improve.

Action-based research about our own practice is the most important development we can make. Well-conceived and sympathetically orchestrated classroom visits can help to move teachers towards that position.

Who does it for the headteacher is another question. Perhaps they have to be open to appropriate assessment and evaluation from colleagues, too.

The effect of the observer's presence

Your presence in a classroom inevitably affects the situation of which you are a part in a number of ways. Three are particularly important.

Projection

Here, the observer imagines they are actually teaching the class and thinks more in terms of what they would do in the circumstances, rather than observing the teacher. The danger is of the observer being projected as a paragon whose lessons never flagged, whose children were never inattentive and who was perpetually kind and understanding. The art of constructive observation is to wrench oneself away from those fantasies and concentrate on helping the teacher.

Compensation

Here, the observer seeks to make up for their own deficiencies. An untidy or badly organised observer may be excessively punitive over this characteristic in others. When the observer's failings are already known to the person being observed, this form of hypocrisy is not only irritating but also reduces the legitimacy of otherwise credible comments.

The power relationship

A powerful headteacher may reduce a newly arrived probationer to a nervous jelly simply because of the huge gap in status. More experienced teachers who nevertheless have a strong sense of hierarchy, will have a different view of a headteacher's visit than others who operate in a more collegial style.

5.3.9 *Motivating Children*

It is not unusual when appointing adults to posts to look for qualities of self-motivation.

Teachers in primary schools cannot rely on self-motivation among their children, many of whom must wonder at their young age why they are there at all. Connie and Harold Rosen, in their book *The Language of Primary School Children* (Penguin, 1976) said

> It is easy to think of many reasons why a young child should not want to write and very difficult to think of reasons why he should.

Every teacher of primary children could, at some stage or another, translate that comment into every curriculum area.

One of the characteristics of poor teaching is to assume that children will bring motivation to their work; some will, but most won't. One of the fundamental tasks of primary teaching is not only to introduce children to a body of facts, or a collection of skills and concepts, but to do so in a way which will encourage children to develop both an intrinsic interest in the subject and a keenness to find out and stay committed.

For some children the subject matter is enough. Every primary teacher will have taught children who irrespective of ability, seemed sparked and inspired by the very nature of one particular subject. This is not true for the majority, though.

The evidence that is available suggests that children's interests and motivation in the primary school are developed much more through personal interaction with their teachers and others than through anything else.

It is not that other influences are not important. It would be foolish to deny the influence of the home, the media or peer groups but teachers have little control over those. What is important is that we should be aware of what is possible in the classroom. Motivating, enthusing and encouraging children is an important function of teaching.

The factors

1 *Fairness*
Children develop a sense of fairness as they move through school. While their own may not always be well-formed they are certainly able to spot fairness or unfairness in others. Their attitude to it is much like the British attitude to speaking French – "I can understand what they are saying but I can't speak it very well myself!"

"It's not fair" is a common phrase in most primary schools. Children are quick to be demotivated by teachers who run unfair classrooms. Children enjoy being in classrooms where

- the demands made are reasonable
- everyone is treated equally (children will be demotivated by teachers even if they treat otherwise unpopular classmates unfairly)
- teachers sort out squabbles in a reasonable way
- teachers emphasise and practise qualities of fairness continually.

2 *Approachability*
Children enjoy being in classrooms run by teachers who are accessible to them and who are interested in what they

have to say. Interestingly, many children are put off by teachers who try and curry favour with their classes. Children seem to expect, almost want, a distance between them and their teachers. On the other hand, the work children have to do is seen as coming 'from the teacher'. There appears to be a common view which says "If she wants me to be interested in her world, then she ought to be interested in mine." Not unreasonable, really.

3 Clarity

Children are motivated by teachers who make what they have to say understandable, whether it is a class lesson, individual help, instructions or a reprimand.

It is sometimes difficult for teachers to realise how much of what is being presented to children each day is new; to adults it often seems commonplace. Just as teachers are demotivated at INSET sessions by presenters of new material who talk too fast, assume understandings or badly structure their session, so children are demotivated by teachers.

4 Excitement

Many adults have been introduced to new subjects and experiences they might otherwise have ignored by the sheer excitement of friends and colleagues. Children like excitement and commitment from teachers and respond to it. A sense of calm in a classroom is undoubtedly important but calmness doesn't have to mean blandness.

A famous teachers' book about spelling was titled *Caught or Taught?* It is a title which could apply very well to the interests and abilities children develop as they move through their primary school. Enthusiasms should not be hidden.

5 Humour

Not surprisingly children enjoy and are motivated by teachers with a sense of humour. It's hardly surprising when you imagine that they are sitting in the same room with one teacher for up to six hours a day. Once again, though, primary children don't want humour all the time; they seem to have an awareness that school is also a place to work. What humour means in this context is not that of a stand-up comedian!

6 Praise and success

Like all of us, children are motivated by success; that is no surprise. Successful work is often important, although very young children sometimes don't understand what it is about their work that their teacher has defined as successful. Success in anything is motivational – walking down the corridor properly, putting the gym equipment away, showing care for others; all of these count.

Praise is obviously the signifier of success and so children are motivated by praise. Unfortunately, there is much evidence to suggest that the ratio between teachers' 'praising statements' and 'critical statements' is heavily weighted in favour of critical statements.

If you dare, tape record yourself working with a class or group of children for 45 minutes and count the praising and critical statements you make. Identify to whom each was aimed, if possible. The evidence will appall you, but might provide the answer to some of your motivational difficulties!

7 Individuality of response

Children are motivated by teachers who care about them as individuals as well as members of a class. Some recent evidence has suggested that 'touching and talking' is an effective way of allowing children to understand and feel care for individuals. Children later – and unknowingly – responded more positively to teachers who gently touched their arm or hair when praising or criticising than they did to teachers who did not touch.

8 A climate of care

Children respond more positively to teachers who are perceived to care not only about them but also about the class, the classroom and the school in general. Such care is reflected in the teachers' attitude to classroom display, tidiness, their colleagues and so on. What is important about primary children's responses to classroom life is that they confirm numerous clichés, from 'the medium is the message' to 'it's the way you tell 'em'.

As children move through the primary school their basic motivational attitudes towards themselves as learners and workers are forming all the time. By the time they leave the primary school they will already be able to confirm themselves as 'no good at maths', 'a scientist', 'always lazy' or 'really hardworking'. Those attitudes will have a profound effect on the rest of their school lives. It is important to realise that they are formed through the interactions with those who have worked with them more than anything else.

5.3.10 *Pastoral Organisation*

Pastoral care can be defined as all of that part of a teacher's responsibility beyond the academic and intellectual development of their pupils. It is primarily concerned with *social, emotional* and *personal* development.

In primary schools any separation between the curricular and pastoral responsibilities of teachers is usually seen as minimal – and rightly so. Apart from sound educational reasons for viewing the child as a whole person, the 'class teacher' organisational structure encourages the development of individual relationships and understandings in the classroom. Nevertheless pastoral problems invariably take up more time than any other difficulties and we need to have clear management structures in place to deal with them.

The role of the class teacher

The following true story (and you will know many more along the same lines) is an interesting example of one teacher's effective response to a problem in her class.

Gemma was a fairly bright nine year old who had completely lost interest in school work. She was doing just enough to get by but her teacher, Ms Miles, knew Gemma was under achieving. Ms Miles decided to have a private talk with Gemma; after an indifferent start it began to emerge that friendship groups were one of the problems. She was particularly worried about Louise who had been her best friend but was now in with another group and seemed to be against Gemma joining in.

Ms Miles decided to watch what was happening in class and to get staff on duty to keep an eye on things during breaks and lunch-times. She also contacted Gemma's parents and asked them to come in for a chat about their daughter's progress.

Gemma's parents were equally concerned and had noticed a deterioration in Gemma's approach to school. After talking together the adults brought Gemma in to let her know their thoughts and to listen to her ideas.

After hearing from other staff and considering all the factors the following action was decided upon:

1 Ms Miles would have a word with the girls about being more positive within the friendship group.
2 At the end of each day Ms Miles would write down all the positive things Gemma had achieved and these comments would go home on a Friday.
3 Gemma's parents would visit Ms Miles on a fortnightly basis to see how things were progressing.

This action was effective and in a very short time Gemma was working hard and enthusiastically again.

The case above illustrates the four key features of the class teacher's role in relation to pastoral care:

- giving time on an individual basis
- gathering accurate information
- involving parent(s), child and teacher in discussion
- taking some sort of positive action.

The role of the year-group coordinator/head of lower school/upper school etc.

In the larger primary school there is often the post of year group coordinator or head of Infant/Junior department (or some other similar title) who frequently has a pastoral overview of a number of classes. Although the class teacher is always the first line pastoral adult, this more senior member of staff can, and hopefully does, play a very useful role by

- leading staff discussion on pastoral matters
- linking personal and social education to pastoral care
- defining management structures for dealing with pastoral problems
- acting as support to class teachers.

The role of the headteacher

In many primary schools the headteacher will play a crucial role when dealing with pastoral matters – particularly in the problem sphere! Many parents will want to see the headteacher rather than the class teacher, deputy or coordinator; they often feel that they will achieve more by going to the top.

There is a danger in the headteacher accepting this role and skating on very thin ice when trying hard to be knowledgeable about the child concerned – especially when the headteacher has only taught the child twice that term.

In any but the most special cases, the headteacher should be the final resort in dealing with pastoral problems.

This is one area where delegation is definitely the order of the day. The people who know the child best should usually be the ones to talk with parents, gather information and make decisions about the child.

The role of ancillary staff

All ancillary staff should be briefed about their possible involvement in children's pastoral development. It often happens that an ancillary helper can make a different relationship with a child to that of the teacher; this can sometimes mean that the child will talk more openly with the ancillary.

Ancillary staff need to be aware of

- the importance of listening to children
- the reflective technique (where a child is prompted into talking, perhaps about difficulties, by repeating the last words of a sentence or phrase spoken by the child)
- the need to identify pastoral problems and discuss them with teaching staff
- the importance of confidentiality.

Regular discussions and a high level of involvement with all ancillary staff can greatly assist the development of positive and effective pastoral care.

Safety nets

No formalised pastoral system is ever perfect and we all know that even the most professional teacher can find an individual child particularly irritating and obnoxious – sometimes with good reason! In accepting this, we do need to devise safety nets for staff. When it's been a wet playtime for the third day and Mr Smith has been up most of the night with his sick child and he suddenly decides he's had enough of Belinda, there should be a strategy in place to help.

Here are some common ones – what actually happens is less important than meeting the main difficulty, which is removing Belinda from the room, and there being an agreed procedure for doing this.

A 'Paired' support – this is where a reciprocal arrangement is agreed to help deal with the very difficult child. Basically, if a pupil is provoking you to the point of distraction, you are able to send him along to a colleague who is aware that this may happen. The other side of the coin is that you are willing to accept children from your colleague's class in similar circumstances.

B Senior member of staff support – this is where a year group coordinator or deputy agrees to take responsibility for very difficult children for a short period of time.

C Headteacher support – headteacher agrees to accept responsibility for the child if A and/or B are inappropriate or unavailable.

In B and C above there is often an in-built assumption that the adult will carry out some pastoral work with the individual concerned and hopefully begin a process whereby the problem will be at least alleviated if not solved.

The key point when considering safety nets is to *play to individual's strengths*. Some of us have a sympathy and patience with certain children which is lacking or in short supply in other colleagues. Some of us have an authority with certain pupils which others lack. These qualities need to be recognised and used to the pastoral advantage of children and the teacher's effective classroom management.

Parental contacts

The role of the parent in pastoral care is vital. The relationship between the child, teacher and parent is not one that can flourish if the school sets up barriers which prevent easy parental involvement – and all too often those barriers are quite unintentional!

We need to set down clear advice for parents about communication with school. First, in the *school brochure* (see over), second in *written communication* and third *verbally*.

SPECIAL EDUCATION NEEDS	Children who have difficulty with learning are given extra help both in the classroom environment and by specialist teachers. Support is also available from the School's Psychological Service, advisory teachers and ancillary helpers.
PASTORAL CARE	Apart from guiding your child's academic studies, we are committed to promoting his or her general development and welfare. The key person as far as your child is concerned is the form teacher, to whom any problem should normally be referred initially. Each year group is also co-ordinated by a more senior member of staff called a Year Group Co-ordinator Tutor who will be involved in more serious or complicated problems, as might the Deputy Heads or the Headteacher.
	At times the school also seeks the advice and assistance of various outside agencies in dealing with more specialist problems. Our Education Welfare Officer liaises at times between home and school and we also have regular contacts with the School Psychological Service, Social Services, the Police and so on.
DISCIPLINE	We insist on good standards of personal and social behaviour from all children in the school. If we are particularly concerned about a child's behaviour we will contact the parents. We do have a system whereby a child is put on 'report' which means that his/her behaviour and attitude to school work is checked upon at each lesson. In extremely rare cases we do have the right to suspend pupils.

An extract from a school brochure

Outside agencies

For all children there will be some contact with outside agencies such as the Area Health Authority, Educational Welfare Officer and Social Services. It is important that those in school dealing with these agencies build up trusting and professional relationships with them. The school doctor who has to wait while children from Class 2 get changed from PE and is never offered a cup of coffee will take away a certain view of that school!

5.3.11 Assessment and Testing – 1

The General Situation

'Assessment' and 'testing' are quite different, although both result in the formation of judgements about children's learning.

Assessment is any activity which leads to the forming of a judgement about the abilities, knowledge or attitudes of someone or something.

Testing is a formal, often standardised procedure which aims to provide specific information within a limited area.

Both assessment and testing take place a great deal in schools. In the case of assessment this is hardly surprising as the purpose of education is to develop the 'abilities, knowledge and attitudes' of young children. Teachers in classrooms could hardly be said to be teaching if they were not making continual judgements about these three aspects of children's lives.

Testing, though, is already more prevalent than many believe. It has been reported recently that 79 per cent of LEAs have some programme of standardised testing in primary schools, most commonly in reading but also in mathematics and 'general ability', which was tested using verbal and non-verbal reasoning tests. Additionally, many schools also tested children with formal material of their own choosing.

The growth in testing appears to be continuous, partly as a response to the increasing democratisation of schools. Pressure has grown on schools to answer two questions from parents:

- What are my child's specific abilities?
- Where does my child stand in relation to other children in the class or age group?

Specific questions have to be answered with specific information. Test results appear to provide that.

Diagnostic or reportage?

Formal testing can be used for two main purposes. In the first case, teachers learn information about children which helps them to plan work more effectively. Such tests diagnose (or appear to diagnose) difficulties and problems which can be remedied. In the second case, formal tests provide a score or a result which can be used to report information, either to local authorities, the government or, as we saw above, to parents.

Advantages and disadvantages

Both assessment and testing have advantages and disadvantages and need to be used appropriately.

Assessment

+ uses a variety of approaches to gather information – talking, questioning, observation, work-sampling

+ builds up a rounded picture of a child's abilities
+ allows for specific contextual information to be taken into account

− doesn't provide evidence of progress relative to other children
− doesn't provide information which

189

enables comparison between schools
- sometimes results in evidence which cannot be easily communicated to others
- depends on a reasonably sophisticated subjective understanding of the whole situation.

Testing
+ can be used for comparative purposes
+ can, because of standardised administration procedures, be used at different sites
+ can help to reveal information

useful for the establishment of national standards
+ provides information in an easily communicable and, apparently, understandable format

- can restrict nature of assessment so that children have to reveal understandings in unfamiliar ways
- may only be used in areas of the curriculum where formal testing works
- may encourage curriculum provision to reflect the test rather than allow the test to monitor the curriculum provision
- may be inappropriate for certain age-groups.

Managing assessment and testing in school

Assessment and testing are an important part of the work of a school. In making decisions about their use certain principles are important.

1   Work from the curriculum to assessment and testing and not the other way round
Tests and assessments are not activities through which children learn, except indirectly as a result of diagnostic testing. Assessment and testing reports or judges the quality of the curriculum offered and children's responses to it. A well thought-out curriculum should precede well-thought-out assessment and testing.

2   Don't use either in the wrong context
When you decide to assess or test understand the advantages and disadvantages of each. Both have limitations; to use them inappropriately simply magnifies them.

3   Accept the limitations
Assessment and testing are often criticised because "they don't tell the whole story". Nothing tells the whole story. The limitations don't render assessments and testing redundant.

4   Understand the response of children
Rightly, the time when primary school children were fed an unrelenting diet of tests leading towards the 11 + have long gone. The corollary is that many primary children are not as used to taking tests as they were. Test conditions which conflict with the normal mode of classroom work can be disturbing.

5   Build assessment and testing into school policies
Notwithstanding that children's work should be curriculum led, assessment and testing are not afterthoughts of a school's curriculum policy. They should be an integral part of it. The

decisions you take about assessment and testing should have the same status as the decisions you take about the content and process of the curriculum.

6 Choose from a selection of tests

There are many tests on the market, many of which claim to do a similar job. Trial tests before you buy them. Make sure they provide you with information you want, have been properly validated, are easy to administer, are reasonably easy to mark and contain effective record sheets.

7 Don't let testing take up too much time

Primary classrooms are busy places, punctuated more than enough by activities other than learning opportunities. Primary children need time to accomplish much of their work; interruptions affect the final quality. Try not to let testing interrupt the day-to-day flow too much.

8 Use 'INSET days' to explore assessment techniques

Assessment is important to schools, adding to the information provided by tests and revealing information where tests are inappropriate.

Assessment techniques, being informal and ongoing, can seem non-problematical but subjective judgements need to be as sophisticated as any testing procedure. 'INSET days' and other INSET opportunities should be used to explore the difficulties with assessment and to provide some solutions.

9 Use children's self-assessment

There is growing evidence that enabling children to assess themselves in the classroom is not only a good motivator but also enhances the quality of information already available to teachers. A number of packs of self-assessment material for children are being published at the present time.

5.3.12 Assessment and Testing – 2

The National Curriculum

The management of the introduction of National Curriculum assessment and testing is to a great extent out of the hands of those who work in schools. At the time of writing an agreed timetable which covers maths, science, technology and English has already been published and made available to schools. Schools will have to statutorily administer the assessment and testing materials which will, inevitably, have to be produced at high speed.

From the point of view of those who work in schools the 'management' of National Curriculum assessment and testing means understanding what is supposed to happen, which organisation is responsible for what, identifying crucial strengths and weaknesses, supporting and making good use of those strengths, and . reporting on the weaknesses through any consultation procedures which might be made available.

What parts of the plan have relevance to primary schools?

By Autumn 1989	Attainment targets formulated for Key Stage 1 (age 5–7 years) in maths, science and, probably, English.
By Autumn 1990	Attainment targets for Key Stage 2 (7/8–11 years) in maths, science and English. Probably, attainment targets for Key Stages 1 and 2 in technology
By Summer 1991	Trial assessments (without reporting) for Key Stage 1 in maths, science and English.
By Autumn 1991	Probably, attainment targets for Key Stage 2 in technology
By Summer 1992	Reported assessments for Key Stage 1 in maths and science and, probably, English Trial assessments (without reporting) for Key Stage 1 in technology
By Summer 1993	Reported assessment for Key Stage 1 in technology
By Summer 1994	Trial assessments (without reporting) for Key Stage 2 in maths, science, English and, probably, technology.
By Summer 1995	Reported assessments for Key Stage 2 in maths, science and English Either trial assessments (unreported) or reported assessments for Key Stage 2 in technology
By Summer 1996	Possibly reported assessments for Key Stage 2 in technology

Who is responsible for what?

The National Curriculum Council (NCC) is responsible for advising the Secretary of State on the curriculum content of each subject area and on the production of attainment targets, statements of attainment and programmes of study.

The *Task Group on Assessment and Testing (TGAT)* was responsible for advising the Secretary of State on the pattern of testing to be implemented in schools in England and Wales. (At the time of writing, Scotland was not included in the National Curriculum proposals. It seems inconceivable, despite some opposition in Scotland, that something very similar won't be imposed there as well).

The *Schools Examination and Assessment Council (SEAC)* is responsible for advising the Secretary of State on the production of assessment and testing material. It aims to produce this material by commissioning outside organisations to devise and trial it.

What form of testing is recommended?

TGAT suggested that

- both informal (assessment) and formal (testing) procedures should be used
- reporting to parents should be based on a combination of both methods
- moderation panels should be created so that schools could unify their subjective procedures as much as possible (although quite how this will work in practice remains to be seen)
- the reporting of tests should be progressive across year groups; in other words that the tests should not be restricted to children of a single year
- the testing should be linked closely to National Curriculum targets to provide overall profiles of attainment
- much of the formal testing and assessment at Key Stage 1 (age 5–7) should be based on tasks which replicate classroom activity as closely as possible and which can be administered as part of the normal classroom day. This will not apply at Key Stage 2.

What are the likely problems?

First, that the timetable will not be adhered to. It depends on agreement about the attainment targets being reached by the deadlines, the production of implementable assessment and testing material by the deadlines and the provision of INSET for all teachers.

Second, that the consultation procedures will become a sham in order that the deadlines can be met. The targets require some of the most sophisticated thinking to take place over very short periods of time. If it appears difficult to do this, political expediency may overtake the real needs of schools, parents and children.

Third, there will be overload on teachers. This could mean that the assessment and testing simply won't get done. It could mean a greater drain on the profession as more teachers leave. It could also mean that other forms of assessment and testing teachers might want to use are put to one side.

Fourth, public acceptability of the scheme could encourage inappropriate testing. There are already doubts over testing at seven because of the different amounts of time children have spent in school and their different range of pre-school educational experiences. Political pressure could force testing on even younger children or could cause testing in areas of the curriculum often thought to be untestable.

Fifth, the INSET load will be too great to organise. The testing and assessment will be carried out by teachers unprepared for it.

So much is still unknown of the core of all this that it is difficult to perceive it in 'management' terms at the present time. What will have to be managed without doubt are

- the school's INSET programme
- information to parents
- teacher morale

Much that is good could result from a well thought-out programme of assessment and testing. To achieve this some in-school management is necessary but, for once, the responsibility lies as much out of schools as it does within them.

5.4 FINANCIAL MANAGEMENT AND BUILDINGS

5.4.1 *Local Management of Schools*

Local Management of Schools (LMS) came about as a result of the Education Reform Act 1988. For most primary schools it means the passing of budgetary control from the LEA to the individual school. Not all the money for running the school is handed over, as some finance is kept centrally by the LEA, but the major finances are the responsibility of the governors and headteacher.

Aims

The major aims of LMS are:

- to give greater flexibility in the spending of the school's budget
- to let the school respond more readily to the changing needs of its pupils and the local community.

Although the financial side of LMS is fundamental, LMS has much wider implications than the allocation of resources.

Three areas of particular concern are these:

- appointments
- dismissals and disciplinary procedures
- marketing.

The first two areas have, in the past, had a high level of LEA involvement, but LMS puts them squarely in the governors' court.

The third, marketing, is concerned with the school's links with the local and wider community – again something not traditionally part of the management function.

The timetable

There are two groups of primary schools affected by LMS – those with more than 200 pupils and those with less than 200. For the smaller school the LEA *may* decide to delegate the budget or keep it centrally. If the LEA doesn't delegate it, it must still run the school's budget to the formula as set up by the LEA and approved by the Secretary of State. The timetable is as follows:

	30th Sept 1989	1st April 1990	1st April 1993	1st April 1994
FORMULA FUNDING	Schemes put forward for approval by LEAs	All schools in scheme plus transition arrangements		End of transitional arrangements
BUDGET DELEGATION		Schools may receive budget	All schools above 200 pupils must receive budget	

The timetable for the introduction of LMS

How is the formula decided?

This can be shown by the following flow-chart:

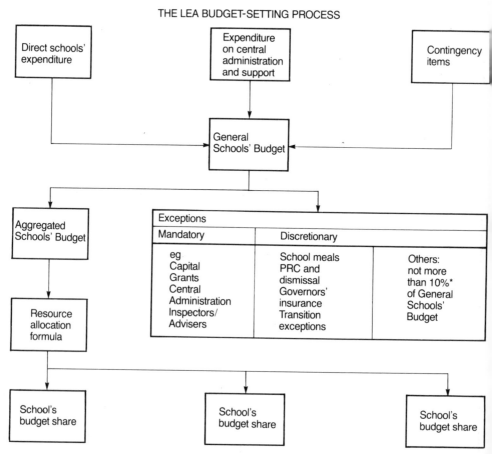

THE LEA BUDGET-SETTING PROCESS

*Expected by the Secretary of State to reduce to 7% after the LEA's 3 year review

General Schools' Budget (GSB)

The whole 'cake' is known as the *General Schools' Budget* and is made up in the following way:

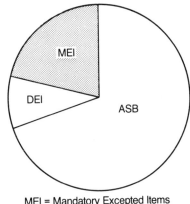

MEI = Mandatory Excepted Items
DEI = Discretionary Excepted Items
ASB = Aggregated Schools' Budget

MANDATORY EXCEPTED ITEMS
(held by LEA)

(a) Central Administration

(b) Inspectors/Advisers

(c) Capital Expenditure

(d) Grants:
  — Education Support
  — Travellers' Children
  — LEA Training
  — Section 11

(e) Home School Transport

(f) EEC Grants

DISCRETIONARY EXCEPTED ITEMS

Not subject to 10%	Subject to 10% (7% after three year)
(a) Transitional arrangements (b) Early retirement (c) Governors' insurance (d) School meals	(a) LEA initiatives (b) Structural repairs (c) Statemented pupils + Ed. Psych. (d) EWO.s (e) Premises insurance (f) Peripatetics (g) Pupil support (h) Special staff costs (cover, safeguarding) (i) Library/museum services (j) School specific contingencies (k) Other approved items

The Aggregated Schools' Budget (ASB)

The ASB is the important bit! It's what's left after the LEA's formula has been applied. These resources are under the governors' control in schools where the budget has been delegated and under LEA control where it hasn't.

At least 75 per cent of this budget is determined by how many children you have in your school and by their ages – this is known in the jargon as *the age-weighted pupil number*.

As formulae vary from authority to authority you cannot say definitively the total items in the ASB but some things are common to all schools. For example

- teaching and non-teaching salaries
- day-to-day running costs of the premises
- equipment, books, goods and services used by the school
- supply teaching budget
- midday supervision.

Management implications

LMS has created pluses and minuses for all teachers who are involved in the management of their schools.

+ flexibility
+ choice
+ independence
+ accountability
+ opportunity
+ freedom from bureaucracy

− additional management tasks

− additional responsibility
− diversion of teacher time from pupils/curriculum
− formula funding based on pupil numbers ignores individual schools' problems.

To make the most of LMS and cushion the negative points we need to manage the total resources effectively. Looking at the area of finance, here are some ways of approaching this task:

A   Decide on

- basic expenditure/set costs
- likely expenditure/estimated costs
- unpredictable expenditure/ contingency costs.

B   Cost out

- school development plan
- resource requirements
- new services.

Compare totals for A and B – in other words *match your overall plan to your budget*.

1 Do this before you begin the year.
2 Keep a close watch on real expenditure v. planned expenditure.

3 Vary the plan if necessary.
4 Involve governors, and all staff.
5 Make sure someone is responsible for an overview.
6 Don't be afraid to seek advice from the LEA.

Conclusion

LMS is hard work, full of challenges and problems, has significant training implications, needs the support of costly technology and has yet to be proved a boon or a burden; it will probably turn out to be a bit of both!

The telephone bill in the school was about £80 a year over the amount allocated. Since the new system of extensions had been installed the bills had rocketed. You see, anyone could dial out and staff were just not putting down all of their private calls. It mattered now because the school had its delegated budget – before the LEA had simply paid the bill. The headteacher decided to solve the problem; he took the telephone out of the staffroom and locked it away in a cupboard!

Result: disaffected teachers, saving of £35.

This story illustrates one of the conceptual difficulties of LMS – the difficulty of looking at the WHOLE before analysing the parts. In the overall budget the saving on telephone calls was negligible *and* caused negative feelings among some staff – a less drastic solution was always possible. If the whole budget had been in deficit looking at every part and going for savings might have been appropriate.

Remember: look at the totality before tinkering with the constituent parts.

5.4.2 Building and Site

At the centre of the management of primary schools are people; but it would be foolish to underestimate the importance of the physical environment. Cold, uninviting class or staffrooms have an obvious effect on staff and pupils, and the wider community make any number of judgements based upon their perception of the way in which a site and building are used.

I'm sorry, St Joe's double-booked, but we've got a sponsored skip starting on the school field in five minutes!

Responsibilities

Since the Education Reform Act (1988) responsibility for the site and building of a school is divided up as follows:

- cleaning and caretaking – LMS (governors)
- internal maintenance – LMS (governors)
- school grounds and playing fields – LMS (governors)
- structural repairs and maintenance – discretionary (could be kept at LEA level or delegated)
- major refurbishments – discretionary (as above)
- overall responsibility – governors.

On a day-to-day level it will usually be the caretaker (sometimes referred to as the custodian) or headteacher who will deal with problems relating to the fabric of the building. You need a clear procedure for reporting damage or deterioration to the site or building – usually a standard form or log book will be adequate. Whatever system you devise make sure everyone is aware of it.

Community use

Increasing use is being made of schools for community use; some have a long tradition of evening classes, societies, youth groups, etc. and under LMS such use is set to increase. We all know of the difficulties community use can bring (well, all those of us who have actually worked in schools), but properly managed you can gain great benefit from such use.

Benefits
- Helps to develop a positive image of the school (see Defining the School's Image pp. 209–211)
- Gives members of the community a chance to see something of the school's work through displays
- Provides income
- Helps security (although see *Problems* below)
- Gives an opportunity for contact with groups and individuals from the local community.

Problems
- Classrooms, hall, etc. can be left in disarray
- Security can be difficult with strangers in the school
- Caretaking, locking up, etc. can create difficulties depending on caretaker's contract
- Parking problems when large functions are on
- Some groups may be 'controversial'
- Double booking

Bookings for community use are the responsibility of the governors although this is usually delegated to the headteacher. This means that you have to be careful about lettings. Often it is the secretary who is the first to receive a request so she needs to be clear about the conditions for groups using the school premises – costs, timings, room availability and so on.

Points to watch out for
- Make sure your school has the right facilities for the hirer – for example, if you only have a small hall with lots of display boards the local five-a-side football club might do better to find another venue
- Make sure your booking form is clearly explained to the hirer. If midnight is the latest locking-up time you don't want a wedding reception that is just getting in full flight as the caretaker comes to turn the key!
- Inform local police if there is going to be a really big function and you anticipate parking problems
- Keep your own simple booking record to avoid double booking and to inform the caretaker
- Discuss and review community use with your caretaker and secretary
- Ensure valuable school items are locked away
- Check that community users are aware of fire exits, access to first aid equipment and emergency telephone
- If you get a request to use the school premises by a group that might be conceived as controversial – for example, a political group advocating racial hatred – make sure you discuss the request with the governors.

You may think "most of this doesn't apply to our school," but be prepared! Under LMS (see Local Management of Schools pp. 195–199) you are positively encouraged to increase, where possible, the community use of your site and buildings.

Making the best of things

Imagine an infant school set in a town but with a good sized field as well as the usual playground and an ornamental garden; the staff decide that some sort of wildlife sanctuary would help the science curriculum. They manage to get some sponsorship and PTA money and construct a small pond – a successful use of the school's environment.

A class of 11-year-olds want to improve their classroom which has high windows, poor display space, crowded tables, etc. Their teacher turns it into a problem-solving exercise and within two weeks the room has been rearranged, plants brought in, windows cleaned and so on. Another improvement in the environment.

We can all think of many such examples but there are some underlying principles when trying to improve the school's site and building:

- set attainable targets
- involve others in identifying areas for improvement
- if a number of areas are identified, draw up a priority list
- make sure the reason for the change/improvement is clear
- if appropriate, get the governors' and/or LEA's permission.

Caring attitudes

Whatever sort of building you work in you need to try and develop a caring attitude towards it from adults and children. Overcrowded and unattractive working conditions are very poor motivators and can inhibit all manner of positive moves in such things as teaching styles, curriculum innovation and shared resources.

As referred to in other sections of this book, *ownership* is a key concept of effective management in the primary school. So you have to make sure that children and teachers feel that they have some stake in the building. Responsibility for designated areas is one way of doing this: another is to allocate resources in such a way that staff have the flexibility to make their classrooms more attractive places.

In one school where graffiti was a problem, a policy of instant cleaning off was begun and in a very short time the scribbling stopped. A clean environment does seem to help perpetuate itself!

Perhaps the best way we develop a caring attitude towards our work place is by example. When everyone begins to bother, care becomes part of the school culture and so we hardly notice the effort being made.

5.4.3 *Budget Allocation*

What are we talking about?

For the purposes of this section, *budget allocation* refers to the allocation of monies specifically designated for such items as books, stationery, consumable stock and equipment. In many LEAs this is known as 'capitation' as in the past it has been the amount provided by LEAs on a 'per capita' basis.

How does Local Management of Schools fit in with this?

Clearly LMS has radically changed the finances given to schools but, in reality, much of the increased devolution is fairly tightly targeted – for example, staff salaries. What might be termed 'curriculum funding' will remain a crucial sum to be divided up.

Who has the responsibility?

The short answer is 'the governors'. There are three common ways in which governors might handle this:

- by forming a sub-committee to oversee all finance and allocate funds themselves
- by delegating 'capitation' funding to the headteacher and working in consultation with him/her
- by delegating 'capitation' funding to the headteacher and keeping a watching brief.

However, the bottom line is that this money can be spent at the discretion of the governing body.

Experience to date indicates that the responsibility invariably falls to the headteacher. Bearing this in mind it is worth ensuring that the governing board, and in particular any finance sub-committee, is kept well informed about capitation spending.

Allocation systems

Four systems of allocation are commonly used in primary schools:

- at the headteacher's discretion
- the 'bids' system
- the 'allowance' system
- the 'bids/allowance' system.

Each has advantages and disadvantages and it will depend on your school's context which is the most appropriate, although you will see from the chart set out on page 204 that we tend to favour a version of the bids system based on a collegial management style (see Collegial Schools pp. 60–62). Only in very exceptional circumstances would we see the first system as a positive managerial position.

CAPITATION ALLOCATION SYSTEMS – PROS AND CONS		
System	*Advantages*	*Disadvantages*
Headteacher's discretion	Headteacher has control	Lack of staff involvement. No sharing of expertise. Encourages patronage.
Bids	Everyone is involved. Needs are identified by staff. Priorities can be drawn up based upon an observable rationale.	Difficulties with long-term planning. Staff cannot be sure of definite allocation.
Allowance	Staff can plan easily. Careful expenditure is rewarded. Long-term planning is easier.	Staff expectations – at least as much as last year! Major initiatives are more difficult. Financial power can be put in the hands of a few teachers.
Bids/Allowances	Flexibility. Mid-term planning help. Basic stock can be taken out of budget before allocation.	Confusion among staff. Major initiatives can be inhibited.

You can add your own points to the chart on the left. Which method is used will depend on the size of school, the relationships, personalities and priorities within that school – not to mention the role of the governing board!

Accounting procedures

In most LEAs the accounting requirements are laid down centrally, and under LMS this is likely to increase, but frequently there is a need to design systems to keep track of spending. In most schools the secretary carries this responsibility but it is, of course, vital that the headteacher and deputy are aware of the budgetary implications of their actions. A readily accessible format for capitation spending is therefore essential. Set out at the top of p. 205 is a sample of one school's Capitation Commitment Record; this school bases its system on subject areas – although this sheet is called 'Humanities, and includes history, geography, social studies, environmental studies and graphicacy.

CAPITATION COMMITMENT RECORD

DEPT: HUMANITIES   YEAR: 1988/89   SHEET NO: 1

DATE	ORDER NO.	SUPPLIER	EST. COST	ACTUAL COST	VARIANCE +	VARIANCE −	CREDITS	BALANCE
14.5.88	W 20824	LONDON MAP CENTRE		119.74				119.74
9.6.88	W 20829	PHILIP GREEN ED.		29.95				149.69
28.7.88	W 40464	G. FOSTER, YORKSHIRE T.V.		82.61				232.30
28.7.88	W 40465/6	FOYLES	C/FWD 178.70 677.85					910.15
28.7.88	W 40467	LONDON MAP CENTRE	49.00					959.15
28.7.88	W 40468	GEORGE PHILIP		31.50				990.65
29.7.88		TRAVEL EXP.	C/FWD 18.10	19.20				1009.85
27.1.89	W 40529	TASKMASTER DLM	14.90					1024.75
10.2.89	W 40536	PHILIP GREEN		47.50				1072.25
	W 40465/6	FOYLES				220.92		851.33
	W 40467	LONDON MAP CENTRE				42.81		808.52
		C/FWD TO 1989/90						191.80
								£616.72

School Fund

There are two key points to remember about School Fund accounts:

- they are mainly 'through' accounts
- they need to be audited every year.

The first point means that usually the School Fund is used to hold money for trips, theatre groups, PTA items, etc., the second point is important because the School Fund is outside the LEA's budget to the school and is, therefore, more open to abuse.

Managing the School Fund should be seen as a very important financial responsibility and a prudent safeguard is to make sure that any cheque account requires two signatures.

GROUND RULES

- Be open about capitation allowance and its procedures for allocation. Involvement of staff leading to a sense of fairness in distribution helps towards achieving shared goals
- Have an overall strategy for spending based upon discussion of the school's needs
- Set up accounting systems that will give you ready access to financial information

5.5.1   *Involving Parents in School*

The range of parental involvement is very broad. It includes

- helping in class (ranging from washing paint-brushes to almost teaching)
- working with a group of children around the school
- helping on outings, visits and school journeys
- getting involved with the PTA or Friends of the School Committee and events
- designing newsletters and brochures
- attending at curriculum evenings
- consultating on specific areas of the school's life
- open evenings

- personal interviews
- sport
- bringing special interests or expertise into the school
- helping children at home.

No doubt you can add examples of your own. You must make your own decisions about the extent parents can be involved at any one time, based on three important factors:

- the school's need to receive feedback from parents and to develop an understanding of the parental view
- the school's requirements for extra help not obtainable elsewhere
- the school's capacity to absorb parents into the school in a variety of ways.

The problems

Despite the undoubted benefits of parental involvement there are problems. In a management sense these are more important since they are the issues which have to be understood, prepared for, accommodated and dealt with.

1 The development of cliques

Some parents see their involvement in school as a special position and talk about it as such outside the school building. Inevitably, such attitudes create resentment amongst other sections of the parent body, bringing difficulties to the school of a different kind.

Even when no clique appears to exist amongst the parent helpers, the group can often be perceived as such by those parents who are not involved.

2 Misuse of information

By definition, parent helpers are allowed 'behind the scenes' of a school to some degree. Sometimes the information that they acquire can be misused. Snippets of confidential information about children, teachers or other parents dropped into conversations over a cup of tea with friends, or misunderstood events of the school being re-interpreted outside, are not uncommon occurrences.

3 Inappropriate behaviour

People who work in a school full-time develop an ethos which works for them. Occasionally parents who come into the school on a voluntary basis may behave in ways not appropriate to that ethos.

4 Poor allocation of tasks

Most teachers and schools are grateful for any help parents can offer. Just occasionally that 'help' may be counter-productive. The parent washing the paint-brushes may leave the brushes and the sink in a worse mess than the six-year-old children; the parent asked to mount a little work may smear glue or paste over everything; the volunteer chairperson of the PTA may not be able to control a meeting and so on.

5 Misuse of staff space

A school which is successful in attracting parental involvement may often have more parents in school during a day than staff. This can result in staff not being able to relax, to talk freely amongst each other or even to grab a cup of coffee before break ends. Some staffs willingly accept parent helpers as they would supply teachers; others are more reticent. This doesn't make them anti-parent necessarily; they are entitled to their own professional privacy. It can, however, make them less enthusiastic about having parents in school.

6 Children of involved parents appear to be favoured

Consciously or unconsciously it is possible to favour in small ways the children of parental helpers in school. Where such favouritism occurs it is quickly noticed by other children and can rebound on the favoured child. Equally, and in the same way as non-existent cliques can be perceived, so some children and parents will believe that the children of involved parents are being favoured whether they are or not.

7 Children can be unduly pressured

The inside knowledge which involved parents pick up isn't only about the staff or other children; it can also be about their own. Such information can be used to pressure children.

These problems may be enough to put anyone off having parental helpers in their school again. The point is that the problems have to be managed; when they are the benefits of parental involvement far outweigh the difficulties which remain.

What can you do?

1   Establish ground rules

If common policies in the school apply to children, staff and supply teachers then they ought to apply to parents, too. It is worth establishing your own particular set of ground rules for parental involvement and then communicating them effectively and pleasantly in a booklet or as a news-sheet. Every parent who offers help should be given a copy; every parent should expect to abide by the rules. Don't be embarrassed by this; most parents will want to fit into your school as well as they can. You might want to specify, amongst other things

- whether parents announce their arrival in school and how
- what parents should do if they can't appear at a meeting or in a classroom
- to what extent they are expected to discipline children before handing over to a class teacher or the headteacher
- how the school tries to instil discipline in children
- which resources are freely available for use and which are not
- what happens at breaktime
- the need for confidentiality.

2   Arrange the first involvement on a temporary basis

Don't commit yourself to accepting help on an open-ended basis until you know the qualities of the offering parent reasonably well or until you are sure of your joint relationship. A half-term time limit or even shorter is quite reasonable.

3   Value help given but always keep new opportunities open

Parents who are involved in school life should be thanked for it but not to the apparent exclusion of everyone else. At the same time that a particular involvement is being valued, the door should always be left open to others.

4   Accept involvement at any level

Some parents, often through their own experiences of school, are still nervous of becoming involved. This does not necessarily signify lack of interest. Others can perhaps only become involved to a very limited extent. Try to accept that parents who offer only very limited involvement usually have good reasons.

5   Take some criticism as inevitable

Not all criticism can be 'managed away'. Parental feelings towards their own child and their child's school often run deep. The involvement of parents at a particular level in the school, or the involvement of particular parents, is always going to create strong feelings amongst a few people. Provided you have done everything in your power to create a fair system and to explain it carefully then ride any other criticisms with a clear conscience.

6   Don't be afraid to interfere

Where you can identify weaknesses in parental involvement in school don't be afraid to interfere. Our experience suggests that the majority of parents want to 'do it right' and are more concerned if problems are not fairly discussed than if they are.

5.5.2 *Defining the School's Image*

'Image' can be a negative word for many people.

> "The problem with these clothes is that they are all image – no quality."

> "These pop stars are all the same. They just give them whichever image is fashionable. They are not real."

Just two comments from members of an INSET discussion about what 'image' meant to them. Yet turning the discussion round in that same meeting it became clear that we all respond to images and carry banks of images around with us.

> "I am looking for another job, yes, but I'd never go and work in that school. You know what it is like as well as I do!"

> "I bought this jacket because I thought I looked good in it. It made me feel good."

> "I don't like him very much. I never think he is telling the truth."

Images are everywhere. We all have them and we all respond to them. The evidence is overwhelming. Sales of books with redesigned covers rise dramatically; we look aghast at the family abum which shows us wearing flared trousers or platform shoes; we like some houses and not others; we present certain wines to friends and drink other, cheaper, wines ourselves.

If images are so prevalent, indeed so normal, it is unlikely that schools exist in a state of supposed purity, image-free. The reality is that your school or classroom will have an image whether you like it or not; that the various groups which form the constituency of your school or class will carry round with them ideas – images – of what it is like, and what its strengths and weaknesses are, what they like about it and what they don't.

As a manager of your school or class you have two options. The first is to allow those images to be formed without input from you. The second is to see defining the image of the school or class as an important and active part of your work. Our attitude is clear. As images are going to form anyway then, as managers, we ought to be as purposeful as we can about defining them.

The compromise

Inevitably, defining the image of a school or classroom results in a compromise. On the one hand you may have your own personal view of what you would like that image to be; on the other hand you have the perspectives of your colleagues, the children, their parents, the governors, the LEA, their inspectors and so on. As we saw in the early part of this book, there is no such thing as a 'parent's' or 'governor's' view either; there are differences within groups as well as between them.

It is important that we have a clear idea of the 'image' we want our school to reflect. Do we want it

- to be authoritarian and/or democratic?
- to provide a practical education and/or a didactic one?
- to appear confident and/or open to doubt?
- to be professionally and/or personally orientated?

and so on.

It is also important that we understand the images our constituency would prefer since meeting those images will create confidence in the school. A recent survey of parental attitudes at one school suggested that parents wanted their children

- to be happy
- to work hard
- to be treated fairly
- not to be bullied
- to receive help when they needed it.

Following this survey, the school felt that the difficulties it had been experiencing in gaining parental confidence in new curriculum methods being introduced was a direct result of their failure to create positive images in the areas their parents appeared to value the most.

Responding to a series of images of your school or classroom on a broad rather than a narrow front is bound to create compromise, but compromises can be effective.

"We had introduced a more practical maths curriculum into the school and the children were doing really well, much more confident and genuinely making better progress. But the parents kept coming up and saying 'Why have you stopped teaching children their tables?' The irony was we hadn't. We were just doing it differently but we couldn't get most of the parents to see that. Some of them started to become critical of the whole maths approach then and we really began to lose their confidence in it and us.

At a staff meeting someone suggested that twice a week, just before the children went home, we all spent ten minutes doing some very obvious work on learning tables. Some of us were very sceptical but we gave it a go. Sure enough, as soon as the children got outside the door they told their mums they'd just been doing tables. It took about three weeks of this before all those who grumbled were coming in saying how pleased they were. Just two lots of ten minutes a week for a term or so and the criticisms of the mathematics stopped. Amazing."

Defining the school or class image – what to do

1   Know what you would like
Your own image of your school or class is important. Think about what you would like and how best those messages can be transmitted.

2   Understand others' points of view
Find out what images others concerned with your school have, too. Yours will have to work alongside theirs. Don't assume you know; spend time really finding out.

3   Think particularly about others' negative images
Are they based on any evidence? Can you do something positive to change them? Are they important enough to worry about?

4   Identify areas of compromise
The images your school or class have are important to you and others. Where are the areas of compromise between your preferred images and those held by others?

As far as possible, it is important to meet the needs of the various groups to whom you are responsible.

5   Think of areas over which you have immediate control
Some things you can affect quite quickly. You might be able to change the appearance and style of your letters, alter the way children come into school from the playground, govern which books are sent home from classroom, increase or decrease the involvement of certain governors in the day-to-day life of the school.

6   Identify other important factors in defining the image of your school
Some things may take longer to change. You may want to increase or decrease the amount of community involvement, alter the presentation of school concerts, redesign and rewrite the brochure, begin to run effective parents' meetings, change the way individual teachers move children about the school and so on.

Create a priority list and work towards it.

7   Work to the strengths of your own personal style
Your personal style will say a lot about your school or classroom. You can't hope to please everyone or to have all the attributes of a perfect human being. Be honest about your strengths and weaknesses and work to your strengths.

8   Make sure that the image reflects the reality
'Image' is a negative word when the gap between it and reality is huge. That is the moment when everyone realises that the image exists on its own, that it doesn't bear any relation to what is really happening. Ironically, at that point, the image has no substance; everyone loses confidence in it.

One of the important images of schools is their honesty. Trade on this. Declare existing weaknesses as professionally as possible and ensure that everyone is aware of all the existing strengths.

We spoke in the previous pages about the inevitability of your school having an image of one sort or another and the consequent importance of being positively involved in its definition. Defining an image of the school which accords with the reality behind it is, in many ways, the first stage of a marketing approach. The second, and equally crucial stage, is communicating that reality and image to anyone likely to be interested in it or helpful to you.

'Marketing' – or approaching it in a structured way – is a very new concept to many primary schools; one with which we are all having to come to terms. Because of that this section of the book is probably the most exploratory of all; there are so few examples in the real world on which to base good judgements.

The independent sector of education has understood the need for marketing for a long time. The need to go out and find customers, maintain their financial security and increase resources or 'go out of business' has concentrated minds wonderfully.

Until recently, most state schools did not share those concerns. Catchment areas, annually guaranteed money from the LEA and resources bought from central supplies allowed, quite rightly in our view, schools to concentrate on the education being provided for children.

All that has changed in recent years and those who work in primary schools find themselves sharing the same concerns as their colleagues in the independent sector. Open enrolment, the weakening of catchment areas, financial devolution and open purchasing markets have suddenly broadened the responsibilities of primary school headteachers to a degree which many are finding uncomfortable.

ST. JOHN'S SCHOOL

INFORMATION FOR PARENTS

What is certain is that primary schools will no longer be able to rely on either a flow of children into the school or an equable redrawing of catchment areas when enrolment patterns change.

What this means is that those who work in primary schools will have to develop plans and strategies for marketing that which they have to offer. What is this likely to mean in practice?

1 Presenting the school differently

Different interest groups which surround the school will be interested in it in different ways. The marketing of the school, through its image, will have to respond to those different needs. Parents will differ from inspectors, inspectors will differ from local business and so on. Some parents will differ from each other, too.

'Presenting the school differently' doesn't mean presenting conflicting messages about the school. That would be totally counterproductive. It does mean working out how to present the same image or message in a way that can be understood by different groups so that the school benefits throughout its constituency.

"When parents come to visit the school I sit them down, give them a cup of coffee, ask them a few questions and listen. I'm trying to find out what they are interested in and what matters to them.

Later, when I take them around the school I show them as much as possible but I concentrate on those areas of the school which I think will be of particular interest. There is no point spending enormous time in the gym with someone who has just talked to me for ten minutes about pottery. It's the kiln they want to see. If I didn't listen over coffee, though, I'd never find this out.

Is it worth it? Well, it impresses people I suppose. What it does best, I think, is make sure that parents send their children here with some enthusiasm, confidence and support."

2 Understanding the purpose of the marketing exercise

Planning is as important in marketing as it is in everything else. Once the perspectives of the targeted group have been identified we have a better idea of the approaches they might prefer. Additionally, what we give, show, send to or talk about to those people has to be focused on the particular purpose we had in mind.

Asking for sponsorship monies from local companies requires a different approach from asking for one of their employees to come and talk to children.

In the first instance companies will need to know

- how much money is required
- over what time scale
- what the money is to be used for
- whether the use is compatible with their own operation
- what publicity might be gained for the company.

In the second instance they might want to know

- what support the employee might receive from the school
- what audio-visual facilities are available
- how long their employee will be away from work
- whether any publicity is possible
- some background information on the work children have done already.

3 Developing a strategy

Successful marketing is rarely the result of a one-off operation. It depends on a combination of the appropriateness of the particular marketing exercise coupled with existing confidence in you and your school.

As this section was being written Marks and Spencer had just announced the successful introduction of a unit trust fund at the same time as other such launches had failed. There will be a number of reasons for this but one will almost certainly be the stock of goodwill Marks and Spencer had created long before they thought of involving themselves in unit trusts.

It is a lesson schools might have to learn. The chances of obtaining money from local companies are likely to be increased if some positive involvement with that company has occurred before the request for sponsorship is made. The chance of maintaining high enrolment into the school will be increased if parents of pre-school children in the area have been aware for some time of what the school stands for and what its achievements are.

4   *Learning new skills*

Developing marketing ability over the next few years will require new skills, particularly in areas such as the media. The importance, for example, of presenting local newspapers and free-sheets with press releases is likely to grow. Writing those press releases in a way which the local papers can use is no more time-consuming than talking to a reporter on the telephone, but it does require the investment of a little time talking to the papers to find out what they want. Good press releases

- free reporters from having to rewrite copy
- increase the chance of exposure in local papers
- maintain some of the control in the hands of the school.

Other skills which could become important in the future include

- responding to media interviews, particularly on local radio
- creating opportunities for local radio and television involvement
- preparing documentation for specific target audiences – some governors, inspectors, local companies
- preparing a marketing plan
- researching the results.

From our present viewpoint the growing importance of marketing seems both exhilarating and appalling at the same time. Few teachers entered the profession with the thought that marketing our schools might become one of our most important activities.

As with everything else, though, situations, ideas and demands change. We do have to respond to those changes as best as we can. If we don't, both we and the schools we work in will suffer. The truth is that it may be the next but one generation of teachers and headteachers who are fully at ease with marketing strategies and marketing language. Those of us at the sharp edge of the changes must still take it seriously.

In a time of uncertainty and doubt one thing we can say for sure is that the role of school governors has changed. The effective management of the new role has got to be a high priority for headteachers and many other staff as well. A clear definition of the new responsibilities is essential knowledge for all teachers and ways of realising the positive potential of governors are a must for all educational managers.

The legal framework

Education (No. 2) Act 1986

- Gives size, constitution and functions of governing body
- Defines *composition* – basically, this gave parents and non-political governors a majority on governing bodies (see 'Constitution of Governing Bodies' overleaf for details)
- Defines the ground rules for *becoming a governor*:
  - minimum age of 18
  - a governor serves for four years
  - parent and teacher governors are elected by secret ballot
  - parents may complete four years even though their children have left school
  - teachers cease to be governors if they leave the school
  - travel and subsistence expenses are allowed.
- Defines *responsibilities of governors*.

1 Appointment of staff

- Headteachers are selected by an LEA and governors' panel which has at least equal numbers of governors
- other staff appointments are the governors' responsibility although they can delegate
- deputy head appointments can be as for headteacher or as for other staff
- job descriptions for redeployed teachers can be written by governors, and the LEA must take this into account.

[NB: some minor changes to this in 1988 Act – see p. 217.]

2 Curriculum

Governors should:

- record and update aims of the school
- consider LEA curriculum guidelines and possibly modify them
- note that headteachers are responsible for delivery of the curriculum and for reconciling any differences between the LEA and governors
- assume responsibility for the existence of sex education in schools
- assume responsibility for the provision of a balanced political education
- ensure that all curriculum documentation is available to parents
- ensure that community and police views are taken into account.

[NB: 1988 Act increases these powers and makes some changes – see pp. 217–218.]

3 Finance

Governors should:

- require LEAs to give a statement of overall running costs of the school
- assume responsibility for a large part of 'capitation'; this can be delegated to the headteacher.

[NB: 1988 Act changes this significantly – see p. 217.]

4 Discipline

- there are strict rules for dealing with suspensions
- only the headteacher has the power to suspend a pupil

- governors may draw up guidelines for pupil discipline
- staff may be temporarily suspended by the headteacher or governors
- dismissal and early retirement may be recommended by governors – only LEA can do this in County Schools
- voluntary aided schools' governors are employers so they undertake formal procedures concerning staff.

5 Governors' meetings and procedures

- no governor can be on more than four boards
- the chairperson is to be elected annually; he/she cannot be an employee of the school
- a quorum is three or one third, whichever is the greater
- any three governors may call a special meeting
- all governors' papers (minutes, reports, etc.) must be available for anyone to consult (except for items deemed 'confidential')
- others may be invited to meetings

- personal involvement in an issue precludes a governor from taking part in discussion
- decisions must be by majority vote
- the clerk must be appointed or dismissed in accordance with published procedures or in agreement with governors
- if the clerk is absent, a governor may step in
- an adjourned meeting with incomplete business must be completed at a later date
- governors' meetings require seven days clear notice unless the chair rules otherwise.

6 Annual meeting for parents

- governors must give an annual report to parents on what they have done during the year and hold a meeting to discuss the report
- resolutions for consideration can be passed if the number of parents present is equal to 20 per cent of the school roll.

Constitution of governing bodies

(Sections 3, 4, and 6 of the Education (No. 2) Act 1986)

County, controlled and special schools

i) *Under 100 pupils:*
   2 parent governors
   2 LEA governors
   1 teacher governor
   The headteacher if he/she wishes
   Either 2 foundation + 1 co-opted (controlled schools) or 3 co-opted (county and special schools)

ii) *100 to 299 pupils:*
   3 parent governors
   3 LEA governors
   1 teacher governor
   The headteacher if he/she wishes
   Either 3 foundation + 1 co-opted (controlled schools) or 4 co-opted (county and special schools)

iii) *300 to 500 pupils:*
   4 parent governors
   4 LEA governors
   2 teacher governors
   The headteacher if he/she wishes
   Either 4 foundation + 1 co-opted (controlled schools) or 5 co-opted (county and special schools)

iv) *Over 600 pupils:*
   5 parent governors
   5 LEA governors
   2 teacher governors
   The headteacher if he/she wishes
   Either 4 foundation + 2 co-opted controlled schools) *or* 6 co-opted (county and special schools)

LEAs have the option to drop the largest category (iv) and treat schools of over 600 pupils the same as those of 300–600, thus establishing 16 as the top size of governing board. This is the only flexibility allowed on numbers.

In making co-options, governors must bear in mind the need for representation of the business community.

Aided and Special Agreement Schools
Regardless of size:
At least 1 LEA governor
In primary schools, at least 1 representative of the minor authority, if any
At least 1 parent governor

At least 1 teacher governor in schools of under 300
At least 2 teacher governors in schools over 300
Foundation governors sufficient to secure majority set out below
The headteacher if he/she wishes.

There shall be a majority of foundation governors of 2 over all other interests in boards up to 18 members and 3 in larger boards. One foundation governor must always be a parent of a pupil.

Commencement dates: county and special schools by September 1st 1988 and voluntary schools by September 1st 1989.

Education Reform Act 1988

This Act did not replace the 1986 Act – in fact most of the 1986 Act has remained unaltered. What has changed is an *increase* in the power of school governors (and central government).

Sections most affecting school governors are concerned with:

1 Finance
- eventually all schools (initially those over 200 pupils) will have control over a major part of their budgets
- the LEA, working within strict governmental guidelines, will produce a formula which determines which budgetary items are kept centrally and which devolved to schools (see Local Management of Schools pp. 195–199)
- major items for governors to decide are: teachers, books, stock, equipment and maintenance.

2 Staffing
- governors make all appointments with advice from the LEA – they may or may not decide to involve the headteacher

- governors recommend dismissal of staff

3 Admissions
- to reduce the 'standard number' (i.e. admissions in 1979–80) governors and LEA must obtain the approval of the Secretary of State
- raising admission numbers does not require this approval.

4 Grant maintained status ('opting out')
- governors of schools with over 300 pupils may apply to be financed directly from the Secretary of State
- this can only be done following a ballot of parents equal to 20 per cent of the school roll and a majority of those voting are in favour
- a second ballot is required if less than 50 per cent vote in the first. The second ballot is binding whatever the turn-out.

5 The National Curriculum
- governors, LEAs and headteachers have a joint responsibility to comply

with the requirements of the National Curriculum (see Primary Schools and the National Curriculum pp. 77–79).

6 Religious worship

- schools must have a daily collective act of worship
- it can be at any time and not for the whole school at once
- it should be broadly 'Christian'

- governors and staff may apply for partial or total exemption from the 'Christian' requirement if the catchment area reflects another or other faiths.

Major point

- The 1988 Act has two major areas where governors are crucially concerned – *Finance* and *Curriculum*.

Involving governors

Peoples' *perceptions* of what happens in our schools are as important as *what* happens. Governors are no exception to this view. They bring the *perspectives* of the business person, the parent, the politician and so on – given their new powers it is vital that their understanding of what goes on in school is as full and accurate as possible.

When involving governors it is important to recognise the two ways in which we operate with them: informally and formally.

School Governors come from a variety of backgrounds

The informal

Even though these may be formally set up, informal functions are relaxed occasions which allow governors to meet informally with staff, parents and other members of the local community. They should provide opportunities for relationships to be deepened and the basis of mutual respect and trust to be laid down.

- It's a good idea to arrange an informal monthly or half-termly meeting between the chairperson of governors and the headteacher to keep communication lines open.
- Some examples of informal governor involvement are as follows:

a) school plays, concerts, parties, Christmas lunch
b) sports day, prize giving, competitions, etc.
c) social occasions with staff, for example, wine and cheese, retirement of long serving staff member
d) PTA type functions, for example, discos, barn dances, 'fairs', etc.

2 The formal

- The termly *governors' meeting* is the most crucial structure for involving governors; this is where much of the decision-making takes place and so headteachers and teachers need to be well-prepared, be seen to be efficient and effective managers and learn new skills in terms of cooperating with non-professionals
- The *sub-committee* structure adopted by many governing bodies (for example, for curriculum, finance, site and building, etc.) is another formal set-up whereby governors can become professionally involved with staff
- Staff appointments will invariably involve governors
- Visits to the school (which can be informal) when governors can see staff and children at work.

All these situations give opportunities for governors to gain insight and make contributions to the life of the school. At all of them staff, and headteachers in particular, need to be:

- well-briefed with the necessary information
- clear about their view on issues
- aware of governors' perspectives.

No one is sure how the governors' new powers will affect schools. In some cases their impact may be minimal, in others it may be radical. Many governors are worried and concerned about their new responsibilities and they need the constructive support of the headteacher and staff.

This bibliography contains two sorts of books. The first is those from which some reference has been made directly or indirectly in the text of our own book. The second is a non-exclusive selection from those which have influenced our thinking about schools and much more.

S J Ball, *The Micro-Politics of the School: Towards a theory of school organisation* (Methuen, London, 1987)

D Bannister, 'Knowledge of Self' in David Fontana (ed) *Psychology for Teachers* (Macmillan, London, 1981)

C H Barry and F Tye, *Running a School* (Temple Smith, London, 1972)

J Burgoyne, 'Self-Management' in P Lawrence and K Elliot (eds) *Introducing Management* (Penguin Books, London, 1985)

T Bush, *Theories of Educational Management* (Harper and Row, London, 1986)

R J Campbell, *Developing the Primary School Curriculum* (Holt, Rinehart and Winston, London, 1985)

R Carter, J Martin, B Mayblin and M Munday, *Systems, Management and Change* (Open University/Harper and Row, Milton Keynes, 1984)

G Claxton, (ed) *Beyond Therapy: The Impact of Eastern Religions on Psychological Theory and Practice* (Wisdom Publications, London, 1986)

C Day, D Johnston and P Whitaker, *Managing Primary Schools* (Paul Chapman Publishing Ltd, London 1985)

C Day, P Whitaker and D Wren, *Appraisal and Professional Development in Primary Schools* (Open University Press, Milton Keynes, 1987)

T Deal, A Kennedy, 'Culture and School Performance', in *Educational Leadership* 40, 1983

J Dean, *Managing the Primary School* (Croom Helm, London, 1987)

DES *Primary Schools: Some aspects of good practice* (HMSO, London, 1987)

P Easen, *Making School-centred INSET Work* (The Open University/Croom Helm, London, 1985)

J Eliot-Kemp and C Rogers, *The Effective Teacher, A Person-Centred Development Guide* (PAVIC Publications, Sheffield City Polytechnic, 1982)

J Eliot-Kemp and G Williams, *Improving your Professional Effectiveness: A Handbook for Managers in Education* (PAVIC Publications, Sheffield City Polytechnic, 1981)

M Fullan, *The Meaning of Educational Change* (Teachers' College Press, New York, 1982)

J Gratue, *Successful Interviewing* (Penguin Books, Business & Management Seminar, London, 1988)

C Handy, *Understanding Organisations* (Penguin Books, London, 1981)

Primary Schools: Some Aspects of Good Practice (HMSO, 1987)

P J Holly and G W Southworth, *The Developing School* (Falmer Press, Lewes, 1989)

C Hooks, *Studying Classrooms* (Deakin University, Australia, 1981)

House of Commons Committee Report, *Achievement in Primary Schools* vol 1 (HMSO, London, 1986)

E Hoyle, *The Politics of School Management* (Hodder and Stoughton, London, 1986)

ILEA, *Keeping the School Under Review: the Primary School* (ILEA, London, 1982)

A McMahon, R Bolam, R Abbot and P Holly, *Guidelines for Review and Internal Development in Schools: Primary School Handbook* (Longman/ Schools Council, York, 1984)

P Mortimore, P Sammons, L Stoll, D Lewis, R Ecob, *School Matters: The Junior Years* (Open Books, Wells, 1988)

NAS/UWT *Commentary on 'The LMS Initiative Guide'* (NAS/UWT, 1989)

D J Nias, G W Southworth and R Yeoman, *Primary School Staff Relationships: a study of school culture* (Cassell, London, 1989)

R T Pascale and A G Athos, *The Art of Japanese Management* (Penguin Books, London, 1982

M Pedlar, J Burgoyne and T Boydell, *A Manager's Guide to Self-Development* (McGraw-Hill, London, 1986)

Peters and N Austin, *A Passion for Excellence: The Leadership Difference* (Fontana Books, New York and London, 1985)

A Pollard and S Tann, *Reflective Teaching in the Primary School: A handbook for the classroom* (Cassell, London, 1988)

D J Pugh, D J Hickson & C R Hinings, *Writers on Organisations* Third edition (Penguin Books, London, 1983)

K Reid, R Bullock and S Howarth, *An Introduction to Primary School Organisation* (Hodder and Stoughton, London, 1988)

C Roberts, *The Interview Game and How It's Played* (BBC Publications, London, 1985)

Rodger and J Richardson, *Self-evaluation for Primary Schools* (Hodder and Stoughton, London, 1985)

Salford Education Department, *Profile '82* (City of Salford Education Department, 1982)

J Sallis, *Schools, Parents and Governors: A new approach to accountability* (Routledge, London, 1988)

G W Southworth, *Staff Selection in the Primary School* (Basil Blackwell, Oxford, 1980)

G W Southworth, 'Primary Headteachers and Collegiality' in G W Southworth (ed) *Readings in Primary School Management* (Falmer Press, Lewes, 1987)

M Stevens, *Practical Problem Solving for Managers* (Kogan Page/BIM, London, 1988)

A J Woodard, *The Head's Legal Guide* (Croner Publications, 1988)

T Wragg, *Teacher Appraisal: a practical guide* (Macmillan, London, 1987)

Acknowledgements

The authors would like to extend special thanks to:

Jean Bateman (Special Needs Co-ordinator, Uplands Middle School) for allowing us to use her work in 4.13 *Special Educational Needs*.

Ken Irvine, Hilary Behenna and Stuart Glynn (headteachers in Devonshire primary schools) and Devonshire County Council for permission to use their material in 5.3.6 *Profiling*.

We would also like to thank the following for permission to quote or reproduce material. We have tried to clear all permissions but this has not been possible in every case. The publishers will be happy to insert full acknowledgements in future editions if notified by copyright-holders.

A.C.E. for permission to reproduce 'The Constitution of Governing Bodies' on pp. 216–217.

Cassell plc for permission to quote from *Reflective Teaching in the Primary School: A handbook for the classroom* by Pollard & Tann.

W & R Chambers Ltd (Publishers) for permission to quote definitions from *Chambers Concise Dictionary* (1988) on pp. 12 and 140.

Paul Chapman Publishing Ltd for permission to reproduce the chart on p. 69 from *Managing Primary Schools* by Day, Johnston & Whitaker.

The LMS Initiative, 3 Robert Street, London WC2N 6BH for permission to reproduce the flow chart on p. 196 (from *Local Management of Schools: A Practical Guide*, section 2 p. 2).

Macmillan Publishers Ltd for permission to reproduce on p. 17 a quote from 'Knowledge of Self' by D Bannister in *Psychology for Teachers* ed. David Fontana (1981).

The Authors

David Playfoot is Headteacher of Uplands Middle School, Sudbury, Suffolk and has previously been Head of a First School in Suffolk and a primary school in Bromley in addition to teaching in several authorities.

Martin Skelton has been a Headteacher of two primary schools and is at present responsible for providing in-service work to schools and local authorities through Fieldwork Ltd.

Geoff Southworth has been a teacher and Headteacher in primary schools in Lancashire. He is now Tutor in Primary Management at the Cambridge Institute of Education.